Supporting children's learning in the early years

Supporting

children's learning

in the early years

Edited by Linda Miller and Jane Devereux

David Fulton Publishers   in association with   The Open University

David Fulton Publishers Ltd
The Chiswick Centre, 414 Chiswick High Road, London W4 5TF

www.fultonpublishers.co.uk

First published in Great Britain in 2004 by David Fulton Publishers

David Fulton Publishers is a division of Granada Learning Limited, part of Granada plc.

British Library Cataloguing in Publication Data
A catalogue record for this book is available from the British Library.

ISBN 1–85346–976–9

Typeset by FiSH Books, London
Printed and bound in Great Britain

Contents

Acknowledgements

We would like to thank all those who have contributed chapters to this Reader or who have approved their reprinting from other publications, and to our colleague, Carrie Cable, for critical feedback on some texts. Grateful acknowledgement is made to the following sources for permission to reproduce material in this book:

Chapter 1: Anning, A. and Edwards, A. (1999) 'Young children as learners', *Promoting Children's Learning from Birth to Five: Developing the New Early Years Professional*. Reproduced by kind permission of Oxford University Press.

Chapter 2: Lansdown, G. and Lancaster, P. (2001) 'Promoting children's welfare by respecting their rights', *Contemporary Issues in Early Years: Working Collaboratively for Children*. Reproduced by kind permission of Paul Chapman Publishing.

Chapter 3: Siraj-Blatchford, I. and Clarke, P. (2000) 'Identity, self-esteem and learning: supporting identity, diversity and language in the early years'. Reproduced by kind permission of Open University Press.

Chapter 4: Wolfendale, S. and Paige-Smith, A. (2000) 'Supporting all children: moving towards inclusion in the early years', *Contemporary Issues in Early Years: Working Collaboratively for Children*. Reproduced by kind permission of Paul Chapman Publishing.

Chapter 5: Paige-Smith, A. (2002) 'Parent partnership and inclusion in the early years', *Exploring Early Years Education and Care*. Reproduced by kind permission of Open University Press.

Chapter 6: Carr, M. (2000) 'A folk model of assessment and an alternative', *Assessment in Early Childhood Settings Learning Stories*. Reproduced by kind permission of Paul Chapman Publishing.

Chapter 7: Clark, A. 'Listening to children'. Reproduced by kind permission of Alison Clark.

Chapter 8: Selleck, D. (2001) 'Being under 3 years of age: enhancing quality experiences', *Contemporary Issues in Early Years: Working Collaboratively for Children*. Reproduced by kind permission of David Fulton Publishers.

Chapter 12: Campbell, R. (2002) 'Young children becoming literate', *Exploring Early Years Education and Care*. Reproduced by kind permission of David Fulton Publishers.

Chapter 16: Cook, D. (2003) 'ICT and curriculum provision in the early years', *ICT for Curriculum Enhancement*. Reproduced by kind permission of Intellect Ltd.

Chapter 18: Turner-Bisset, R. (2000) 'Meaningful history with young children', *Looking at Early Years Education and Care*. Reproduced by kind permission of David Fulton Publishers.

Chapter 19: Dowling, M. (2000) 'Emotional well-being', *Young Children's Personal, Social and Emotional Development*. Reproduced by kind permission of Paul Chapman Publishing.

Chapter 20: Elfer, P. (1996) 'Building intimacy in relationships with young children in early years settings', *Early Years Journal* **16** (2). Reproduced by kind permission of Taylor & Francis Ltd, http://www.tandf.co.uk/journals.

Chapter 21: Robson, S. (1996) 'The physical environment', *Education in Early Childhood: First Things First*. Reproduced by kind permission of David Fulton Publishers.

Chapter 22: Lindon, J. (1999) 'The future of childhood', *Coordinate: The Journal of the National Early Years Network*. Reproduced by kind permission of the National Children's Bureau.

Chapter 23: Anning, A. and Edwards, A. (1999) 'Creating contexts for professional educare', *Promoting Children's Learning from Birth to Five: Developing the New Early YearsPprofessional*. Reproduced by kind permission of Open University Press.

Every effort has been made to contact all the copyright holders of material included in the book. If any material has been included without permission, the publishers offer their apologies and will be happy to make acknowledgment in any future edition of the book.

Part 1
Supporting learning

Linda Miller

Introduction

> Practitioners in today's early childhood institutions are maybe facing some of the most demanding challenges in the history of their profession...Profound and interrelated change in our social, economic, political and technological environments, combined with a fundamental shift in the nature of work and employment patterns, are impacting on the lives of children and families
>
> (Oberhaumer and Colberg-Schrader 1999 cited in Abbott and Hevey 2001: 179)

The readings in this book *Supporting Children's Learning in the Early Years* have been selected as a representative sample of a large and growing body of research and scholarship relating to the field of early years education and care, and reflect changing views about children and the people who care for and educate them, and the settings in which this takes place. The book is primarily aimed at the 310,000 childcare workers or early years practitioners working in settings such as nurseries, playgroups, out-of-school childcare or as childminders and nannies, identified in the Labour Force Survey 2001–2 (Moss 2003: 2), and also teaching assistants working with young children in school settings. The book is divided into three sections:

1. Supporting learning.
2. Early years curriculum.
3. Positive learning environments: children and adults.

The chapters within each section illustrate the new demands and challenges that early years practitioners face in a rapidly changing field. However, we also hope that they will interest and stimulate a wider audience.

   The last decade has been both a challenging and exciting time to be working with young children. Young children and their families have been firmly fixed on the political agenda, although professionals and experts differ in their views regarding the rate and significance of the progress made (Moss 2003; Pugh 2001). A range of initiatives has been part of this drive to achieve progress.

Developments include the establishment in England of a new Foundation Stage of early education, with similar plans undertaken for Wales; a framework in England for those working with children under three; a National Childcare Strategy in England and Wales to expand and improve services for children from birth to 14 and recommendations for Scotland that parallel many of the changes proposed (Scottish Executive 2000); more family-friendly workplace policies; the Introduction of Early Years Development and Childcare Partnerships in England and Wales, with similar commitments in Scotland and Northern Ireland; the establishment of Early Excellence Centres; the Sure Start initiative to develop services for children under 4 and the production by the Qualifications and Curriculum Authority in England (QCA 1999) of a national 'climbing frame' of qualifications covering vocational and occupational qualifications and a route to higher level qualifications. Both the Welsh Qualifications Authority and the Northern Ireland Qualifications Authority have linked with QCA to accredit qualifications within this framework. As Pugh (2001) notes, this rate of change has been astonishing and, whilst much remains to be done, much has been achieved.

The developments outlined above are opening up new roles, responsibilities and opportunities for early years practitioners, which will require higher levels of knowledge and skills. Yet childcare remains heavily gendered work and childcare workers are still overwhelmingly female; cross-national comparisons illustrate the relative lowly position of such workers in the United Kingdom (Moss 2003). Nevertheless they are charged with one of the most important jobs imaginable, that of supporting the learning and development of young children. As Abbott and Hevey (2001) note, Britain 'gets its childcare on the cheap' (p.181), but there is a drive to improve the qualifications and status of this workforce. The above-mentioned 'climbing frame' of qualifications in early years education, childcare and playwork (QCA 1999) and the development of Sure Start Unit Recognised Early Years Sector-Endorsed Foundation Degrees (DfES 2001) in England, will confer a new Senior Practitioner status and open up progression routes that have previously been unavailable to the majority of early years practitioners. This will be an important step in providing the knowledge and skills needed for working with young children and their families in a rapidly changing political and educational climate. We hope that this book will be part of this supporting structure.

Supporting learning

The chapters in this section are about supporting children's learning in the widest sense. In all four countries of the United Kingdom published curriculum documents for children aged three to five have been introduced (Miller *et al.* 2003), which offer a generic framework for practice in many early years settings. Angela Anning and Anne Edwards in chapter 1 'Young children as learners' describe how a group of practitioners rose to the challenge of working with unfamiliar guidance to focus upon the children as learners and on the 'how' rather than the 'what' of learning. They go on to consider some contrasting theoretical perspectives on the development of children's learning and how these same practitioners were able to transform this knowledge into action in their settings. Children are most likely to learn if they feel safe, protected and are well nurtured; chapter 2 'Promoting children's welfare by respecting their rights' explores these issues in relation to children's rights. Gerison Lansdown and Penny Lancaster consider the limitations of a welfare approach to children's rights, which they argue has been detrimental to their well being. The chapter gives voice to the children themselves on important issues that affect their lives and argues that children need to be recognised as subjects of rights. The authors go on to explore a rights-based model of children's welfare. Chapters 3, 4 and 5 raise issues and present challenges to those working with young children in responding appropriately to diversity and recognise that genuine inclusion and equality of opportunity are not easy to achieve. In chapter 3 'Identity, self esteem and learning' Iram Siraj-Blatchford and Priscilla Clarke examine issues for young bilingual children and provide evidence of the importance of self-esteem in children's learning and identify strategies for effective practice. Implementing policy to meet the diverse needs of children requires the expertise of well informed practitioners. Statutory requirements and policy documents pose a challenge to early years practitioners as they need to be understood and sensitively interpreted and implemented in early years settings. Chapter 4 'Supporting all children – moving towards inclusion in the early years' by Sheila Wolfendale and Alice Paige-Smith considers special educational needs within an inclusive framework. The chapter discusses notable developments in special needs and early years and offers a celebration of achievements as early years issues have become prominent on the education agenda. In the next chapter 'Parent partnership and inclusion in the early years' Alice Paige-Smith describes through parents' voices the gulf between parents' views of inclusion and professionals' views. She charts the establishment of a support group for parents as they strive to achieve inclusion for their children with disabilities or difficulties in learning. 'Why' questions can be difficult for early years practitioners who may feel vulnerable about their position. However, such questions are at the heart of what practitioners do as they seek to understand children's learning; in particular in relation to withstanding the pressures of externally guided assessment, which is increasingly about accountability and a focus on outcomes rather than children's learning. In chapter 6 'A folk model of assessment – and an alternative' Margaret Carr explores some complex ideas and documents the development of her thinking about assessment. She describes how she moved from a deficit model to a 'credit 'model of assessment, which enhances children's disposition to learn. She now agrees with Mary Jane Drummond's definition of assessment which is, 'the ways in which, in our everyday practice, we observe children's learning, strive to understand it, and then put our understanding to good use' (1993: 13). In the final chapter in this section Alison Clark describes the Mosaic approach to 'Listening to children' and builds on a strong tradition of using observation as a key approach to understanding what children think, know and can do. The chapter places children firmly at the centre by exploring innovative approaches to listening to their perspectives on their daily lives and provides insights that go beyond children's learning.

References

Abbott, L. and Hevey, D. (2001) 'Training to work in the early years: developing the climbing frame', in Pugh, G. (ed.) *Contemporary Issues in the Early Years: working collaboratively for children*, 3rd edn, 179–93. London: Paul Chapman Publishing.

Department for Education and Skills (DfES) (2001) *Statement of Requirement.* London: DfES.

Drummond, M. J. (1993) *Assessing Children's Learning.* London: David Fulton Publishing.

Miller, L., Hughes, J., Roberts, A. and Staggs, L. (2003) 'Curricular guidance and frameworks for the early years', in Devereux, J. and Miller, L. (eds) *Working with Children in the Early Years.* London: David Fulton Publishing.

Moss, P. (2003) *Beyond Caring: the case for reforming the childcare early years workforce.* London: Daycare Trust.

Pugh, G. (2001) 'A policy for early childhood services?', in Pugh, G. (ed.) *Contemporary Issues in the Early Years: working collaboratively for children*, 3rd edn, 9–22. London: Paul Chapman Publishing.

Qualifications and Curriculum Authority (QCA) (1999) *Early Years, Education, Childcare and Playwork Sector: a framework of nationally accredited qualifications.* London: Qualifications and Curriculum Authority.

Scottish Executive (2000) 'Regulation of early education and care: the way ahead' (online), http//www.Scotland.gov.uk/library2/doc15/reec-00.asp (accessed 22 August 2002).

Chapter 1

Young children as learners

Angela Anning and Anne Edwards

The what, who and how of learning

In this chapter Anning and Edwards report on the findings of a project involving collaboration between higher education, local authority officers and early years practitioners in creating an informal community of practice.

Those of us who are involved in the education of young children need to focus on helping children to become learners, to enjoy learning and to feel that they are people who are able to learn. This is no small challenge but it is a safe bet that investment in children's dispositions to learn will pay dividends.

Our research partnership was stimulated by the publication of *Desirable Outcomes* (DfEE/SCAA 1996) which, when we started, represented government policy on the pre-compulsory education phase of provision for children. The emphasis in the document was clearly on the *what* of learning.

How different is the emphasis placed by Schweinhart and Weikart (1993: 4) when they discuss the lasting change that occurred as a result of High Scope interventions with disadvantaged children in the USA in the 1970s:

> The essential process connecting early childhood experience to patterns of improved success in school and community seemed to be the development of habits, traits and dispositions that allowed the child to interact positively with other people and with tasks. This process was based neither on permanently improved intellectual performance nor on academic knowledge.

Schweinhart and Weikart point to dispositions – that is, orientations towards the world around us – which ensure that children approach activities from which they might learn in ways that allow them to be open to the learning opportunities in them. Schweinhart and Weikart's emphasis is on helping children to see themselves as people who can learn. Their focus is on the *who* of learning – that is, on creating learners.

Desirable Outcomes (DfEE/SCAA 1996) also appeared to differ in emphasis from 'The Rumbold Report' on quality in early years provision (DES 1990) despite the report's obvious influence on it.

The emphases can be summarised as:

1. identifying *what* children are to learn;
2. creating children *who* are learners;
3. attending to *how* children learn and *how* adults support their learning.

There is, however, a danger in selecting just one of these emphases as the basis of practice. Recent thinking about learning suggests that the *what, who* and *how* of learning are crucially interlinked. For example, a disposition to learn in the domain of mathematics is nurtured by previous success with mathematics. This success is, in turn, connected to children's developing capacities to deal with mathematical concepts and the support that adults give them.

A sociocultural view of learning: learning and context

Sociocultural approaches have a lot in common with Piagetian ideas, about learning. They acknowledge that learning occurs as a result of active involvement with the environment; and that children construct, that is build up, increasingly complex understandings over time, so very young children will operate, at times, with misconceptions about the world. Sociocultural approaches are even more clearly rooted in Vygotskian perspectives on learning and therefore emphasise how adults can support children as they learn; how children learn what is important in their culture through interactions with more experienced members of that culture; and how language carries the meanings and values of a particular culture when it is used in that culture. Let us, therefore, look at four of the key features of a sociocultural approach to understanding learning.

1. the situated nature of learning (i.e. we learn to do what we think the context demands of us);
2. the relationship between our sense of who we are and what we do (i.e. between our identities, dispositions and our actions);
3. an understanding that learning occurs through interaction with others (i.e. through language and imitation);
4. an understanding that learning occurs through interaction with objects (i.e. through using objects in the same way as others do).

Learning is situated

Sociocultural psychology tells us that learning is a process of being able to *participate* increasingly effectively in the world in which we find ourselves. At birth, that world is fairly straightforward, albeit heavily emotionally charged, consisting of the presence or absence of sources of food and comfort. It soon becomes more complicated so that, for example, young children learn that although rowdy behaviour might be fine in the garden it is not appropriate in the supermarket. By the time children are ready to enter compulsory schooling they should have some idea of how to participate as pupils, rather than members of a family, when at school; and how to begin to think as, for example, mathematicians and historians when given tasks which demand specific approaches.

In summary, action and therefore learning is heavily situated. Learners look for cues in contexts for guidance on how to participate. One challenge for early years professionals has always been how to ensure that children learn all that they can from the experiences provided. So much depends on how children see, interpret and respond to the learning opportunities available to them. As Schweinhart and Weikart (1993) indicate, a disposition to interact positively with people and with tasks seems to be a crucial indicator of long-term success as a learner. A sociocultural perspective on learning goes a little further than simply promoting a positive approach to experiences by suggesting that children's actions need to be within the bounds of what is considered appropriate. So, for example, young learners learn to sit and listen to stories; to use pictures as clues to the meanings of text; that stories have endings; and so on.

Alison's development of the construction area in her centre in order to provide 3- and 4-year-old children with opportunities to participate positively and appropriately with materials, illustrates these ideas in practice. Having resourced the area with books about boats, small- and medium-size wooden blocks, 'engineers' helmets, tape measures, paper and pencils, staff encouraged children to work in pairs to build boats. Once finished, the boats were measured and the measurements recorded by the children. The children were encouraged to participate – i.e. think and act – as designers and mathematicians and to participate in a process from planning to recording. The children tackled the activities in ways that reflected their own physical and intellectual development and achieved a sense of success through completing the activities. They left the construction area with memories of an experience in which thinking and acting as designers and mathematicians was associated with their own effectiveness.

Identities and dispositions

One way of looking at disposition, so that we can become clearer about how adults can support children's dispositions to respond positively and appropriately, is to connect disposition to children's developing sense of who they are and what they can do. For example, if a child's identity includes a belief that she is good with numbers, she will find herself attracted to number activities. At a more detailed level, if that identity includes a capacity to see mathematics as sets of patterns then the child will seek out the patterns in the learning opportunities provided. In other words, she will have a disposition to engage with aspects of the mathematics available in the experience provided for her.

The children in Alison's construction area were, through their role play, developing dispositions to design and evaluate as part of the construction process. They were able to operate at levels which reflected their capabilities and their successes were supported and recognised by the adults.

Dispositions are rooted in our sense of our likely effectiveness. The challenge for educators is to assist the development of a sense of effectiveness through careful and sensitive support while children acquire the capabilities and understandings which will underpin their effectiveness. Here we connect the *how* and the *what* to the *who* of learning and need to examine the relationships that support early learning.

Learning often occurs in interaction with others

The learning trajectory followed by most children from birth to 5 can be summarised as a gradual and parallel shift from interdependence to independence and from a focus on personal meanings to a focus on public meanings. Hence, the role of carers of young children is to support them as they acquire the capacity to participate in their social worlds. The responsibilities of adults therefore change in relation to the development of children's capacities to cope effectively with the world around of assisting children to understand the external world in the way that it is understood by other members of society.

The intersubjective phase

Initially children experience the world, and participate in it, through their relationships with their main caregivers who bring them into involvement with some of the basic features of social life by highlighting particular behaviours. The most important of these behaviours is the turn-taking that underpins, for example, language development. Young babies are not, however, entirely passive participants in these relationships.

Colwyn Trevarthen's (1977) detailed analyses of videotaped interactions between mothers and babies in their first few months of life has drawn attention to the finely-tuned patterns of interaction that occur and the extent to which these interactions can be mutual and not simply a matter of infants responding to their mothers.

The close relationship between infant and caregiver which Trevarthen observed and which enables an infant to experience the world in the physical and emotional safety provided by the relationship is characterised by *intersubjectivity*. Inter-subjectivity demands considerable attention to the emotional state of infants and a capacity to slow down and tune into young children's ways of experiencing the world so that children are brought into interaction with the world. A key feature of the adult role in an intersubjective relationship, in the western world, appears to be to act *as if* the infant has intentions and is able to make evaluations. We see this behaviour in the conversations that mothers have with infants about feeding – for example, 'You want your bottle now don't you, I can tell'. This *as if* behaviour appears to prepare the child for her or his later intentional and purposeful interactions with the world.

What we know of intersubjectivity is reason enough for ensuring that key worker systems are safeguarded, particularly for infants. If education is to be a feature of provision from birth we need to attend carefully to the subtle and demanding nature of work with babies.

Millie and Amy in their inner-city nursery worked cautiously and carefully in this area through the use of 'action songs'. They collected songs from the nursery workers and the parents involved in the nursery. They then produced a song book with, alongside each song, suggestions for ways of holding the babies and for actions associated with the lyrics. The songs were sung both at home and at the nursery. In both settings the infants were held in similar ways and were involved in consistent sets of patterns and responses with both sets of caregivers.

Learning to look outwards

Once infants have gained some sense of their own intentionality – for example, that adults will respond to them – and they are secure in their capacity to engage in various forms of conversational turn-taking, they are ready to begin to look beyond the familiar patterns of meaning making found in their intersubjective relationships. This is an important stage in the move towards being able to deal with the social world and the public meanings that operate within it. Again adults can help or hinder this stage in a child's developmental behaviour.

The key concept here is a *joint involvement episode* (JIE) (Schaffer 1992). In a JIE an adult and a child pay joint attention to, and act together on, an object. An object may be, for example, a toy or part of the environment. As children get older the object may be, for example, a play on words or a joke. The important point is that JIEs direct children's attention to objects and events outside their relationships with their caregivers while giving them opportunities to act on these objects within the security and fund of expertise available in their caregiver relationships.

During our workshop discussions of evidence from the projects we gave both intersubjective meshing and JIEs the label of 'good one-to-ones' and were particularly excited by the way JIEs provided a framework for understanding the role of adults in interactions around objects with children from their second year of life. Jenny's project with babies and books, which aimed at encouraging mothers to interact with their babies and toddlers as they shared books, illustrates the continuum of 'good one-to-ones' that was a feature of several of the projects.

Working independently (with just a little help)

This phase marks the final stage in the shift to children's independent action and use of public meanings when they communicate with others in the pre-school years. It is frequently the most difficult for adults to manage as it requires them to maintain sensitivity to children's need for support together with an ability to intervene without inhibiting the flow of children's meaning making in context. In the previous two stages, adults have provided a supporting structure for children's actions and meaning making as part of their close relationships with children. Now the support has to increasingly occur outside relationships that have forms of dependency at their core. We therefore need to look carefully at how adults provide support, or *scaffolding*, at this stage of children's development as learners.

Saffolding has been defined as 'the contingent control of learning' by an adult with a child (Wood 1986). This definition is important because the word 'contingent' reminds us that scaffolding as support needs to be sensitively in response to (that is, contingent upon) the learner's need for assistance. The responsive nature of scaffolding is particularly relevant when working with very young learners who are gaining confidence as effective participants in the world around them and are developing dispositions to engage with the learning opportunities provided.

Scaffolding learning is an interactive process and demands close observation and continuous assessment of children as they participate in the learning contexts provided for them. In some ways scaffolding can be seen as a form of *guided participation*. Scaffolding or guided participation is, however, not simply based on interactions between adults and children. Children's participation in an activity is also, in part, shaped by the resources available and the expectations for the use of the resources in a particular setting.

The children in Alison's construction area were guided into particular ways of participating as builders with blocks by the selection of materials available to them (for example, the sizes of the blocks available, tape measures, role play clothing and paper for recording); and by staff who brought resources to their attention and encouraged them to plan, complete, measure and record. The adult is managing to ensure that the child remains in control of the activity and provides support which is tailored to the learning focus of the construction area.

Learning occurs through the manipulation of the tools of a culture

This feature of a sociocultural approach to understanding learners and learning provides a useful framework for looking at resource-based preschool provision. Cultural tools (Rogoff 1991; Wertsch 1991) include the meanings carried in the language we use – for example, referring to children as 'little' allows them to get away with breaking rules and is a reason for their being sent to bed before their older brothers and sisters. Tools can be intellectual and include the way we think about activities – for example, the children in Alison's centre were encouraged to plan and evaluate. Also, cultural tools are the objects or artefacts with which we surround ourselves and with which we interact in culturally specific ways. For example, although pieces of wooden puzzles make good missiles, we offer them to children as puzzles and expect them to use them as such. Similarly, children are guided into participation in preschool settings by learning the accepted way of using familiar materials, such as sand or water, while in the nursery. We can bring all three features of cultural tools together when we consider how adults help children work with the materials that are available to them in most preschool settings.

In order for children to understand how material resources are used and learn the ways of thinking associated with them they need to experience those resources in conversation with those who do have some understanding. So when first given a wooden puzzle children need to work on it with someone who will use it as a puzzle and not a missile store. While jointly assembling the puzzle, through trial and error or the sorting of pieces, children learn how members of their knowledge communities tackle such tasks. They learn not only the meanings of words 'here is another blue piece', but also how to approach the task by sorting, planning, testing and completing, and they do this, as Bruner (1996: 57) suggests, through 'discourse, collaboration and negotiation'. The role of adults in guiding children into being competent users of the cultural tools of their society is therefore crucial.

How children develop as thinkers

In the previous section we explained how children learn through acting on and trying to make sense of the world around them. We also emphasised that they are enabled in their meaning making by the support of sensitive others who are alert to their current ways of seeing, interpreting and responding. In this section we shall look at some of the features of the meaning making process and pay some, but fairly brief, attention to developmental aspects of children's thinking. We shall focus on children as individual and as social thinkers.

Children as individual thinkers

The frameworks offered by Piaget for understanding how children process the information they glean from their experiences fall into the 'best bet' category. We shall therefore start with them. The key words are *schema, assimilation, accommodation* and *equilibration.* Through these key concepts Piaget's work helps us understand just how learners construct understandings of their worlds.

Schema are the mental structures into which we organise the knowledge we hold about the world. For example, 3-year-old Naomi playing in the water area might think that big things sink and small things float. She will have a sinking/floating schema, which although not in tune with expert knowledge, does work. The schema will change once she experiences enough counter evidence and needs another way of organising that knowledge to make sense of the world.

Assimilation occurs when we take in information which does not demand that we alter our existing schema. For example, another large object that sinks will not require Naomi to adjust her schema. Assimilation can also occur when we experience something that is so beyond our capacity to understand it that we cannot engage with its full cultural meaning and therefore there is no impact on our schema.

From such examples it should be evident that young children frequently find themselves in situations where they simply don't have the knowledge that would allow them to make sense of an object or experience. We see this when children make 'music' with a keyboard, or mark-make when recording orders in the 'cafe'. We also see it when they turn an object to their own purposes and ride a broom handle or hand out leaves as 'cakes'. Much of children's play is therefore assimilation and it is through this kind of imaginative play that children become familiar with the rituals and objects that are part of their worlds. Children need a great deal of assimilation-oriented play, as the familiarisation with objects and how they might be acted upon is an essential part of meaning making.

Accommodation is what happens when we adjust our existing schema to take in new information. This is often simply a case of refining existing schema so that, for example, a child acknowledges through his language and behaviour that there is a schema that both he and adults call 'hat' and that his shorts do not belong to it. Sometimes the adjustment is quite radical, demanding new schema, such as when Naomi recognises that some large objects float and some small objects sink. A strictly Piagetian interpretation might argue that Naomi would manage the reorganisation of her schema without adult help. A more educationally-oriented interpretation, and one we would advocate, would suggest that the adults' role is to provide the language support that helps the children to label their new understanding.

Importantly, accommodation only occurs when the difference between existing schema and the new information is not too great. (Hence the importance of the opportunity for familiarisation through imaginative play.) Problem-solving play is particularly valuable for encouraging accommodation of new information, as during this kind of play children are able to work using their existing schema on materials that have been selected to give them the opportunity to refine those schema. One should not, therefore, see assimilation and accommodation as distinct phases in a learning cycle which can be planned for. Rather they occur together as a child tests out existing understandings and has to adjust them to be able to cope with new information. The meaning-making process can, in this way, be seen as a search for a balance between what is understood and what is experienced.

Equilibration is the term used by Piaget to explain the constant adjustments made to schema by learners as they encounter events which disturb their current understandings and lead them to new explanations and a reorganisation of the relevant schema.

Concluding points

We have focused on learning as a process of increasingly informed participation in the world and have discussed how adults can guide young children's participation in the learning opportunities available in preschool settings. This guidance is seen in adults' sensitive interactions with children and through their careful resourcing of areas of activity. We have emphasised a play-based approach to helping children develop as confident thinkers.

References

Bruner, J. S. (1996) *The Culture of Education.* Cambridge, MA: Harvard University Press.

DES (Department of Education and Science) (1990) *Starting with Quality. Report of the Committee of Enquiry into the Quality of the Educational Experience Offered to 3 and 4 Year Olds.* London: HMSO.

DfEE/SCAA (Department for Education and Employment/School Curriculum and Assessment Authority) (1996) *Desirable Outcomes for Children's Learning on Entering Compulsory Education.* London: DfEE/SCAA.

Rogoff, B. (1991) 'Social interaction as apprenticeship in thinking: guided participation in spatial planning', in L. Resnick, J. Levine and S. Teasley (eds) *Perspectives on Socially Shared Cognition.* Washington: APA.

Schaffer, H. R. (1992) 'Joint involvement episodes as contexts for cognitive development', in H. McGurk (ed.) *Childhood and Social Development: contemporary perspectives.* Hove: Lawrence Earlbaum.

Schweinhart, L. and Weikart, D. (1993) *A Summary of Significant Benefits: The High Scope Perry Pre-School Study Through Age 27.* Ypsilanti, MI: The High Scope Press.

Trevarthen, C. (1997) 'Descriptive analyses of infant communicative behaviour', in H. R. Schaffer (ed.) *Studies in Mother Infant Interaction.* London: Academic Press.

Wertsch, J. (1991) 'A sociocultural approach to socially shared cognition', in L. Resnick, J. Levine and S. Teasley (eds) *Perspectives on Socially Shared Cognition.* Washington: APA.

Wood, D. (1986) 'Aspects of teaching and learning', in M. Richards and P. Light (eds) *Children of Social Worlds.* Cambridge: Polity Press.

Chapter 2

Promoting children's welfare by respecting their rights

Gerison Lansdown and Y. Penny Lancaster

The responsibility for decisions that affect children has traditionally been vested with those adults who care for them. It has been presumed that adults are better placed than young children to exercise responsibility for decision-making and that they will act in children's best interests. This welfare model of adult/child relationships constructs the child as a passive recipient of adult protection and good will, lacking the competence to exercise responsibility for his or her own life.

In recent years, we have begun to question the adequacy of this approach and re-examine the assumptions on which it is based:

- that adults can be relied on to act in children's best interests;
- that children lack the competence to act as agents in their own lives;
- that adults have the monopoly of expertise in determining outcomes in children's lives.

The limitations of a welfare approach

1. Adults can abuse their power over children

Adults in positions of power over children can exploit and abuse that power to the detriment of children's well being. During the 1970s the extent and scale of violence perpetrated by parents on their own children was brought home forcefully in this country with the case of Maria Colwell, an eight-year-old girl who was returned from care to live with her parents who subsequently beat her to death.[1] No opportunity then existed for her views and concerns to be taken seriously by those responsible for the decision. During the 1980s, the phenomenon of sexual abuse within families, as a day-to-day reality for many thousands of children, hit the public consciousness in this country with the Cleveland scandal into sexual abuse of children.[2] There was, and probably still

---

1 *Remember Maria*, John H. Howells, Butterworths, 1974
2 *Report of the Inquiry into Child Abuse in Cleveland*, HMSO, 1988

is, considerable resistance to the recognition that parents and other adult relatives could and do rape and assault their children. Particularly shocking has been the realisation that even babies and toddlers are not exempt from such abuse. It challenges the very notion that children are safest within their families and the comfortable assumption that parents can always be relied on to promote the welfare of their children.

In the 1990s, it became apparent not only that children in public care in a number of local authorities had been subjected to systematic physical and sexual abuse by staff in children's homes, but that these practices had been surrounded by a culture of collusion, neglect, indifference and silence on the part of the officers and elected members within those authorities. One of the most forceful lessons to emerge from a subsequent series of public inquiries into abuse of children in institutional care has been the extent to which those children were systematically disbelieved in favour of adult accounts and denied access to any advocacy to help them articulate their concerns. Indeed, if and when they did complain, they risked further abuse.[3] The adults involved could, with impunity, behave in ways entirely contrary to the children's welfare.

We can no longer disregard that children can be both physically and sexually abused by the very adults who are responsible for their care, within families and in state institutions. It is necessary to move beyond the assumption that reliance on adults to promote the well-being of children, because of their biological or professional relationship with the child, is an adequate approach to caring for children.

2. Adults do not always act in children's best interests

Actions detrimental to the wellbeing of children do not merely occur when adults deliberately abuse or neglect children. During this century, politicians, policy-makers and professionals have been responsible for decisions, policies and actions that have been inappropriate or even harmful to children, while claiming to be acting to promote their welfare. For example, the separation of young children from parents in the war evacuations, the exclusion of mothers from hospital when their small children were sick, in pain and frightened, and the placement of children in care in institutions which stigmatised them and denied them opportunities for emotional and psychological wellbeing. There is now public recognition that children were more harmed than helped by these practices.

Current public policy continues to place disabled children in special schools on grounds of the 'efficient use of resources'.[4] There is concern that the emphasis on attainment targets for preschool children will jeopardise their play opportunities. And there is growing evidence that the massive expansion in out

---

3   *The Pindown Experience and the Protection of Children: the report of the Staffordshire Child Care Enquiry,* Levy, A. and Kahan, B., Staffordshire County Council, 1991 and *The Leicestershire Inquiry 1992,* Kirkwood, A. (Leicestershire County Council 1993), *Lost In Care,* the Tribunal of Inquiry into abuse of children in care in Clywd and Gwynedd, Sir Ronald Waterhouse, DH/Welsh Office, 2000

4   Section 316, Education Act, 1996

of school clubs in order to promote work opportunities for mothers is being developed more as a resource for parents than as a service designed to meet the best interests of children.[5]

3. Parents' rights are protected over those of children

Public policy often supports the rights and interests of parents ahead of those of children, even when the consequences of so doing are detrimental to the welfare of children. In 2000, the Government issued a consultation paper setting out proposals to change the law on physical punishment of children in order to comply with the findings of the European Court of Human Rights that the law in this country failed to protect a child from inhuman and degrading treatment under Article 3 of the European Convention on Human Rights.[6] The consultation set out three questions for consideration. Should the defence of 'reasonable chastisement' be removed from certain forms of physical punishment such as hitting children around the head in ways that might cause brain injury, or damage to the eyes and ears? Should the defence cease to be available against a charge of actual bodily harm? And should the defence be restricted to those with parental responsibility?[7] The consultation document failed to ask the central and most significant question – should parents be allowed to hit their children at all? Although there was considerable pressure on the Government to change the law to remove the defence of 'reasonable chastisement' for parents and to give children the same protection from all forms of assault as adults,[8] the Government refused to do so.

A consultation exercise conducted by Willow and Hyder with 70 children aged 5–7 provides graphic evidence of the humiliation, pain and rejection they experience when their parents hit them. When asked what they understood by a 'smack', they all described it as a hit. Comments such as 'it feels like someone banged you with a hammer', 'it's like breaking your bones', 'it's like you're bleeding' and 'it hurts, it's hard and it makes you sore' were amongst those used to describe how it felt. Their eloquent accounts contrast starkly with the widely promulgated view from parents that such punishment is delivered with love, does not cause real hurt and is only applied *in extremis.*[9]

International law recognises that the continued practice of hitting children represents a breach of their human rights.[10] The Committee on the Rights of the Child has criticised the UK Government for its failure to introduce legislation to protect children from physical punishment by parents and recommended a review of the law to introduce appropriate protection.[11] The Government is not

---

5 Child-centred after school and holiday childcare, Smith and Barker, Children 5–16 research
   programme, ESRC, 2000
6 A v UK, ECHR, 1998
7 *Protecting children: Supporting parents*, DH, 2000
8 *Children are Unbeatable*, Epoch, 2000
9 *It Hurts you Inside*, Willow and Hyder, National Children's Bureau/Save the Children, 1998
10 Article 19, UN Convention on the Rights of the Child
11 CRC/C/Add.34 February 1995

willing to consult on a proposal to end all physical punishment of children because to do so would be seen to interfere with the rights of parents. It is not the welfare of children which informs the law and its proposed reform, but the need to assuage adult public opinion.

4. Children's interests are often disregarded in public policy

Children's interests are frequently disregarded in the public policy sphere in favour of more powerful interest groups. For example, in 1979 one in ten children were living in poverty, and by 1991 the proportion had increased to one in three.[12] Notably, it was children who bore the disproportionate burden of the increase in poverty: no other group in society experienced an increase on a comparable scale. The detrimental consequences on children's life chances were profound – on educational attainment, physical and mental health, emotional wellbeing, and employment opportunities. Countless housing estates have been built in which the needs of children have been completely disregarded – no play spaces or facilities, dangerous balconies, and lifts with controls out of the reach of small children.[13] Public spaces are seen to be 'owned' by adults. Yet these are the adults on whom children rely to promote their best interests, to protect them. At a collective level our society has failed to promote and protect the welfare of children.

Moving beyond a welfare perspective

Once it is acknowledged, not only that adults are capable of abuse of children, but also that children's welfare can be undermined by conflicting interests, neglect, indifference and even hostility on the part of adults, then it becomes clear that it is not sufficient to rely exclusively on adults to define children's needs and be responsible for meeting them. The welfare model has failed children. Children need to be recognised as subjects of rights, a concept that has gained force in recent years, culminating in the adoption by the UN General Assembly in 1990 of the UN Convention on the Rights of the Child. The Convention is a comprehensive human rights treaty, encompassing social, economic, and cultural as well as civil and political rights. Acknowledgement of children as rights-bearers rather than merely recipients of adult protective care introduces a new dimension in adult relationships towards children. It does not negate the fact that children have needs but argues that, accordingly, children have rights to have those needs met.

---

12 *Households below average income* 1979-1990/1, HMSO, 1993
13 *Planning with children for better communities,* Freeman, Henderson and Kettle, The Policy
   Press, 1999

Implications of respecting children's human rights

One of the underlying principles of the Convention is that the best interests of the child must be a primary consideration in all actions concerning the child.[14] And the best interests of children are achieved through the realisation of their rights. This injects two fundamental challenges to traditional approaches to children's welfare.

First, the rights embodied in the Convention provide a comprehensive framework through which to analyse the extent to which policies or services promote the best interests of children, both in respect of individual children and children as a body.[15] It becomes necessary to ask, for example, in respect of child protection, whether service interventions, which seek to protect the child from abuse, also respect the child's right to privacy, to respect for the child's views and evolving capacities, to continuity in family life, to contact with immediate and extended family. In a proposed local housing development, have the rights of children to adequate play facilities and to safe road crossings been fully considered? Unless such a holistic rights-based approach is taken, there is a risk that a decision or intervention is made which responds to one aspect of the child's life and in so doing fails to acknowledge other rights or needs. Indeed, it may inadvertently impact adversely on the child.

Second, if children are subjects of rights, then they themselves must have opportunities to be heard. Article 12 of the Convention stresses that children have the right to express their views on matters of concern to them and to have those views taken seriously in accordance with their age and maturity. Respecting this right to be heard enables children to move beyond their traditional status as recipients of adult care and protection and become social actors entitled to influence decisions that affect their lives.[16] And it applies to all children capable of expressing their views, however young. Children are entitled to be actively involved in those decisions that affect them as individuals – in the family, in schools, in public care, in the courts, and as a body in the development, delivery, monitoring and evaluation of public policy at both local and national levels. Their active participation raises the potential for improved decision-making. In addition, children who from an early age experience respect for their views and are encouraged to take responsibility for those decisions they are competent to make, will also acquire greater confidence to challenge abuses of their rights, and to contribute towards their own protection.

The welfare model of childcare has perpetuated the view that children lack the capacity to contribute to their own wellbeing or that they have a valid and valuable contribution to make. Yet failure to involve children in decisions that affect their own lives is the common thread that underpins many of the mistakes

---

14 Article 3, UNCRC

15 See *Implementation Handbook on the Convention on the Rights of the Child*, Hodgkin and Newell, UNICEF, New York, 1998

16 See, for example, *Taking Part*, Gerison Lansdown, IPPR, 1996 and *Hear! Hear!*, Carloyne Willow, LGIU, 1997

and poor judgements exercised by adults when acting on children's behalf. There is now a growing body of evidence that children, in respect both of individual decisions that affect their lives and as a body in the broader public-policy arena, have a considerable contribution to make to decision-makers.[17] Far from being 'in waiting' until they acquire adult competencies, young children when empowered to do so can act as a source of expertise, skill and information for adults and contribute towards meeting their own needs.

Towards a rights-based model of promoting young children's welfare

The Listening to Young Children project

Coram Family's 'Listening to Young Children' project was established in 2000 when listening to children was increasingly being recognised as important and valid. The primary aim of the project was to understand when 'listening' works for young children and to identify the nature of the relationships and opportunities that enable children under the age of eight to articulate their feelings, experiences, concerns and anxieties.

Underpinning this was the acknowledgement that young children have something worthwhile to say about their lives, they are capable of expressing their viewpoint and, when provided with information, they are competent to make informed decisions. In seeking to move from a model of promoting young children's welfare to an approach that is rights-based the project viewed young children as active players in their environment, people who already have a significant contribution to make in matters that affect their lives.

Although a rights-based approach addresses traditional power relations, young children have not advanced to the status of *the* expert, having the expertise to be the sole decision-makers in their lives. Rather it is about advocating that young children participate in processes that have been traditionally undertaken by adults. Inclusion in decision-making processes is not premised on the exclusion of others – parents, carers or other significant people in their lives. Participation in this sense is about pulling up another chair alongside those already present within these processes so that the *voices* of young children are also heard.

An ethical package

Central to the project has been the respect that Article 12 of the UN Convention on the Rights of the Child affords young children. The project

---

17 See for example, *Children's Consent to Surgery*, Priscilla Alderson, OUP, 1993, *Children's Rights in the Balance: the participation–protection divide*, Kathleen Marshall, Stationery Office, 1997, *Children in Charge: the child's right to a fair hearing*, ed. Mary John, Jessica Kingsley, 1996

utilised the three elements in Article 12 to translate the rhetoric of respect into rights-based practice:[18]

- Respecting children's right to appropriate information
- Respecting children's diverse views
- Respecting children's right to participate in matters that affect their lives

Methodology

The methodology of the project has been multi-layered.

Younger children

Young children participated in the planning, designing and evaluation processes of the project. Their perspectives contributed to developing an understanding of why, when and how listening works for children under the age of eight, of how they are making sense of their world and the kind of listeners they need to be heard.

Children as consultants

We met regularly with older children to gather their views on how we should conduct the research, the obstacles that might exist and methods that might be useful, and facilitated training sessions so that they could participate as research assistants.

Parent focus-group discussions

Gathering views from parents – for example, on the use of the video camera in helping them increase their understanding of their child's competency – was underpinned with the value of respecting parents' existing skill as their child's first educator.

Professional forums

'Listening to Young Children' facilitated discussions with professionals from the education, social and health sectors, so that there was a platform for an exchange of ideas on how to promote listening policy and practice.

---

18 The ethical package is described in Coram Family's forthcoming publication: Lancaster, Y. Penny and Broadbent, Vanessa (2003) *Listening to Young Children*, Open University Press

Summary

The UN Convention on the Rights of the Child has played a significant role in calling for children's views to be taken seriously. Article 12 in particular details the importance of children being given opportunities to express their opinion about issues that are important to them. The view that young children are competent to express their opinions and participate in decision-making processes evokes a range of feelings amongst parents, and professionals alike – anxious that it challenges traditional ways of organising family life and that the authority they have to act in the best interests of their children may be undermined. The Listening to Young Children project has developed a rights-based resource, *Listening to Young Children*[19] using the visual arts to promote the welfare of young children, but within a framework that secures that the rights of others are likewise upheld. The resource supports parents and practitioners to relate more effectively with the young children they work with and/or care for.

Conclusion

There is a continuing resistance to the concept of rights for children in this country. It is a resistance shared by many parents, politicians, policy makers and the media. It derives, at least in part, from a fear that children represent a threat to stability and order if not kept under control. Further, it reflects the strong cultural tradition that children are 'owned' by their parents and the state should play as minimal a role as possible in their care.

Promoting the rights of children is about moving away from the discredited assumption that adults alone can determine what happens in children's lives without regard for children's own views, experiences and aspirations. It means accepting that children, even very small children, are entitled to be listened to and taken seriously. It means acknowledging that as children grow older they can take greater responsibility for exercising their own rights. A commitment to respecting children's rights does not mean abandoning their welfare. It means promoting their welfare by adherence to the human rights standards defined by international law.

---

19 See Coram Family's forthcoming publication: Lancaster, Y. Penny and Broadbent, Vanessa (2003) *Listening to Young Children*, Open University Press

Chapter 3

Identity, self-esteem and learning

Iram Siraj-Blatchford and Priscilla Clarke

In all of our modern multicultural societies, it is essential that children learn to respect other groups and individuals, regardless of difference. This learning must begin in the very earliest years of a child's education. In this chapter we identify the groups that are often disadvantaged owing to the poor understanding many early years staff have of them. We argue that there is a need to challenge the hidden oppression that is often imposed upon particular individuals and groups. While most early childhood settings appear to be calm and friendly places on the surface, we argue that there may be a great deal of underlying inequality. This may occur through differential policies, interactions, displays, or through variations in the curriculum or programme that the staff offer to some individuals or groups. These are important issues to be considered because they concern the early socialisation of all of our children. In the early years children are very vulnerable and every adult, and other children as well, has the power to affect each child's behaviour actions, intentions and beliefs.

Children can be disadvantaged on the grounds of diversity in ethnic background, language, gender and socio-economic class in both intentional and in unintentional ways. The structures through which inequity can be perpetuated or measured are related to societal aspects such as employment, housing or education. For instance, we know that women earn less than men, as a group, and that working-class people live in poorer homes. We are concerned with the structural inequalities that create and support an over-representation of some groups in disadvantaged conditions. However, we do caution against the assumption that all members of a structurally oppressed group, for example, *all girls*, are necessarily oppressed by those members of a structurally dominant group, for example, all boys. Because of the interplay between social class, gender, ethnicity and disability, identities are multifaceted. We therefore argue that children can hold contradictory individual positions with respect to the structural position that their 'group' holds in society. Interactional contexts are also often highly significant.

We will end the chapter by identifying the salient features of effective and ineffective practice in challenging oppression and in promoting respect for children, for parents and for staff in early child care and education settings (Siraj-Blatchford 1996).

The complexity of identity

A number of authors have written about the origins of inequality, about the implications for practice, and the need for a truly inclusive pedagogy and curriculum in the early years (see Davies 1989; Lloyd and Duveen 1992; Siraj-Blatchford 1992, 1994; Clarke 1993; Siraj-Blatchford and Siraj-Blatchford 1995). We argue here that children can only learn to be tolerant, challenge unfair generalisations and learn inclusiveness and positive regard for diversity if they see the adults around them doing the same. Children will often imitate adult behaviour whether it is positive or negative, but they need to learn to discuss what they already know, just as we do (Brown 1998).

The way children feel about themselves is not innate or inherited, it is learned. A number of researchers (Lawrence 1988; Siraj-Blatchford 1994) have shown that positive self-esteem depends upon whether children feel that others accept them and see them as competent and worthwhile. Researchers have also shown the connection between academic achievement and self-esteem. Purkey (1970) correlates high self-esteem with high academic performance. Positive action to promote self-esteem should form an integral part of work with children and ought to be incorporated into the everyday curriculum. Roberts (1998) argues that the process by which all children develop their self-esteem and identity rests heavily upon the type of interactions and relationships people form with young children.

Identity formation is a complex process that is never completed. The effects of gender, class and other formative categories overlap, in often very complicated ways, to shape an individual's identity. While we do not attempt to discuss this complexity in detail, it is important for practitioners to be aware of the nature of shifting and changing identities. No group of children or any individual should be essentialised (in other words, defined and bound within this definition as if it were impossible for any individual to escape this) and treated as having a homogeneous experience with others of their 'type'.

It is important to highlight the complexity of identity formation in children. To ignore it is to ignore the child's individuality. It illustrates why each minority ethnic child and every girl or child with disabilities does not perceive themselves in the same way. In fact, children from structurally disadvantaged groups often hold contradictory positions, which is why we might find in our classrooms black and other minority ethnic children who are very confident and academically successful in spite of the structural, cultural and interpersonal racism in society. Similarly, we will find working-class boys who do not conform to a stereotype and are caring and unaggressive and African-Caribbean boys who are capable and well behaved. We should not be surprised at any of this (Siraj-Blatchford 1996).

The sexism, racism and other inequalities in our society can explain why at a structural level certain groups of people have less power while others have more. But at the level of interaction and agency we should be critically aware of the danger of stereotyping and should focus on individual people. This is not to suggest that we should ignore structure, far from it, we need to engage in developing the awareness of children and staff through policies and practices that explain and counter group inequalities. We will turn to the point of practice later. What we are suggesting is that educators need to work from a number of standpoints to fully empower the children in their care. Children need to be educated to deal confidently and fairly with each other and with others in an unjust society (Siraj-Blatchford 1992, 1994, 1996).

Recent research has focused on the under-sevens. Many educators have begun to ask how it is that young children who are in our care learn about and experience class bias, sexism and racism. We know that children pick up stereotypical knowledge and understanding from their environment and try to make their own meanings from this experience. Outside experiences can come from parental views, media images and the child's own perceptions of the way people in their own image are seen and treated. In the absence of strong and positive role models children may be left with a negative or a positive perception of people like themselves.

Many parents and staff conclude from children's behaviour that they are naturally different, without considering their own contribution to the children's socialisation. Difference, therefore, is also a matter of social learning, as well as physiology. This has implications for practice and the kinds of activities to which we should make sure all children have access, regardless of their gendered or other previous experiences.

Identity and achievement

Cultural identity should be seen as a significant area of concern for curriculum development (Siraj-Blatchford 1996). All children and adults identify with classed, gendered and racialised groups (as well as other groups), but what is especially significant is that some cultural identities are seen as less 'academic' than others (often by the staff and children). We know that children can hold views about their 'masterful' or 'helpless' attributes as learners (Dweck and Legett 1988). Dweck and Leggett (1988) therefore emphasise the importance of developing 'mastery' learning dispositions in children. There is evidence that children who experience education through taking some responsibility for their actions and learning become more effective learners. They are learning not only the content of the curriculum but the processes by which learning takes place (Siraj Blatchford 1998). Roberts (1998) argues that the important area of personal and social education should be treated as a curriculum area worthy of separate activities, planning and assessment.

The 'helpless' views' adopted by some children can be related to particular areas of learning and can lead to underachievement in a particular area of the curriculum. Children construct their identities in association with their perceived cultural heritage (Siraj-Blatchford 1996). Recently we have heard a good deal in the British press about (working-class) boys' underachievement. The results from the school league-tables suggest that some boys do underachieve in terms of basic literacy, but it is important to note that this is only certain groups of boys and not all boys. In the UK working-class white boys and African-Caribbean boys are particularly vulnerable. Similarly, children from some minority ethnic groups perform poorly in significant areas of the curriculum while other minority ethnic groups achieve particularly highly (Gillborn and Gipps 1997).

It is apparent that certain confounding identities, for instance, white/working-class/male, can lead to lower outcomes because of expectations held by the children and adults. In asserting their masculinity, white working-class boys might choose gross-motor construction activities over reading or pre-reading activities. Similarly, some girls may identify more strongly with home-corner play and favour nurturing activities over construction choices. Class, gender and ethnicity are all complicit here and the permutations are not simple, but they do exist and do lead to underachievement. The answer is to avoid essentialising children's identities, but it also requires educators to take an active role in planning for, supporting and developing individual children's identities as masterful learners of a broad and balanced curriculum (Siraj-Blatchford 1998).

Diversity, equality and learning

Four main conditions need to be satisfied for learning to take place; we want to argue here that we need an understanding of the first two to lay the foundations for learning:

- the child needs to be in a state of emotional wellbeing and secure;
- the child needs a positive self-identity and self-esteem;
- the curriculum must be social/interactional and instructive;
- the child needs to be cognitively engaged.

It is widely recognised that an integrated, holistic and developmental approach is needed to learning, teaching and care with children from birth to 7. Many adults believe children remain innocent, but even the very youngest children are constantly learning from what and who is around them. They learn not only from what we intend to teach but from all of their experiences. For example, if girls and boys or children from traveller families are treated differently or in a particular manner from other people then children will learn about the difference as part of their world-view. To deny this effect is to deny that children are influenced by their socialisation. The need for emotional, social, physical, moral, aesthetic and mental wellbeing all go hand in hand.

The early years curriculum should therefore incorporate work on children's awareness of similarities and differences, and to help them to see this as 'normal'. For instance, research evidence produced by David Milner (1983) has shown that children have learned positive and negative feelings about racial groups from an early age. Milner suggests that children as young as three demonstrate an awareness of a racial hierarchy in line with current adult prejudices (1983: 122) Some children can be limited in their development by their view that there are people around them who do not value them because of who they are. This would suggest that early years staff need to offer *all* children guidance and support in developing positive attitudes towards all people. A focus on similarities is as important as dealing with human differences (see Siraj-Blatchford and Macleod-Brudenell 1999). The early years is an appropriate time to develop this work with young children.

How do young children who are in our care experience and learn about social class or linguistic prejudice, sexism or racism? How does this affect their learning more generally? These are questions that staff need to address. We know that children adopt biased (both good and bad) knowledge and understanding from their environment. This can be from parental views, media images, and the child's own perceptions of the way people are seen and treated. The most common form of prejudice young children experience is through name-calling or through negative references by other children (or adults) to their gender, dress, appearance, skin colour, language or culture. Educators may hear some of these remarks and it is vital that these are dealt with appropriately as they arise. The following childlike remarks have deep consequences for the children who utter them, and for those receiving them:

'You're brown so you're dirty.'
'Girls can't play football.'
'Don't be a sissy.'
'Boys can't skip.'
'She's got dirty clothes.'

Early years educators are often worried about their lack of experience and their lack of knowledge and understanding in dealing with these matters. They often display a profound sense of inadequacy when faced with prejudice from children. They may also doubt whether name-calling is wrong and they might even see it as 'natural behaviour' (Siraj-Blatchford 1994).

Students, teachers, childminders and playgroup workers have often asked how they can deal with class, gender and ethnic prejudice. The first step is to recognise that the problem exists. As Davey (1983) has argued, we have to accept that a system of racial categorisation and classification exists and that, until it is finally rejected by everyone, it will continue to provide an irresistible tool by which children can simplify and make meaning of their social world. It would be a great mistake to assume that this is only a 'problem' in largely multi-ethnic settings. Strategies which allow children to discuss, understand and deal with oppressive behaviour aimed at particular groups such as minority ethnic children, girls, the disabled and younger children are essential in all settings. We suggest that educators should always make opportunities for stressing similarities as well as differences.

Promoting positive self-esteem

Early childhood educators have an instrumental role to play in this development. Staff need to help children learn to guide their own behaviour in a way that shows respect and caring for themselves, other children and adults, and their immediate and the outside environment. Values education goes hand-in-hand with good behaviour management practices. The way that adults and children relate to each other in any setting is an indication of the ethos of that setting. To create a positive ethos for equity practices, staff in every setting will need to explore what the ethos in their setting feels like to the users, such as parents, children and staff. Staff need to explore what behaviours, procedures and structures create the ethos, what aspects of the existing provision are positive and which are negative, and who is responsible for change.

Children need help from the adults around them in learning how to care for each other and to share things. To help the children in this respect, the educator must have the trust of the children and their parents: Young children's capacity to reflect and see things from another person's point of view is not fully developed. Most small children find it difficult to see another person's view as equally important. Children need a lot of adult guidance to appreciate the views and feelings of others. This can be learnt from a very early age. In her research on the relationship between mothers and their babies, and relationships between very young siblings, Judy Dunn (1987) suggests that mothers who talk to their children about 'feeling states' have children who themselves 'become particularly articulate about and interested in feeling states' (1987: 38). Consideration for others has to be learnt.

We believe that children need educators who will consciously:

- encourage positive interactions;
- encourage discussion about how they and others feel;
- encourage attention to other points of view;
- encourage communication with others;
- try to ensure that they learn constructive ways to resolve differences;
- promote co-operation, not competition.

(Adapted from Stonehouse 1991: 78)

Of course educators cannot expect children to behave in this way if they do not practise the same behaviour themselves. If children see us showing kindness, patience, love, empathy, respect and care for others, they are more likely to want to emulate such behaviour. For many educators the experience of working actively with children in this way may be underdeveloped, especially when it comes to dealing with incidents of sexism or racism. Each setting, as part of their equity policy, will need to discuss the issue of harassment and devise procedures for dealing with it. According to Siraj-Blatchford (1994) staff can take some of the following actions in dealing with incidents of name-calling:

Short-term action

- If you hear sexist, racist or other remarks against other people because of their ethnicity, class or disability, you should not ignore them or you will be condoning the behaviour and therefore complying with the remarks.
- As a 'significant other' in the children's lives, they are likely to learn from your value position. Explain clearly why the remarks made were wrong and hurtful or offensive, and ask the abused children and the abusers how they felt so that the children can begin to think actively about the incident.
- Do not attack the children who have made the offending remarks in a personal manner or imply that the children are wrong, only that what was said is wrong.
- Explain in appropriate terms to the abusers why the comment was wrong and give all the children the correct information.
- Support and physically comfort the abused children, making sure that they know that you support their identity and that of their group and spend some time working with them on their activity.
- At some point during the same day, work with the children who made the offending remarks to ensure that they know that you continue to value them as people.

Long-term action

- Target the parents of children who make offensive discriminatory comments to ensure that they understand your policy for equality, and that you will not accept abuse against any child. Point out how this damages their child.
- Develop topics and read stories which raise issues of similarities and differences in language, gender and ethnicity and encourage the children to talk about their understandings and feelings.
- Create the kind of ethos that promotes and values diverse images and contributions to society.
- Involve parents and children (depending on the age of the children) in decision-making processes, particularly during the development of a policy on equality.
- Talk through your equality policy with all parents as and when children enter the setting, along with the other information parents need.
- Develop appropriate teaching and learning strategies for children who are acquiring English so that they do not get bored, frustrated and driven to poor behaviour patterns.

(Adapted from Siraj-Blatchford 1994)

Working towards effective practice

The identity (or ethos) of the early childhood setting is very important (Suschitzky and Chapman 1998). We identify six stages of equity oriented practice, stage one being the least desirable and least developed practice in the area. These are based on our own and other colleagues' experiences within and observations of a very wide range of early years settings. The six stages are not meant to be prescriptive or definitive, but they are intended to stimulate discussion and thought among early years staff and parents. Different kinds of beliefs and practices are identified that promote or hinder the implementation of equity practices that allow children, parents and staff to feel either valued or devalued.

Stage 1

Discriminatory practice – where diversity according to gender, class, ability or cultural and racial background is seen as a disadvantage and a problem, and no effort has been made to explore positive strategies for change. There is a separatist, or overtly racist, sexist and/or classist environment. We may observe some of the following:

- Staff believe that all children are 'the same' and that sameness of treatment is sufficient regardless of a child's gender, social class, special needs or ethnicity.
- Parents are blamed for children not 'fitting in' to the way the setting functions and that if parents are dissatisfied with the service they should take their children elsewhere.
- Inflexible curriculum and assessment procedures which do not reflect a recognition for the need for positive minority ethnic or gender role models, multilingualism in society or sufficient observations that detect special needs.
- There is no policy statement of intent, or policy documents relating to equal opportunities. British culture, child rearing patterns, etc., are universalised.

Stage 2

Inadequate practice – where children's special needs are recognised according to disability but generally a deficit model exists. If children who perform poorly also happen to be from a minority ethnic group this is seen as contributory. Gendered reasons may be given for poor achievement. Alternatively the parents are blamed for being inadequate at parenting. We may observe some of the following:

- There is a general acceptance that staff are doing their best without actually undertaking staff development for equality issues except for special needs.
- It is recognised that extra resources should be provided for children with English as an additional language, but it is felt that this is a special need which

should be met by an English as an Additional Language (EAL) teacher or assistant, and that 'these' children will find it difficult to learn until they have acquired a basic grasp of English.

- Staff encourage children to play with a range of resources but no special effort is being made to encourage girls to construct or boys to play in the home corner.
- Staff do not know how to, or do not want to, challenge discriminatory remarks because they feel the children pick these up from home, and they do not feel they can raise these issues with parents.

Stage 3

Well meaning but poorly informed practice – where staff are keen to meet individual children's needs and are receptive to valuing diversity. We may observe some of the following:

- Token measures at valuing diversity can be observed, for example, multilingual posters, black dolls and puzzles and books with positive black and gender role models may be found but are rarely the focus of attention.
- There is an equal opportunities policy statement but this does not permeate other documents related to parent guides, curriculum or assessment.
- Staff respond positively to all parents and children and appreciate diversity as richness but are not well informed about their cultures or about anti-racist, sexist or classist practice.
- Bilingual staff are employed as extra 'aides' or 'assistants'.

Stage 4

Practice that values diversity generally where some attempts are made to provide an anti-discriminatory curriculum and environment. We may observe some of the following:

- There is a centre policy on equal opportunities which includes promoting gender, race and other equality issues.
- Staff are inhibited through worries about parents raising objections to anti-racist or anti-sexist practice.
- Resources are applied which promote anti-discriminatory work and special activities to promote racial harmony and gender and race equality are practised. All children are observed carefully to detect any special learning needs.
- Children's home languages are valued and attempts are made to encourage parents to support bilingualism at home.

Stage 5

Practice that values diversity and challenges discrimination, where equal opportunities is firmly on the agenda. We may observe some of the following:

- The centre staff have made a conscious effort to learn about inequality through staff development and someone is allocated with responsibility for promoting good practice in the area.
- There is a policy statement on equal opportunities and a document which applies the statement of intent to everyday practice, curriculum evaluation and assessment and to the positive encouragement of anti-discriminatory activities.
- Staff observe the children's learning and interactions with equality in mind and develop short- and long-term plans to promote self-image, self-esteem, language and cultural awareness.
- Staff are keen to challenge stereotypes and confident to raise issues with parents and support them through their learning if they hold negative stereotypes.
- Bilingual staff are employed as mainstream staff.

Stage 6

Challenging inequality and promoting equity, where staff actively try to change the structures and power relations which inhibit equal opportunities. We may observe some of the following:

- Staff value the community they work in and encourage parents to be involved in decision making. Bi/multi-lingualism is actively supported.
- The management take full responsibility for promoting equal opportunities and try positively to promote their service to all sections of the community.
- Management actively seek to recruit more male and minority ethnic staff.
- The equal opportunities policy is monitored and evaluated regularly and staff are confident in their anti-discriminatory practice.
- Equality issues are reflected across curriculum, resources, assessment and record keeping and the general ethos of the centre.
- Parents and children are supported against discrimination in the local community.
- Staff know how to use the UK Sex Discrimination Act, Race Relations Act, the Warnock Report, Code of Practice, the Children Act and the United Nations Convention on the Rights of Children to achieve equality assurance

(Adapted from Siraj-Blatchford 1996)

A positive self concept is necessary for healthy development and learning and includes feelings about gender, race, ability, culture and language. Positive self-esteem depends on whether children feel that others accept them and see them as competent and worthwhile. Young children develop attitudes about themselves and others from a very early age and need to be exposed to positive images of diversity in the early years setting. Children need to feel secure and to learn to trust the staff that care for them in order to learn effectively.

References

Brown, B. (1998) *Unlearning Discrimination in the Early Years*. Stoke-on-Trent: Trentham Books.

Clarke, P. (1993) 'Multicultural perspectives in early childhood services in Australia', *Multicultural Teaching*, Stoke-on-Trent: Trentham Books.

Davey, A. (1983) *Learning to be Prejudiced*. London: Edward Arnold.

Davies, B. (1989) *Frogs and Snails and Feminist Tales*. St Leonards, NSW: Allen & Unwin.

Dunn, J. (1987) 'Understanding feelings: the early stages', in J. Bruner and H. Haste (eds) *Making Sense: the child's construction of the world*, 26–40. London: Routledge.

Dweck, C. S. and Leggett, E. (1988) 'A social-cognitive approach to motivation and personality', *Psychological Review* **95** (2): 256–73.

Gillborn, D. and Gipps, C. (1997) *Recent Research on the Achievements of Minority Ethnic Pupils*. London: HMSO.

Lawrence, D. (1998) *Enhancing Self-esteem in the Classroom*. London: Paul Chapman.

Lloyd, B. and Duveen, G. (1992) *Gender Identities and Education*. London: Harvester Wheatsheaf.

Milner, D. (1983) *Children and Race: ten years on*. London: Ward Lock Educational.

Purkey, W. (1970) *Self-concept and School Achievement*. London: Paul Chapman.

Roberts, R. (1998) 'Thinking about me and them: personal and social development', in I. Siraj-Blatchford (ed.) *A Curriculum Development Handbook for Early Childhood Educators*, 155–74. Stoke-on-Trent: Trentham Books.

Siraj-Blatchford, I. (1992) 'Why understanding cultural differences is not enough', in G. Pugh (ed.) *Contemporary Issues in the Early Years*. London: Paul Chapman.

Siraj-Blatchford, I. (1994) *The Early Years: laying the foundations for racial equality*. Stoke-on-Trent: Trentham Books.

Siraj-Blatchford, I. (1996) 'Language, culture and difference', in C. Nutbrown *Children's Rights and Early Education*, 23–33. London: Paul Chapman.

Siraj-Blatchford, I. (1998) (ed.) *A Curriculum Development Handbook for Early Childhood Educators*. Stoke-on-Trent: Trentham Books.

Siraj-Blatchford, J. and Siraj-Blatchford, I. (eds) (1995) *Educating the Whole Child: cross-curricular skills, themes and dimensions in the primary schools*. Buckingham: Open University Press.

Siraj-Blatchford, J. and MacLeod-Brudenell, I. (1999) *Supporting Science, Design and Technology in the Early Years*. Buckingham: Open University Press.

Stonehouse, A. (1991) *Opening the Doors: childcare in a multicultural society*. Melbourne, Victoria: Australian Early Childhood Association Inc.

Suschitzky, W. and Chapman, J. (1998) *Valued Children, Informed Teaching*. Buckingham: Open University Press.

Chapter 4

Supporting all children – moving towards inclusion in the early years

Sheila Wolfendale and Alice Paige-Smith

Introduction

This chapter provides a review of recent developments in special needs in the early years. A number of concepts, principles and values are examined which are put into the context of special needs legislation and policy evolution, and a number of issues are explored.

Values and principles

In this chapter we acknowledge and celebrate achievements in special needs/early years, commensurate with early years issues becoming higher on the education agenda. So a number of notable developments will be chronicled. At the same time we want to demonstrate a broad responsibility on the part of all early years practitioners towards the distinctive learning and developmental needs of all children, in creating opportunities for them to flourish.

Rights and opportunities

It is a fairly recent phenomenon that special needs and disability areas have been perceived to come within the orbit of equal opportunities, belatedly joining 'race, sex and class' as major educational and social issues. The language of the Warnock Report (1978), the Education Act 1981 and its accompanying Circular 1/83 was not couched in equal opportunities terms but these in part paved the way for the perspective propagated within the Education Reform Act 1988 that pupils with special educational needs have a fundamental, inalienable entitlement to the National Curriculum. These rights to access to all available curriculum and educational opportunities became a bedrock principle permeating educational thinking including that of those working in preschool and multidisciplinary settings (Cameron and Sturge-Moore 1990).

The broadest universal context for these developments was the moral imperative provided in the International Convention on the Rights of the Child (Newell 1991). This convention adopted by the United Nations General Assembly in 1989 has been signed by the majority of countries. It is a set of international standards and measures that recognises the particular vulnerability of children, brings together in one comprehensive code the benefits and protection for children scattered in scores of other agreements and adds new rights never before recognised. Once the Convention was signed and ratified by 20 countries (and this was attained), it had the force of international law.

This will and should have implications at every level of policy, decision-making, provision and practice of children from birth, if the fundamental premise is to protect and guarantee children's rights. A number of Articles within the Convention are explicitly geared towards special needs and disability.

The placing of special needs in the early years on the agenda

Significant developments to 1996

a) The public and legislative agenda: focus on education.

Government reports on early years in the 1970s and 80s include:

- **The Warnock Report** in 1978 gave under fives and special needs a higher profile by recommending it as a priority area in terms of teacher training and increased provision. Emphasis was given to the proven effectiveness of intervention programmes, including Portage. The Warnock Report paved the way for the legislation that amended existing law on special education, namely the Education Act 1981 (implemented from 1 April 1983), which conferred new duties on local education and health authorities in respect of identifying and assessing young children with possible special needs.
- **The Education Reform Act 1988** had implications for the education of four-year-olds in infant schools (Dowling 1995) and for the applicability of the National Curriculum for young children with special educational needs.
- **The Education Act 1993**, Part 3 of which referred exclusively to special educational needs. This strengthened a number of parental rights and clarified the assessment process. Schools were also required by law to have written acccountable SEN policies.
- **The 1994 Code of Practice** constituted a set of guidelines to which LEAs and schools must have 'due regard' in the planning and delivery of SEN services.

Parent Partnership:
The 1994 Code of Practice acknowledged the importance of partnership between LEAs, child health and social services in working together to meet the needs of children under five with SEN. Parents of children under five with SEN

were able to express a preference for a particular maintained school to be named in their child's statement.

The 1993 Education Act also introduced the Special Educational Needs Tribunal (SENT) for parents who seek redress against decisions over their children's SEN with which they disagree. There is plenty of evidence, for example from Ofsted reports, that schools, progressively from 1994–5 were indeed having 'due regard' to the Code of Practice.

The period, around the mid-1990s, also saw increased manifestation of inter-agency co-operation, as witnessed by the introduction of Children's Services Plans which require local agencies to dovetail and co-ordinate their provision for children with special needs and disabilities (Roffey 1999).

b) The parents' agenda

The various Acts have enshrined and latterly strengthened a number of parental rights. Many parents themselves have translated rhetoric and principles into a number of realities and practical action, which include:

- Finding a collective voice: a number of local, regional and national parents' groups emerged, and parents of children with SEN have begun to share their views and concerns more widely (Gascoigne 1995; Wolfendale 1997a).
- Empowerment, via the emergence of parent advocacy, representation, self-help, and parent-professional coalitions (Armstrong 1995; Garner and Sandow 1995; Hornby 1995).
- Participating in assessment processes (Wolfendale 1993).
- Parents as educators, as in Portage and other home-based early learning schemes.

The 1994 Code of Practice set out a number of key principles for establishing and facilitating parent-professional partnership, and illustrated how this can be effected throughout the implementation of the Code. The 'message' was further reinforced via the existence of Department for Education and Employment grant (GEST) from 1994 to 1997 to LEAs and schools to set up and maintain Parent Partnership Schemes.

Significant developments in early years and special needs from 1997

This section of the chapter outlines the changes in policy and practice initiatives which have placed an emphasis on inclusion in the early years.

A political and policy-driven educational agenda for special needs, with reference to early years

Several months after the Labour Government came to power in 1997, it published a Green Paper (DfEE October 1997) which signalled an intention to reframe SEN policy and practice. On the basis of this 'manifesto' and responses to consultation, a year later the SEN Programme of Action was published (DfEE 1998). This landmark publication heralded a number of significant changes, chief amongst which were: revision of the 1994 SEN Code of Practice; revision of the SEN Tribunal procedures; enhancement of parent partnership; investment in early years. The guiding principles include 'promoting the inclusion of children with SEN within mainstream schooling wherever possible...' (p.8).

Of especial relevance to early years providers and practitioners is the cross-reference to Early Years Development and Childcare Plans and Partnerships and to the advent of Sure Start, both of which are discussed later in this chapter, as are several other areas mentioned in the Programme of Action, such as parents, multi-agency working, and the revised Code of Practice.

The Green Paper and Programme of Action are, of course, manifestations of a 'top down' approach, yet much of the substance of these documents reflects existing 'on the ground' practice, so that there is consonance between public policy and local execution. Indeed, the documents were welcomed by local SEN policy-makers and practitioners. The 2001 Special Educational Needs and Disability Act (SENDA) supersedes the 1981 Education Act and has increased children's rights to be educated in mainstream schools. Inclusion in mainstream under the 1981 Act used to have to take into consideration that a child's placement had to take into account 'the efficient use of resources'; this condition has been removed by SENDA.

The 2001 SEN Code of Practice

The two-fold rationale for revising the Code of Practice is that (a) procedures, especially the five-stage model, are thought to need improving and streamlining, and (b) many post-Code SEN and related developments and initiatives need to be incorporated into a revised Code of Practice. The 2001 Code deals with principles, partnership with parents, identification, assessment, review and provision across all age-phases, and multi-agency work. There is a whole new section on Pupil Participation.

Early years workers will welcome incorporation of and cross-reference to Early Years Development and Childcare Partnership; to the newly-designated (since 1999) Foundation stage of education for children aged 3–5 years and associated QCA curriculum guidance to an on-entry-to-school Baseline Assessment, mandatory since September 1998 and replaced by the Foundation Stage Profile during 2003 (QCA 2003). All early education settings which receive government funding are expected to have regard to the Code of Practice. They are also expected to identify a member of staff to act as the special educational needs co-ordinator: this role may be shared among individual childminders or playgroups and the co-ordinator of the network. The responsibilities vary from liaising with parents and professionals to organising the child's individual education programme (DfES 2001: 34, para 4.15). The SEN Toolkit (DfES 2001) provides additional guidance to the 2001 Code of Practice and contains information on issues and action on supporting children and managing individual education programmes.

The 2001 Code of Practice does away with the staged approach described earlier in this chapter and replaces it with two clear action points: School Action and School Action Plus. For early years, these are designated Early Years Action and Early Years Action Plus. This approach is described as 'a graduated response so as to be able to provide specific help to individual young children' (para 4.10, p.33), and 'once practitioners have identified that a child has SEN..., the provider should intervene through Early Years Action' (para 4.11, p.33) and if further advice and support are needed, then Early Years Action Plus is triggered, leading to statutory assessment. Figure 4.1 represents and illustrates a whole range of SEN responsibilities on the part of schools, early years settings, practitioners, policy-makers and parents in the immediate post Code of Practice era. It illustrates interconnections as well as individual and collective responsibilities in the area of SEN.

An agenda for the early years

This section contextualises the preceding SEN discussion, by drawing readers' attention to the broader early years terrain, of which SEN is a part.

After the Labour Government took office in May 1997, it set out its National Childcare Strategy, of which increased childcare provision is a major plank, and proceeded to set up local Early Years Development and Childcare Partnerships, which bring together maintained, private and voluntary sector providers with local education authorities, social services departments, health services and parent representatives in the planning and provision of services in the early education sector, including delivery of services to meet SEN.

All early years government-funded providers must (a) have regard to the SEN Code of Practice, and (b) have a written SEN policy. Also, one of the criteria by which Early Excellence Centres are thus designated is that of meeting and providing for special needs (DfEE 2000).

Radical changes to assessment are also changing the early years landscape. The Qualifications and Curriculum Authority (QCA) created a Foundation Stage for children aged three to the end of the academic year in which they are five, and has developed and trialled a set of Early Learning Goals (ELG). In 2000 the ELG were applied within all government-funded nursery/early years settings from September 2000 and the QCA issued a pack of curriculum guidance for the foundation stage (QCA 2000) to support practitioners in supporting children to work towards and attain the ELG. A page-long section in the Guidance (pp.18–19) is devoted to discussion as to how practitioners can meet additional, extra needs of some young children. This advice is sensible but couched in general terms and unfortunately makes no cross-reference to the 2001 Special Educational Needs Code of Practice to assist early years workers through procedures for identifying and assessing SEN.

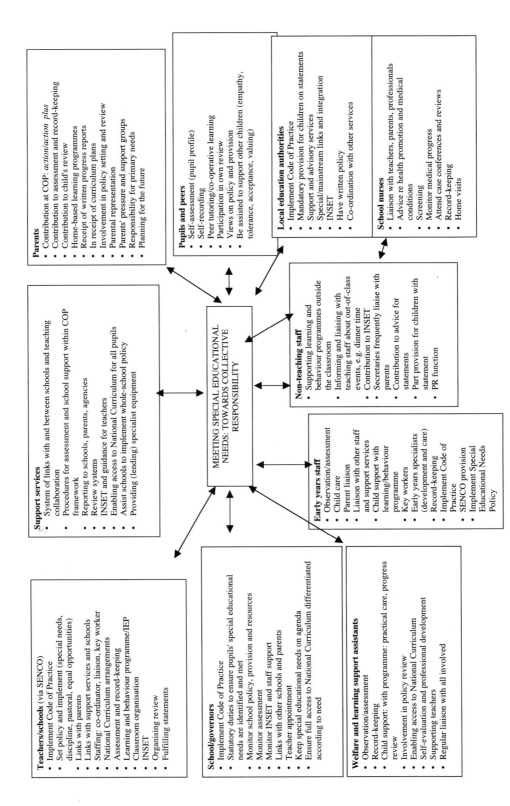

Parents
- Contribution at COP: *action/action plus*
- Contribution to assessment and record-keeping
- Contribution to child's review
- Home-based learning programmes
- Receipt of written progress reports
- In receipt of curriculum plans
- Involvement in policy setting and review
- Parental representation
- Parents' pressure and support groups
- Responsibility for primary needs
- Planning for the future

Pupils and peers
- Self-assessment (pupil profile)
- Self-recording
- Peer tutoring/co-operative learning
- Participation in own review
- Views on policy and provision
- Be assisted to support other children (empathy, tolerance, acceptance, valuing)

Local education authorities
- Implement Code of Practice
- Mandatory provision for children on statements
- Support and advisory services
- Special/mainstream links and integration
- INSET
- Have written policy
- Co-ordination with other services

School nurses
- Liaison with teachers, parents, professionals
- Advice re health promotion and medical conditions
- Screening
- Monitor medical progress
- Attend case conferences and reviews
- Record-keeping
- Home visits

Support services
- System of links with and between schools and teaching collaboration
- Procedures for assessment and school support within COP framework
- Reporting to schools, parents, agencies
- Review systems
- INSET and guidance for teachers
- Enabling access to National Curriculum for all pupils
- Assist schools to implement whole-school policy
- Providing (lending) specialist equipment

MEETING SPECIAL EDUCATIONAL NEEDS: TOWARDS COLLECTIVE RESPONSIBILITY

Non-teaching staff
- Supporting learning and behaviour programmes outside the classroom
- Informing and liaising with teaching staff about out-of-class events, e.g. dinner time
- Contribution to INSET
- Secretaries frequently liaise with parents
- Contribution to advice for statements
- Part provision for children with statement
- PR function

Early years staff
- Observation/assessment
- Child care
- Parent liaison
- Liaison with other staff and support services
- Child support with learning/behaviour programme
- Key workers
- Early years specialists (development and care)
- Record-keeping
- Implement Code of Practice
- SENCO provision
- Implement Special Educational Needs Policy

Teachers/schools (via SENCO)
- Implement Code of Practice
- Set policy and implement (special needs, discipline, pastoral, equal opportunities)
- Links with parents
- Links with support services and schools
- Staffing: co-ordinator, liaison, key worker
- National Curriculum arrangements
- Assessment and record-keeping
- Learning and behaviour programme/IEP
- Classroom organisation
- INSET
- Organising review
- Fulfilling statements

School/governors
- Implement Code of Practice
- Statutory duties to ensure pupils' special educational needs are identified and met
- Monitor school policy, provision and resources
- Monitor assessment
- Monitor INSET and staff support
- Links with other schools and parents
- Teacher appointment
- Keep special educational needs on agenda
- Ensure full access to National Curriculum differentiated according to need

Welfare and learning support assistants
- Observation/assessment
- Record-keeping
- Child support: with programme: practical care, progress
- Involvement in policy review
- Enabling access to National Curriculum
- Self-evaluation and professional development
- Supporting teachers
- Regular liaison with all involved

Figure 4.1 Collective responsibility for SEN

The 2001 Code of Practice refers to on-entry-to-school Baseline Assessment (BA), another key area of early years assessment. The inclusion of a special needs dimension into Baseline Assessment schemes (QCA 1997) is one of the key accreditation criteria that BA schemes had to meet, to be accepted and accredited by the QCA. That is, scheme providers (mostly LEAs) had to be able to demonstrate that their assessment schemes were sensitive enough to identify early-appearing learning or behaviour difficulties, and areas of concern to do with learning and adjustment (Wolfendale 2000b). Replacing the BA is the Foundation Stage Profile (QCA 2003) which is based on practitioner observations recorded using a set of 13 assessment scales that are related to the early learning goals.

A cornerstone of the present Government's drive to tackle child poverty and social inclusion is the ambitious, long-term Sure Start programme (Russell 2000). The Government has invested £452,000,000 to set up 250 Sure Start projects across England within the life of the current Parliament. The programme aims are to improve the health, wellbeing, and therefore life-chances of children before and after birth, offering services such as family support, advice on parenting, increased/better access to health care and other services.

Each programme has to make a clear statement on special needs and developing ways of working with families that complement existing services. There is also a clear commitment to the early identification of special educational needs and social inclusion. Each programme has to set out:

- the different provision and services available to young children with special educational needs and their families
- arrangements made by existing service providers for early identification, assessment and support for young children with special educational needs
- details of specialist provision and services.

In addition to the SURE START programme is the £435,000,000 set aside in 2003 for a three-year programme to fund Children's Centres for at least 650,000 children under 5 living in disadvantaged areas in England. This initiative will add services to Sure Start local programmes, Neighbourhood Nurseries and Early Excellence Centres, as well as developing nursery schools and other settings (DfES 2003).

We can see that there is a whole mosaic of early childhood developments and policies and a significant number of local initiatives, some of which, although related to the theme of this chapter, are outside its scope and parameters. For example, the reader is referred to Wade and Moore (2000) for a description of Bookstart, an early years family literacy approach, and to Mortimer (2000) for models and ideas for developing individual behaviour plans in the early years, and Wolfendale (2000a) for discussion on intervention and for accounts of providing for young children with special needs and disabilities, some in inclusive settings.

Promoting partnership with parents in SEN

The 'parents' agenda' was introduced earlier in the chapter, along with a brief résumé of notable earlier developments. Contributors to a book examining the impact of the (1994) SEN Code of Practice upon parent partnership (Wolfendale 1997a) felt that, although much had been achieved in parent–professional, home–school co-operation, there was still a long way to go.

There is now further accumulating evidence of progress towards a working partnership that is in the best interests of children with SEN. Two research reports, both commissioned by the DfEE (Department for Education and Employment) provided considerable data on the service delivery of the burgeoning LEA-based Parent Partnership Services (PPS). Wolfendale and Cook (1997) and Vernon (1999) describe a wide range of activities by PPS staff, which include provision of information about SEN to parents (leaflets, resources, handbooks), direct casework, advocacy, conciliation, and oversight of Named Persons Schemes (typically volunteers who work with and support parents whose children are going through statutory assessment and beyond).

The provision of PPSs within LEAs has been seen by governments (pre- and post-1997) as an effective vehicle to provide parent-focused services, which at best epitomise partnership (see Wolfendale and Cook 1997 for discussion on partnership criteria) and at the least offer information, support and sympathy. The present Government is committed to extending PPS and, via legislation, ensuring that all LEAs will have these, as well as a system for independent parental support (replacing Named Persons) and conciliation arrangements. The Code of Practice sets out a helpful table summarising the roles and responsibilities of LEAs, schools, independent parental supporters and voluntary groups in promoting partnership with parents (DfES 2001, 2.31, p.26; and see Wolfendale 2002).

In fact, a Government-driven ideological commitment to enhancing and supporting the parental contribution to all child-focused services is pervasive across services and agencies, with an especial emphasis upon the early years. Parents/carers must be represented on local Early Years Development and Childcare Partnerships; Sure Start (see above) is essentially family-focused, and the Government is equally committed to expansion of parenting education and support programmes (Wolfendale and Einzig 1999) and has created the National Family and Parenting Institute, operational from 1999 (address in references), which has a remit to be a voice for families, to raise awareness of the importance of parenting and family relationships, and to undertake a range of activities to realise these and other aims.

Towards a systemic and equitable approach to meeting special needs in the early years

Inclusion

The inclusion ideology is now subscribed to by Government departments, local agencies, and an increasing number of schools (Sebba and Sachdev 1997;

Alderson 2000) although definitions and models of inclusion still do vary (Widdows 1997).

Practical handbooks aimed at supporting early years workers to implement inclusive policies include the Preschool Learning Alliance publication (1999) and Dickens and Denziloe (1998) who provide a myriad of practical proposals as to how to operate inclusive practice. From an overarching strategy framework for implementing inclusive practice the reader is referred to the CSIE Index for Inclusion as a comprehensive resource (CSIE 2000). The SEN and Disability Rights in Education Act (2001) is expected to reinforce a commitment towards inclusive practice. The guidance on the statutory framework for inclusion *Inclusive schooling – children with special educational needs* (DfES 2001) provides case study examples of ensuring inclusion in schools and local education authorities. The values and ethos required for inclusive settings are also specified. However, it remains the case that notwithstanding increased commitment to this principle, there has to be commensurate matched funding to support the introduction of physical and other human resources that are needed to change long-standing separatist practices.

Judging quality and effectiveness of provision for young children with SEN and their families

Service providers nowadays expect to be assessed and judged as to the quality and effectiveness of what they offer. The system that has applied for several years is that of Ofsted, which has now unified its early years inspection regimes under the jurisdiction of its Early Years Directorate, which has been responsible for the registration and inspection of about 80,000 childminders and 25,000 early years settings from September 2001. A number of early years quality assurance models have been proposed (see Wolfendale 1997b for a brief review) and what all these signify is that a principled approach to early years provision must include transparency and accountability procedures.

A performance and evidence-based approach to service delivery and evaluation is increasingly taking hold (NCB Highlight 170 1999).

> Children and their families have a right to expect that our interventions in their lives will be based on the best available knowledge.
>
> (Macdonald and Roberts 1995: 3)

Provision that comes under the aegis of local Early Years Development and Childcare Partnerships is expected to conform to providing evidence of effectiveness and thus build in suitable monitoring and evaluation procedures. The ambitious SURE START programme (see earlier) has a number of aims, targets and objectives, the realisation or not of which will be key planks of the national and local evaluation strategy.

To support SURE START workers, the DfEE-based SURE START Unit produced a handbook *A Guide to Evidence-based practice* (SURE START 1999) which provides a description and review of around 20 early intervention programmes, and commentary on the research and evidence-base of each. The preface states:

Evaluation is necessary to know whether services are succeeding in their objectives and to discover which aspects of the way they function are contributing to, or detracting from, that success.

(p.4)

A handbook which uses a similar formula but which includes a greater number and range of services is Utting (1999).

Summary

We have witnessed, and many readers are participating in, radical changes and developments which impact directly upon the lives, learning and wellbeing of all young children, including those deemed to have special needs. Those of us who are committed to equality of opportunity can only hope that these changes are now irreversible, and that they will provide the building blocks for further improvements and innovations in provision and services for young children.

References

Alderson, P. (2000) *Young Children's Rights: exploring beliefs, principles and practice*. London: Jessica Kingsley Publishers.

Armstrong, D. (1995) *Power and Partnership in Education*. London: Routledge.

Cameron, J. and Sturge-Moore, L. (1990) *Ordinary everyday families: Under Fives Project*. MENCAP London Division, 115 Golden Lane, London, EC1Y 0TJ.

Code of Practice on the Identification and Assessment of Special Educational Needs. (1994) London: DFE/HMSO.

CSIE (2000) *Index for Inclusion*. Centre for Studies on Inclusive Education, 1 Redland Close, Elm Lane, Redland, Bristol, BS6 6UE.

Department of Education and Science (1978) *The Warnock Report, Special Educational Needs*. London: HMSO.

Department of Education and Employment (DfEE). London: Stationery Office:
- *Excellence for all children, meeting SEN* (1997, October).
- *Meeting SEN, a programme of action* (1998).
- *Early Excellence Centres: First Findings* (1999, Autumn).
- *SEN Code of Practice on the Identification and Assessment of Pupils with SEN and SEN Thresholds: good practice guidance on identification and provision for pupils with SEN* (2000, July).

Department of Education and Skills (DfES). London: Stationery Office:
- *Inclusive schooling* (2001).
- *SEN Toolkit* (2001).
- *SEN Code of Practice* (2001).

Department for Education and Skills (DfES) *Children's Centres Give Children a Sure Start – Clarke*, Press Notice, 25 March 2003, 0044. http://www.dfes.gov.uk/pns/DisplayPN.cgi?pn_id=2003_0044.

Dickens, M. and Denziloe, J. (1998) *All together – how to create inclusive services for disabled children and their families: a practical handbook for early years workers.* London: National Early Years Network.

Dowling, M. (1995) *Starting School at Four: a joint endeavour.* London: Paul Chapman Publishing Ltd.

Garner, P. and Sandow, S. (eds) (1995) *Advocacy, Self-Advocacy and Special Needs.* London: David Fulton Publishers.

Gascoigne, E. (1995) *Working with Parents as Partners in SEN.* London: David Fulton Publishers.

Hornby, G. (1995) *Working with Parents of Children with Special Needs.* London: Cassell.

Macdonald, G. and Roberts, H. (1995) *What Works in the Early Years? Effective Interventions for Children and their Families in Health, Social Welfare, Education and Child Protection.* Barkingside, Essex: Barnardo's.

Mortimer, H. (2000) *Developing Individual Behaviour Plans in Early Years.* Tamworth: NASEN.

Newell, P. (1991) *The UN Convention and Children's Rights in the UK.* London: National Children's Bureau.

Preschool Learning Alliance (1999) *Inclusion in preschool settings.* 69 Kings Cross Road, London, WC1X 9L.

Qualifications and Curriculum Authority (QCA) (1997) *The National Framework for Baseline Assessment; criteria and procedures for the Accreditation of BA schemes.* London: QCA.

Qualifications and Curriculum Authority (QCA) (2000) *Curriculum Guidance for the Foundation Stage.* London: QCA.

Qualifications and Curriculum Authority (QCA) (2003) *Foundation Stage Profile.* London: QCA.

Roffey, S. (1999) *Special Needs in the Early Years.* London: David Fulton Publishers.

Russell, P. (2000) 'Developing a comprehensive and integrated approach to early years services for children with SEN opportunities and challenges in current Government initiatives', in Norwich, B. (ed.) *Early Years Development and SEN, Policy Paper 3.* Tamworth: NASEN.

Sebba, J. and Sachdev, D. (1997) *What works in Inclusive Education.* Barkingside, Essex: Barnardo's.

Sure Start (1999) *A Guide to Evidence-based Practice* (2nd edn) London: DfEE.

Utting, D. (ed.) (1999) *A Guide to Promising Approaches.* London: Communities that Care.

Vernon, J. (1999) *Parent Partnership and SEN: perspectives on developing good practice*, Research Report 162. Suffolk: DfEE Publications.

Wade, B. and Moore, M. (2000) 'Starting Early with Books', Ch.8 in Wolfendale, S. and Bastiani, J. (eds) *The Contribution of Parents to School Effectiveness.* London: David Fulton Publishers.

Widdows, J. (1997) *A Special Need for Inclusion.* London: Children's Society.

Wolfendale, S. (1993) 'Involving Parents in Assessment', Ch.9 in Wolfendale, S. (ed.) *Assessing Special Educational Needs.* London: Cassell.

Wolfendale, S. and Cook, G. (1997) *Evaluation of SEN Parent Partnership Schemes,* Research Report 34. Suffolk: DfEE Publications.

Wolfendale, S. (ed.) (1997a) *Working with Parents of SEN Children after the Code of Practice.* London: David Fulton Publishers.

Wolfendale, S. (ed.) (1997b) *Meeting Special Needs in the Early Years, directions in policy and practice.* London: David Fulton Publishers (reissued 2000).

Wolfendale, S. and Einzig, H. (eds) (1999) *Parenting Education and Support, new opportunities.* London: David Fulton Publishers.

Wolfendale, S. (ed.) (2000a) *Special Needs in the Early Years: snapshots of practice.* London: Routledge.

Wolfendale, S. (ed.) (2002) *Parent Partnership Services for Special Educational Needs; celebrations and challenges.* London: David Fulton Publishers.

Helpful references

Lewis, A. and Lindsay, G. (eds) (2000) *Researching Children's Perspectives.* Buckingham: Open University Press.

National Family and Parenting Institute, Unit 431, Highgate Studios, 53-79 Highgate Road, London, NW5 1TL.

National Children's Bureau Highlight No. 170 (1999) *Evidence-based Child Care Practice.* London: NCB.

Sayeed, Z. and Guerin, E. (2000) *Early Years Play: a happy medium for Assessment and Intervention.* London: David Fulton Publishers.

Wilson, B. (1998) *SEN in the Early Years.* London: Routledge.

Wolfendale, S. (ed.) (2000b) 'Special Needs in the Early Years: policy options and practice prospects', in Norwich, B. (ed.) *Early Years Development and SEN,* Policy Paper 3. Tamworth: NASEN.

Chapter 5

Parent partnership and inclusion in the early years

Alice Paige-Smith

Introduction

In this chapter I consider different perspectives towards parents of children with learning difficulties and disabilities and how the concept of parent partnership has developed. An analysis of policy documents which describe parent partnership indicates that there has been a shift in perspective from a 'supportive' model in the 1970s towards a 'rights' model represented in the Special Educational Needs Code of Practice (DfES 2001). Parents are considered to have the right to participate in their child's education and to indicate their choices in their child's schooling. Local Education Authorities are instructed in the Code to provide parents with independent advisers to support them in making these choices. This shift will be outlined in this chapter by considering the conflicting attitudes between parents and professionals and how one particular group of parents supported and became involved in the education of their children in the early years.

Parents and professionals

Since the 1981 Education Act there has been a repositioning of 'special educational needs' in the early years within an inclusive framework (Wolfendale 2000). Issues of inclusion in the early years were firstly recognised in the Green Paper *Excellence for All Children, Meeting Special Educational Needs* (DfEE 1997) and the subsequent Programme of Action (DfEE 1998) announced initiatives such as Sure Start (Wolfendale 2000). Alongside these developments there has been a growth in expertise for practitioners working in the early years with children who experience difficulties in learning or have disabilities (Wolfendale 2000). The notion of 'parent partnership' in the early years has also been recognised in the curriculum guidance for the Foundation Stage (QCA 2000).

The 1981 Education Act represented a major change in the education of children; the term 'special educational needs' replaced previous categories of learning difficulties that had been based on assessments by professionals. This term came out of discussions during the Warnock Committee in 1978 which recognised that 20 per cent of all children would experience difficulties at some time during their school career. The Committee also acknowledged that input from parents was important during the assessment process. A statement of special educational needs was recommended by the Warnock Report (DES 1978) as a way of assessing a child's needs and provision, and in 1981 parents were given the legal right to participate in this process. Approximately two per cent of children have statements of their special educational needs.

However, while the 1978 Warnock Report had a chapter dedicated to parent partnership this could be considered to have a patronising attitude towards parents. Professionals are considered to be the people who know or are the 'experts' on the child. This theme recurs throughout the education of children with learning difficulties and disabilities and the notion of parent partnership has developed as a way of recognising the tensions that exist between parents and professionals. An example of the attitudes towards parents is in this extract from the Warnock Report (DES 1978):

> Parents must be assisted to understand their child's difficulties. They must also be helped to adopt attitudes to him most conducive to his feeling that he is accepted and has the same status in the family as any brothers or sisters.
>
> (Department of Education and Science 1978: Section 7.19)

Parents are considered to need help in order to understand and accept their child. Models of how parents 'parent' their child who has a disability or learning difficulty have been proposed by professionals (Mittler and Mittler 1982; Cunningham and Davis 1985). These may neglect the difference in the power relationship between parents and professionals and also the relationship with the child.

Professionals and prejudicial attitudes

Incidences of prejudicial attitudes towards disability and difficulties of learning abound in the literature on parents' experiences. Professional practice may fail to consider the best interests of the child where his or her opinions differ from those of the parents. Doctors have been criticised for the way they break the news to the parent that they have a disabled child because they prejudge the child:

> When my son was two he was diagnosed at a London hospital. I [the father] saw the doctor. He just told me that my son was an imbecile, then closed the interview by ringing for the next patient.
>
> (Furneaux 1988: 9)

The parents of this child were told by a paediatrician to 'put him away and forget you ever had him' (Furneaux 1988). These parents found the doctor's judgements painful to experience. They did not perceive their child in the same way as their doctor. Birth and the early years are considered to be hard for parents especially if they have a child with a learning difficulty or a disability. They are recognised to go through stages of shock through to acceptance during the diagnosis of their child's learning difficulty or disability (Cunningham 1982). Some parents have attempted to redefine what this period of time is like for them. They stress the negative attitudes of other people towards their child, including professionals (Goodey 1992). The lack of sensitivity which parents face at the time of the diagnosis of their child's learning difficulty or disability in the early years has been acknowledged by the guidelines *Right from the Start* (Scope 2003) produced by Scope – a disability charity whose focus is cerebral palsy – a number of voluntary bodies and the Department of Health (DfES 2003). These guidelines support professionals in how to break the news of disability and the advice 'promotes a culture of respect for children and parents' (DFES 2003).

Parents – challenging ideologies

Challenging perceptions of disability or of difficulties of learning is an experience common to parents of children born with Trisomy 21 (so-called Down's syndrome). Chris Goodey (1992) researched how parents' experiences clashed with the professionals' perceptions of parenting a child with Trisomy 21. Contrary to the myth that the child is automatically rejected by the parent who 'mourns the death of the normal child that didn't emerge', Goodey reports that parents feel the expectation of rejecting their child is imposed on them. Parents are subjected to ideologies of how disability is perceived, in the first instance, by professionals, like doctors and nurses, and others, such as family members. He suggests in his research, carried out with 18 families, that parents challenge perceptions of disability and difficulties in learning held by professionals in the medical field. He claims that parents become 'includers' through their experiences and contact with members of the 'excluded' group, and their power to change prevailing views is negated by the institutionalised power of professionals, who define and dominate practice. Goodey, as a parent of a child with Trisomy 21, is advocating inclusion as a belief, or a philosophy. He suggests that an inclusive philosophy may be held by parents and others who have experienced a 'shift in human values'.

Parents' experiences and views – ensuring inclusion

What are parents' experiences if they have a child with learning difficulties or disabilities: what are their experiences in the early years: how do these relate to their involvement in education and their choice of inclusion? Robina Mallett set up a parents' group in the West of England to support parents and provide information for them. She has articulated what it is like to be a parent – she could be considered to be a 'professional parent' as she provides advice, information and support for other parents:

The title a professional acquires gives status, recognition of the body of knowledge they have achieved and perhaps reinforces self-confidence. The social standing of a parent of a child with 'special needs' seems to depend, to an extent, on the disability experienced. This can range between 'super human' to 'ineffectual parent'. Wherever the judgement rests we may be perceived uncomfortably – other parents feeling sorry for us or suspecting we resent their 'better fortunes'. We are (accidentally one hopes) frequently called 'special needs parents'!

(Mallett 1997: 29)

Other parents have set up parents' groups since the 1981 Education Act and I interviewed eight parents to find out what their experiences had been and why they had become involved in setting up parents' groups (Paige-Smith 1996). The experiences of these parents indicate that they had similar philosophies and attitudes towards their children; these influenced the choice of schooling for their children. Jane's experiences illustrate the barriers in ensuring inclusion and how some of these barriers were overcome.

Jane's experiences

Jane had set up a parents' campaign and support group with other mothers whose children attended a preschool playgroup: they wanted their children to attend mainstream schools rather than a special school, which was the practice of the local education authority. When Jane's son was a year old he was diagnosed as having cerebral palsy. Jane joined a local playgroup funded by social services and MENCAP. This playgroup had been established in her town for children referred by social services because the children experienced difficulties in learning or had a disability. When all the mothers from the playgroup met they realised they had a common concern:

We all got together one day and the biggest thing we were concerned about was education. Talking together we all found that we had a common concern about our kids – that when they reach five, where are they going to go?

Jane

This group of parents became concerned about the practice of sending all children with disabilities or learning difficulties to special schools. Jane was not satisfied with the prospect of this for her son:

If a child had spina bifida, say, or cerebral palsy, or a physical disability they would be bussed or taxied to Coventry which is the nearest school. So, for young children, often as young as four, because they often liked them to go to nursery, they would be spending up to two hours travelling. We thought that was appalling, given all the problems our kids have anyway, you know, isolation, to spend all that time travelling – and it's very expensive.

(Jane)

The mothers from the playgroup arranged for a parents' group from Coventry to visit and talk to them. They were impressed with this group and decided to set up a campaign and support group in order to try to ensure the inclusion of their children into mainstream school. Jane described how the parents' group emerged out of a group of parents who shared similar views on what they wanted for their children. The group, which began with a group of mothers meeting informally, turned into a structured group with a set of aims. They gathered and disseminated information to support their campaign, they decided on a name and met every week. The parents were asking for support for their children to attend mainstream school; however, the local authority wanted the children to attend special schools:

> They were saying 'I'm sorry but I have got no money'. I mean it always came down to resources. They said, 'look the special school, is there – there is separate funding for that and for mainstream'. They didn't have a policy, the authority didn't even have a written policy, they were just hoping that they could carry on as normal. They were saying, 'we've got the set up and that is it, basically'.
>
> (Jane)

The parents' group responded to the 'deadlock' situation with the local authority by providing individual support for parents by attending meetings with them to talk to education officers. The group also ensured that people with disabilities at open meetings provided information on disability awareness issues. As people came to talk at the meetings from different parts of England the parents recognised that inclusion varied according to location. This knowledge strengthened the aims of the group and reduced their sense of isolation.

Jane put her son's name down at the nursery at the local school where her eldest son attended. However she found the head teacher hostile to her son attending her school, and she was very concerned about the prejudicial attitudes towards her son's disability:

> The head teacher said 'O.K. well, we'll see when the time comes'. Anyway when the time did come the letter that was sent out to welcome new parents to the nursery, I didn't have one. So I went to her and said, 'O.K. what's going on?' – she was quite frightened of us actually, and she avoided me for quite a long time, and I cornered her in the hall in the school and I got very upset about it and I drafted a letter to the governors and she wouldn't have him and I said 'Why won't you take Alexis?' I mean it's awful when you are actually saying 'Well he's quite a nice boy really' and all this kind of shit. You know, having to sort of persuade people to take your children to school, and she [the headteacher] said: 'Well he'd take up too much space, and maybe later, when he'll be walking by that time', because he had a rollator then, he wasn't walking at that time.
>
> (Jane)

The head teacher told Alexis' father that she feared she would get a flood of handicapped children in the school if she let Alexis and another child with disabilities in. Alexis' parents were told by an education officer that 'he wouldn't want his son in a classroom with a handicapped child in it'. These prejudicial attitudes meant that Alexis' parents were unable to trust professionals:

> They would say lots of things and then they would completely deny that they said that and so we had a policy that we would take a tape recorder in to meetings, or I

would go along and take notes, and they didn't like that at all, that really got up their nose. But of course, they would say things in one breath and then say they'd never said them. I mean you couldn't trust them at all.

(Jane)

The authority had an 'unwritten' policy of refusing full-time support in mainstream. Alexis was finally granted 10 hours' support in mainstream because of his difficulties in reading and writing. Jane feels that his support benefited the whole class and the class teacher because she had an 'extra pair of hands'. The decision to make this support available to her son was made by an education officer. Jane thought that the authority had 'backstepped' on their decision not to provide support because of the cost of transporting her son to special school.

Jane managed to ensure that her son was integrated into his local school. However, three other parents from the group tried for three years to get their children into their local mainstream school. It proved harder for these parents because, Jane suggests, their children were categorised as having 'severe learning difficulties'. The appeal process experienced by these parents has been written about by Will Swann (1987). The barriers to their inclusion were the local authority's inability to provide support in mainstream for these pupils and the lack of flexibility of the special schools to provide support in mainstream for these pupils.

The parents continued to work through encouraging disability awareness in their local community. The group were also involved in the national parents' group Network '81. The two groups found that they had a common aim for parents, children and young people.

Parental Involvement

Robina Mallett (1997) has written about her involvement in setting up the parents' group in the West of England and the services and support that are provided for parents. Jane's experiences also illustrate how parents' collective experiences can lead to their empowerment and involvement in decision making concerning their child's education. Major changes have occurred in the development of parents' rights since the 1981 Education Act, as the Special Educational Needs and Disability Act (2001a) has recognised children's rights to attend mainstream school and parents' rights to assert this choice. The power of Local Education Authorities, and hence professionals, to segregate children in special schools has been reduced through the changes in education law which have been campaigned for by disabled people and parents' groups (Rieser 2001).

In the curriculum guidance for the Foundation Stage (QCA 2000) there is a section on 'Parents as partners' which recognises that each setting should develop an effective partnership with parents which consists of:

- A two-way flow of information, knowledge and expertise

Practitioners should:

- show respect and understand the role of the parent

- listen to parents' accounts of their child's development and any concerns they have
- make parents feel welcome
- use the knowledge and expertise of parents and other family adults to support learning
- keep parents fully informed about the curriculum
- talk about and record children's progress and achievements
- extend relevant learning and play activities such as reading and sharing books, so that they continue at home.

(QCA 2000: 9)

The guidance for children with special educational needs and disabilities also suggests that:

Early years practitioners have a key role to play in working with parents to identify learning needs and respond quickly to any area of particular difficulty, and to develop an effective strategy to meet these needs, making good use of individual education plans, so that later difficulties can be avoided.

(QCA 2000: 18)

The foundation stage documentation for England does suggest that there are links between parental involvement and the curriculum of the child. It is suggested that parents should be informed about their child's experiences and their progress and that activities should be extended into the home. The involvement of parents in their children's learning is also emphasised in the Scottish Curriculum Framework for Children 3–5 which recognises the need for staff to value the role of parents in their young child's learning in order to create a 'genuine partnership' between parents and staff (SCCC 1999). The Northern Ireland Curricular Guidance for Pre-School Education (NICCEA 1997) suggests that the child's first educator is the parent, and that adults working with preschool children should be partners with parents. The Welsh Desirable Outcomes for Children's Learning before Compulsory School Age suggests that a feature of good practice is that parents should be acknowledged as educators, requiring partnership with practitioners: 'based on shared understanding, mutual respect and discussion' (ACCAC 2000: 9). Individual Education Programmes provide a way of recording and evaluating children's learning if they have learning difficulties or disabilities that can be shared with the parents. The English Foundation Stage documentation also recognises the value of parents' views and that practitioners should listen to parents. Robina Mallett, who set up the parents' group in the West of England, suggested that:

Parents often are the only people who know everything that has happened to the child. They actually carry a body of knowledge that the other professionals haven't shared in whether they are carrying messages from the medics about diagnosis and things which just haven't been shared. It is often as if the parent is the *key worker* in what is going on. Some will be able to cope with that, others can't. What they actually know should be respected. They know that their children need encouragement... they know when they get tired, they know their likes and dislikes and how much they like being teased or joked with.

(Robina)

Conclusion

The Special Educational Needs Code of Practice (DfES 2001) does recognise this perspective and parents are considered to hold 'key information' and to have a 'critical role to play in their children's education' (DfES 2001: 16). Effective communication with parents by professionals, according to this document, should draw on parental knowledge and expertise in relation to their child. However, in the section on key principles in communicating and working in partnership with parents, the role of parents as participants in supporting their children's learning is not emphasised. The section on the roles and responsibilities of schools and, in particular, the Special Educational Needs Co-ordinator, notes that parents should be encouraged to participate, but that they may need 'emotional support', indicating that there may be conflict experienced by parents (DfES 2001: 26). The role of local education authorities and parent partnership has been outlined in the Code of Practice (DfES 2001), LEAs are instructed to provide 'access to an independent Parental Supporter for all parents who want one' as well as 'accurate, neutral information on their rights, roles and responsibilities within the SEN process, and on the wide range of options that are available for their children's education' (DfES 2001: 21).

The Code of Practice (2001) does acknowledge the ways in which parents should be provided with information and support in order to understand their rights and roles in the education of their child with a learning difficulty or a disability. The 1978 Warnock Report suggested that parents should be 'helped' to adopt the right attitudes towards their child; the shift in the past 20 years has been towards a 'rights' model of parent partnership. Perhaps this shift is due to the actions of parents and parent groups who have campaigned for changes in the attitudes and perspectives of professionals.

This chapter is based on the chapter 'Parent partnership in the early years' in *Exploring Early Years Education and Care* (2002) eds Miller, L., Drury, R. and Campbell, R., London: David Fulton Publishers, pp. 90–100.

References

ACCAC (2000) *Desirable Outcomes for Children's Learning before Compulsory School Age.* Cardiff: Qualifications, Curriculum and Assessment Authority for Wales.

Cunningham, C. (1982) *Down's Syndrome: an introduction for parents.* London: Souvenir Press.

Cunningham, C. and Davis, H. (1985) *Working with Parents: frameworks for collaboration.* Milton Keynes: Open University Press.

Department of Education and Science (1978) *The Warnock Report, Special Educational Needs.* London: HMSO.

Department of Education and Science (1981) *The Education Act 1981.* London: HMSO.

Department for Education and Employment (1997) *Excellence for all Children: meeting special educational needs*. London: Stationery Office.

Department for Education and Employment (1998) *Meeting Special Educational Needs: a programme of action*. London: DfEE.

Department for Education and Skills (2001) *Special Educational Needs Code of Practice*. Nottinghamshire: DfES Publications.

Department for Education and Skills (2001a) *The Special Educational Needs and Disability Act*. London: HMSO.

Department for Education and Skills (2003) *Disabled children to get more support*, DfES Press Notice 2003/0078, info@dfes.gsi.gov.uk

Furneaux, B. (1988) *Special Parents*. Milton Keynes: Open University Press.

Goodey, C. (1992) 'Fools and heretics: parents' views of professionals' in Booth, T. *et al. Policies for Diversity in Education*, 165–76. London: Routledge.

Mallett, R. (1997) 'A parental perspective on partnership' in Wolfendale, S. (ed.) *Working With Parents of SEN Children After the Code of Practice*, 27–40. London: David Fulton Publishers.

Mittler, P. and Mittler, H. (1982) *Partnership with Parents*. Stratford-on-Avon: National Council for Special Education.

Northern Ireland Council for the Curriculum, Examinations and Assessment (1997) *Curricular Guidance for Pre-School Education*. Belfast: NICCEA.

Paige-Smith, A. (1996) 'Choosing to campaign: a case study of parent choice, statementing and integration', *European Journal of Special Needs Education* **11**, (3), 321–29.

Qualifications and Curriculum Authority (QCA) (2000) *Curriculum Guidance on the Foundation Stage*. London: Qualifications and Curriculum Authority/DfEE.

Rieser, R. (2001) 'New Act a turning point: disability, special educational needs and the law' *Inclusion Now* **2**, 4–5.

Scope (2003) *Right from the Start – template*. London: Scope.

Scottish Consultative Council on the Curriculum (1999) *Curriculum Framework for Children 3–5*. Dundee: SCCC.

Swann, W. (1987) 'Statements of intent: an assessment of reality', in Booth, T. and Swann, W. (eds) *Including Pupils with Disabilities*. Milton Keynes: Open University Press.

Wolfendale, S. (2000) 'Special needs in the early years: prospects for policy and practice', *Support for Learning* **15** (4), 147–51.

Chapter 6

A folk model of assessment – and an alternative

Margaret Carr

When I was a beginning kindergarten teacher, twenty years ago, I believed that assessment was about checking to see whether the nearly-school-age children had acquired what I considered to be the requisite skills for school: the list included early writing (writing their name), self-help skills, early mathematics (counting), turn-taking scissor-cutting. I therefore looked out for the gaps in a school-readiness repertoire, keeping a checklist, and used some direct teaching strategies to do something about them in the months before school. I did not find the process interesting or helpful to me, but I certainly saw it as linked to my reputation as a competent early childhood teacher with the children's families and with the local schools.

There are a number of assumptions about assessment here, and twenty years later I don't hold any of them. My interest has been captured by children like four-year-old Emily, an articulate and confident child, who, when her friend Laura tells her that she has done a jigsaw 'wrong', shouts angrily 'No! Don't call me wrong. If you call me wrong I won't let you stroke my mouse.' I am intrigued by processes in the kindergarten whereby Jason changes the simple activity of 'marble-painting' into a complex and difficult process, teaches Nell (who normally avoids this kind of difficulty) and then Nell teaches Jinny and Nick. In one activity in one centre I frequently hear 'good girl' from the adults but I never hear 'good boy', although boys are participating too. I pursue Myra and Molly who are practising a language that I have called *girl-friend-speak*, a language that involves reciprocal and responsive dialogue but appears to exclude Lisa. I interview Danny about what he finds difficult, and he tells me that it is drawing the triangular back windows of cars. I read a story to two-year-old Moses and he puzzles about whether the ducks have feet under the water, and what kind of feet they are. I hear Trevor advising his friend that if he finds something difficult he should just leave it. I puzzle about whether there is learning going on both above and 'under the water', what kind of learning it is, how we might assess it, and whether, as early childhood educators, it is any of our business.

I have called those twenty-year-old ideas of mine about assessment my 'folk' model of assessment. David Olson and Jerome Bruner (1996) point out that these everyday intuitive theories and models reflect deeply ingrained cultural beliefs and assumptions. In the case of my folk model of assessment, the assumptions were about: the *purpose* for assessment (to check against a short list of skills that describe 'competence' for the next stage of education), *outcomes of interest* (fragmented and context-free school-oriented skills), *focus for intervention* or attention (the deficits), *validity* of assessment data (objective observations of skills, reflected in a checklist, are best), *progress* (hierarchies of skill, especially in literacy and numeracy), *procedures* (checklists) and *value* (surveillance of me as a teacher). I developed these assumptions as I grew up, from my own experience of teachers and assessment at school and university, from my perception of the experience of my own children in early childhood settings and in school, and from the views of my family and peers. Teacher education had done nothing to shift them.

Later, together with a group of practitioners who wanted to explore some alternative assessment practices, I had the opportunity to try to integrate our ideas about learning and teaching with a different set of assumptions about assessment. Table 6.1 lists the assumptions of my folk model about assessment, and sets alongside them the assumptions of an alternative model. These alternative assumptions are outlined in this chapter.

Table 6.1 assumptions in two models of assessment: a folk model and an alternative

Assumptions about	My folk model about assessment	An alternative model
Purpose	To check against a short list of skills that describe 'competence' at school entry	To enhance learning
Outcomes of interest	Fragmented and context-free school-oriented skills	Learning dispositions
Focus for intervention	Deficit, gap-filling, is foregrounded	Credit, disposition enhancing, is foregrounded
Validity	Objective observation	Interpreted observations, discussions and agreements
Progress	Hierarchies of skills	Increasingly complex participation
Procedures	Checklists	Learning stories
Value to practitioners	Surveillance by external agencies	For communicating with four audiences: children, families, other staff and self (the practitioner)

Purpose

An assumption that I was making twenty years ago was that assessment sums up the child's knowledge or skill from a predetermined list. Harry Torrance and John Pryor (1998) have described this assumption as 'convergent' assessment. The alternative is 'divergent' assessment, which emphasises the learner's understanding and is jointly accomplished by the teacher and the learner. These ideas reflect not only views about assessment, but views about learning and teaching as well. I think I was holding a convergent and a divergent view of learning at the same time. In convergent mode I checked the children's achievement against a short list of skills that described 'competence' at school entry. When my checklist indicated a gap in the requisite skills, I devised ways of directly teaching them. In divergent mode I was implementing a play-based programme to enhance the learning I valued at this site, but I did not see a role for assessment or documentation in that.

I don't have any examples of those convergent assessments. However, I do have an example of my working in more divergent mode at that time. Some years after the event I wrote about the invention by one of the four-year-olds at the kindergarten of an accessible carpentry drill (Carr 1987). I had observed one of the children wielding a G-clamp upside down to 'drill' a dent in the carpentry table. Normally a G-clamp has a cap on the end of the thread so that it doesn't mark the inside of the table when it is clamped on, but this clamp had lost the cap, and the thread had a pointed end. He called out: 'Look, Margaret, I'm drilling a hole.' We discussed how he had transformed a G-clamp into a carpentry drill, and evaluated this invention as potentially providing an extremely helpful artefact for enhancing the children's carpentry. Our drills at that time were of the egg-beater variety, where children had to keep the drill upright while they both pressed down and rotated the handle in a vertical plane. In the new 'drill', the thread maintained the pressure while the child could use both hands to turn the horizontally aligned handle at the top to drill the hole. I later persuaded a parent to weld a threaded bit onto the G-clamp, and set it into a block of wood, and it did indeed enhance the children's problem-solving and planning processes in carpentry. I wrote the story of one of the boys making a boat by drilling two 5mm holes in a block of wood, sawing and hammering in short lengths of dowel (for masts), and then floating it in the water trough (it fell to the side; later modifications to the design to get it to float the right way up were not recorded); and of one of the girls drilling holes in 'wheels' cut from an old broom handle, attaching them with flat-headed nails to the side of a piece of wood, and pulling it along as a car or cart. I had taken photos for the families, but it did not occur to me to write up either the invention or the carpentry as part of an assessment procedure. I think now that documenting that learning at the time would have given the children and the families, and me, some new insights into the goals of our early childhood programme, and of how they might be recognised and developed in other activities.

I was therefore only documenting part of the curriculum, and I was documenting it for an external audience. This may be true for many early childhood educators, and as demands for external accountability press more insistently on the profession, surveillance begins to encroach on intuitive and responsive teaching. The alternative model tries to connect external accountability and responsive teaching together: it advocates the documenting of learner outcomes and it is embedded in episodes of responsive teaching. However, it defines learner outcomes rather differently from the convergent checklist that I employed twenty years ago.

Outcomes of interest

My folk model of documented assessment viewed learning as individual and independent of the context. Learner outcomes of interest were fragmented and context-free school-oriented skills. The alternative model says that learning always takes some of its context with it, and that, as James Wertsch (1991) has suggested, the learner is a 'learner-in-action'. This viewpoint derives mainly from Lev Vygotsky's (1978) notion of 'mediated action'. It takes a view of learning that focuses on the relationship between the learner and the environment, and seeks ways to define and document complex reciprocal and responsive relationships in that environment. Emphasising this view of learning, Barbara Rogoff (1997, 1998) has described development as the 'transformation of participation'.

A number of other writers have emphasised the context- and culture-specific nature of learning. Jerome Bruner (1990: 106), for instance, has described this emphasis as a 'contextual revolution' in psychology. Attention has shifted from internal structures and representations in the mind to meaning-making, intention and relationships in the experienced world. This development is of great interest to early childhood practitioners. The traditional separation of the individual from the environment, has been replaced by attaching social and cultural purpose to skills and knowledge, thereby blurring the division between the individual and the learning environment. One way to look at a range of learning outcomes is to describe them as an accumulation. Table 6.2 sets out four outcomes along an accumulated continuum of complexity.

Table 6.2 Learning outcomes along an accumulated continuum of complexity

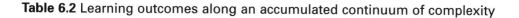

LEARNING OUTCOMES
(i)   Skills and knowledge
(ii) Skills and knowledge + intent = learning strategies
(iii) Learning strategies + social partners and practices + tools = situated learning strategies
(iv) Situated learning strategies + motivation = learning dispositions

Skills and knowledge

The focus here is on skills and knowledge 'in the head', acquired by the learner. In early childhood there are a number of basic routines and low-level skills that might be, and often are, taught and tested: cutting with scissors, colouring between the lines, saying a series of numbers in the correct sequence, knowing the sounds of letters. Often complex tasks are seen as learning hierarchies with the assumption that smaller units of behaviour need to be mastered as prerequisites for more complex units later on.

Learning is seen as linear and sequential. Complex understandings can occur only by adding together simpler, prerequisite units of knowledge. Measurement-driven basic-skills instruction is based on a model of learning which holds that 'basic skills should be taught and mastered before going on to higher-order problems' (Shepard 1991: 2–3). Shepard asks (p. 7) 'What if learning is not linear and is not acquired by assembling bits of simpler learning?' We (Carr and Claxton 1989: 133) pointed out that this model of learning encourages didactic adult-controlled teaching strategies which ignore the particular, the situational and the social dimensions of learning.

This basic skills model of learning is often used to predict children's prospects at school. The literature on 'school readiness' does not, however, persuade us that particular items of skills and knowledge, unattached to meaningful activities, predict achievement at school.

Teachers and schools may construct a package of entry skills that, through teacher expectation effects, can become critical. But, while skills and knowledge matter a great deal, they will be fragile indeed if institutional arrangements in classrooms and early childhood settings do not embed them in motivating circumstances and imbue them with social and cultural meaning.

Skills and knowledge + intent = learning strategies

Skills that are attached to meaning and intent have been called 'learning strategies'. Nisbet and Shucksmith suggest that a learning strategy is a series of skills used with a particular purpose in mind: 'Strategies are different from skills in that a strategy has a purpose' (1986: vii). Learning strategies are often associated with the idea that children are 'learning to learn'. Nisbet and Shucksmith described strategies like planning ahead, monitoring one's progress to identify sources of difficulty, asking questions. Cullen (1991) describes the continuity of learning from early childhood to school in terms of learning strategies, as she observed children using the same strategies in play in their kindergarten and then in reading lessons at school. She described these as 'repeated patterns of behaviour and language which indicate an active, strategic approach to learning' (Cullen 1991: 45–6). Cullen noted that in the different context of the primary school classroom, however, such abilities or strategies may not be demonstrated. They will not appear if, for instance, there is little opportunity for the child to use a creative approach to choosing resources appropriate to the task in hand, or for the child to see herself as a resource for others.

Learning strategies + social partners and practices + tools = situated learning strategies

At the third level of accumulation, the purpose or intent is linked to social partners and practices, and tools. The learning strategies are *situated*. The focus is on the individual-in-action in which the action is mediated by social partners, social practices and tools (the technology and languages available). This is sometimes called a 'situative' approach, and the outcomes at this level can be called situated learning strategies. The emphasis is on learning as participation in sociocultural activities. Mediated *action* is, as Elizabeth Graue and Daniel Walsh (1995) commented, 'located within specific cultural and historic practices and time'. They compare this to a behavioural approach in which 'behaviour is stripped of these local characteristics; it is mechanical description without narration'. Writing about cognition, Gavriel Salomon comments that distributed cognition elaborates on the notion that 'People appear to think in conjunction or partnership with others and with the help of culturally provided tools and implements' (Salomon 1993: xiii).

This notion of thinking or learning being distributed across social practice and partners and tools introduces the idea of learning as a product of reciprocal relations between the environment and the mind, of the learning process as a *transaction*. Individual learners engage in activities and their participation changes the activities while at the same time they are changed by those activities. Jason changes the marble-painting activity and becomes a tutor in the process; Moses calls on adults and toys and videos not only to help him develop his fund of knowledge about animals, but to use animals as a metaphor or mechanism for making sense of and manipulating his two-year-old world.

Situated learning strategies + motivation = learning dispositions

The fourth level of accumulation adds *motivation* to stimulated learning strategies to form learning dispositions (Katz 1993). A vivid way to describe this accumulation of motivation, situation and skill is to say that a learner is 'ready, willing and able' to learn. Lauren Resnick (1987: 40–2) commented that shaping the disposition is central to developing the ability, and that much of the learning to be a good thinker is learning to recognise and even search for opportunities to apply one's capacities. She added (p. 42) that 'dispositions are cultivated by participation in social communities that value thinking and independent judgement'. If we take the example of communication, or expressing one's ideas, then *being ready* is being motivated or inclined to communicate, *being willing* is recognising that the situation is an appropriate one in which to express one's ideas, and *being able* is the communication skills and understandings that will be needed for this occasion. Kathy Sylva writes about the 'will and skill to do' as a legacy of effective preschool education (1994: 163) and inclination, sensitivity to occasion, and ability have been described as the three components of thinking dispositions by David Perkins, Eileen Jay and Shari Tishman (1993). Guy Claxton (1990: 164) has commented that in societies where knowledge, values and styles of relationship are undergoing rapid change: 'it can be strongly argued that schools' (and early childhood settings') major responsibility must be to help young people become ready, willing and able to cope with change successfully: that is, to be powerful and effective learners.' Coping with change means coping with changing situations: social partners, social practices and tools. Learning dispositions that take account of the situation can be defined as participation repertoires from which a learner recognises, selects, edits, responds to, resists, searches for and constructs learning opportunities. These can be referred to in a number of ways, as:

- learning dispositions
- being ready, willing and able
- inclination, sensitivity to occasion, and ability
- participation repertoires.

Summary of outcomes of interest

The four levels make up a conceptual hierarchy, not a developmental one. We can assess children's learning at any of the four levels of accumulation. However, assessment that is appropriate for level one outcomes (skills and knowledge) is not appropriate for level four outcomes (learning dispositions). As Elliot Eisner (2000: 346) has pointed out, 'tests are poor proxies for things that really matter'. We will have to devise something very different. On occasion, it will be appropriate to assess (perhaps to measure) narrow outcomes, but I would argue that if we only assess at the first three levels, then we will be taking a narrow and impoverished view of children's learning. The fourth level deserves our primary attention.

Focus for intervention

In my folk model, assessment was designed to highlight deficits. This notion of the developing child as incomplete, a jigsaw with parts missing, means that the areas in which the child is 'unable' become the sites of greatest educational interest. The deficit model says either 'we'll find the missing pieces' or 'don't worry, the missing pieces will turn up in their own time'.

The alternative approach is a credit model, disposition enhancing. The relevant community decides what domains of learning disposition are important, and in a credit model the examples of successful participation that will contribute to the inclination or *being ready* are foregrounded. They are the sites of educational interest because we want their occurrence to be frequent enough to become an inclination.

Deficit-based assessment is 'how you've been brought up'; a credit-based approach 'turns you around'. Foregrounding achievement is not primarily a matter of encouraging self-esteem; it is a matter of strengthening learning dispositions and of encouraging a view of the self as a learner. Early childhood practitioners frequently foreground the occasion or the situation in order to evaluate their programmes, and assessment often places skills and knowledge in the foreground. Procedures for foregrounding the inclination are less familiar.

Notions of validity

The notion that an external 'objective' measure or standard exists for all outcomes (if only we can find it) was another feature of my folk model of assessment. I looked for performances that could be scored independently by people who had no additional knowledge about the student. In the alternative approach, however, assessment of the complex outcomes outlined above (learning dispositions, the learner-in-action and -in-relationships) is a central puzzle. To be valid, these assessments must go beyond anecdote, belief and hope. They will require interpreted observations, discussions and agreements. This process of assessment is like action research, with the practitioner/ researcher as part of the action. Assessment procedures in early childhood will call on interpretive and qualitative approaches for the same reasons a researcher will choose interpretive and qualitative methods for researching complex learning in a real-life early childhood setting. These reasons include an interest in the learner-in-action or -in-relationships, and an interest in motivation – in understanding the learning environment from the children's point of view. A number of people's opinions will be surveyed, including the children's, and often the assessments will be tentative.

   Both research and assessments, in trying to 'make sense' of data and turn in a plausible story, always run the risk of over-simplification: losing the rich and often ambiguous complexity of young children's behaviour. Knupfer warns that to 'tell the story' of a child's learning: 'We can run the risk of not fully addressing the perplexities, the contradictions, and the conflicting perspectives if we attempt to create cohesion at the expense of complexity' (1996: 142). Discussions with and observations by a number of interested parties, including the child, can be a source of what Graue and Walsh (1995) have called 'thick' description, acknowledging contradiction, ambiguity, inconsistency, and situation-specific factors.

Ideas about progress

The folk model of assessment with which I began included the notion that all learning could be described as a progression through a hierarchy of skills. Piagetian stage theory, and the strong influence of the early intervention movement in early childhood, have provided a firm foundation for the viewpoint that skills and understandings have an 'early' stage and that the task of early childhood education is to ensure that specific developmental skills are taught in an orderly sequence.

A particular hierarchy or sequence implies a single *endpoint*, but views about the domains of intelligence have changed substantially. In recent years, that single developmental path has given way to alternatives. The notion of multiple ways of thinking and knowing has challenged what Shirley Turkle and Seymour Papert (1992: 3) have called the 'hegemony of the abstract, formal, and logical' in particular to give renewed value to the concrete and the 'here and now', originally seen in Piagetian terms as an immature stage of development. Seymour Papert (1993) emphasised action and 'concreteness' and criticised what he called the 'perverse commitment to moving as quickly as possible from the concrete to the abstract' (p. 143). The value of Piaget's work, he maintained, is that he gave us valuable insights into the workings of a non-abstract way of thinking.

Cross-cultural studies have also challenged beliefs in the universality of one particular endpoint, individual rationalism, indicating that any valued endpoint is a cultural construction, not a developmental inevitability. Some West African communities define stages of development to full selfhood using social signposts. Children are assigned different roles at different stages of life, and progress is defined as increased authority and shared responsibility within the social community (Nsamenang and Lamb 1998). Margaret Donaldson, in *Human Minds*, has suggested two major pathways of development: the intellectual and the emotional. In the 'value-sensing' emotional pathway the imagination is central. She reminds us (1992: 259) that education is about increasing what she calls the 'modal' repertoire: 'It is about suggesting new directions in which lives may go.'

Therefore, new voices have suggested that responsibility, care and intuition are endpoints too. Relationships have been emphasised as central to the trajectory from early childhood experience into later learning, and these relationships may be more than mediating variables, means to cognitive ends. Reciprocal relationships and opportunities for participation, valuable in the here and now of an early childhood setting, are also pivotal to the first messages about the self as a learner that children receive in early childhood settings, messages that have an enduring effect on their capacities to learn in later years. What do they tell us about progress? Writers using ecological and sociocultural frameworks have provided some theoretical guidelines. The theoretical perspectives that I have found useful for this question of progress are as follows. Jean Lave and Étienne Wenger (1991) described development and progress as a shift in participation from the edge (periphery) of the activities of a community to taking on a more central role. Barbara Rogoff (1997) described development as transformation of participation. Her list of features for the evaluation of learning and development from this perspective included: changing involvement and role, approaches to participation flexibly shifting from home to an early childhood setting, an interest in 'learning' versus an interest in protecting the status quo, and the taking of responsibility in cultural activities including 'flexibility and vision' in revising ongoing community practices. Bonnie Litowitz (1997) has also emphasised participation as responsibility and resistance (transaction and reciprocity): the child may bring a very different view from the adult to an activity or a task. Urie Bronfenbrenner (1979: 60, 163, 212) has said that learning and development are facilitated by the participation of the developing person in *progressively more complex activities and patterns of reciprocal interaction,* and by *gradual 'shifts in the balance of power' between the learner and the adult.* His theory also maintains that development and learning are about the learner taking on roles and relationships in an *increasing number of structurally different settings.*

As practitioners and I worked together on assessment projects to implement some of these alternative theoretical approaches, to help the children they were working with, and to share ideas with families, five features of participation emerged. They are:

- taking an interest in aspects of the early childhood setting that might be the same or different from home; coping with transition and changing situations;
- being involved, at an increasingly complex level;
- persistence with difficulty or uncertainty: an interest in 'learning' and a capacity to risk error or failure;
- communicating with others, expressing a point of view, an idea or an emotion;
- taking increasing responsibility in a range of ways.

Procedures

It seems, then, that my checklist was not the only, or the best, way to document learning in early childhood. One of the advantages of a checklist is that it takes little time, whereas qualitative and interpretive methods using narrative methods – learning stories – are time-consuming. Practitioners using storied approaches of assessment, however, become part of a rich tradition of ethnographic and case study observations in early childhood. Susan Isaacs' observations in the 1930s are, in Mary Jane Drummond's words (1999: 4), 'transformed into a geography of learning, as she charts the children's explorations of both their inner and outer worlds'. However, although I commented earlier that a practitioner is like an action researcher, assessment of ongoing learning in an early childhood centre by practitioners is rather different from observations by a visiting researcher. Staff have had to develop ways in which these more story-like methods can be manageable. Practitioners have had to become increasingly skilled at recognising 'critical' moments and memorising the events while jotting down the conversations, and assessment has become less likely to take them away from the 'real' action of teaching and enjoying working with children. Situated frameworks call for the adult to be included in the observations as well, and for many practitioners this is unusual and difficult.

Value to practitioners

Twenty years ago I saw documented assessment as only valuable to me when my reputation with outside agencies was at stake. It was as if in my mind I had a 'league table' of early childhood centres, and I wanted to be reassured that my children were achieving up there with the others from the early childhood centre down the road. Also, I did not want to be blamed by the school and the families for any child's low level of preparation for school. However, as I have worked together with practitioners on different ways of doing assessment that have linked more closely to curriculum implementation, a number of more valuable reasons for documented assessment have emerged. Value for practitioners has included:

• to understand, get to know, be 'in tune' with individual children
• to understand children by using the documentation as a catalyst for discussion with others
• to share information with others in this setting
• to reflect on practice
• to plan for individuals and groups.

Other values included involving the children in self-assessment, discussing the programme with families, and sharing experiences with families.

Concluding comments

This chapter has outlined a shift in my views of assessment, along seven dimensions, from a 'folk' model of twenty years ago, to my current understanding of what the much more complex parameters of an alternative model might look like. I have come around to Mary Jane Drummond's definition of assessment. She says that assessment is: 'the ways in which, in our everyday practice, we observe children's learning, strive to understand it, and then put our understanding to good use' (1993: 13). Assessment then has four characteristics: it is about everyday practice (in this place), it is observation-based (including talking to children), it requires an interpretation, and it points the way to better learning and teaching.

It is ironic that at the dawn of the twenty-first century, at the same time as we are becoming aware that a key feature of children's learning is that it is situated in activity and social practice, governments are requiring national curricula and universal measures of individual achievement. Early childhood programmes are often besieged by school curricula and school entry assessments as well. At the beginning of this chapter I asked whether assessing learning in early childhood is any of our business. It has become our business as early childhood educators and practitioners to respond to these demands and in doing so, in many cases, to reframe the purpose, the outcomes, the items for intervention, the definitions of validity and progress, the procedures, and the value for practitioners. Reframing the rules and redefining curriculum and achievement may simply be exchanging one form of surveillance for another. But we have a responsibility to ensure that the new communities we are constructing for children, in childcare centres, kindergartens and amongst childminders for instance, are ethical and safe environments in which all children learn. Early childhood practitioners therefore have to make some assumptions about learning, assessment and evaluation (as well as about ethics and safety) that are informed and reflective.

The alternative assumptions about assessment outlined in this chapter have emphasised two major views about learning outcomes. The first view is that learning can be described as transformation of participation, that it is situated in social practice and activities, and includes responsibility and resistance. The second view is that learning of interest will include motivation, and that learning dispositions, that add motivation to situated learning strategies, are very complex outcomes.

References

Bronfenbrenner, U. (1979) *The Ecology of Human Development*. Cambridge, Mass.: Harvard University Press.

Bruner, J. (1990) *Acts of Meaning*. Cambridge, Mass.: Harvard University Press.

Carr, M. (1987) 'A preschool "drill" for problem-solving'. *Investigating* **3** (1), 3–5.

Carr, M. and Claxton, G. (1989) 'The costs of calculation'. *New Zealand Journal of Educational Studies* **24** (2), 129–40.

Claxton, G. (1990) *Teaching to Learn*. London: Cassell.

Cullen, J. (1991) 'Young children's learning strategies: continuities and discontinuities'. *International Journal of Early Childhood* **23** (1), 44–58.

Donaldson, M. (1992) *Human Minds*. London: The Penguin Press.

Drummond, M. J. (1993) *Assessing Children's Learning*. London: David Fulton Publishers.

Drummond, M. J. (1999) *Comparisons in Early Years Education: history, fact and fiction*. CREPE Occasional Paper. University of Warwick, Centre for Research in Elementary and Primary Education.

Eisner, E. (2000) 'Those who ignore the past...: 12 "easy" lessons for the next millenium'. *Journal of Curriculum Studies* **32** (2), 343–57.

Graue, M. E. and Walsh, D. J. (1995) 'Children in context: interpreting the here and now of children's lives'. In J. A. Hatch (ed.), *Qualitative Research in Early Childhood Settings*. Westport, Connecticut: Praeger, 135–54.

Isaacs, S. (1932) *The Nursery Years: the Mind of the Child from Birth to Six Years*. London: Routledge and Kegan Paul.

Katz, L. G. (1993) *Dispositions: Definitions and Implications for Early Childhood Practices*. Perspectives from ERIC/ECCE: a monograph series. Urbana, Illinois: ERIC Clearinghouse on ECCE.

Knupfer, A. M. (1996) 'Ethnographic studies of children: the difficulties of entry, rappart, and presentations of their worlds'. *Qualitative Studies in Education* **9** (2) 135–49.

Lave, J. and Wenger. E. (1991) *Situated Learning: Legitimate Peripheral Participation*. Cambridge: Cambridge University Press.

Litowitz, B. E. (1997) 'Just say no: responsibility and resistance'. In M. Cole, Y. Engeström and O. Vasquez (eds) *Mind, Culture, and Activity: seminal papers from the Laboratory of Comparative Human Cognition.* Cambridge: Cambridge University Press.

Nisbet, J. and Shucksmith, J. (1986) *Learning Strategies.* London: Routledge and Kegan Paul.

Nsamenang, A. Bame and Lamb, M. E. (1998) 'Socialization of Nso children in the Bamenda grassfields of northwestern Cameroon'. In M. Woodhead, D. Faulkner and K. Littleton (eds) *Cultural Worlds of Early Childhood.* London and New York: Routledge in association with The Open University.

Olson, D. R and Bruner, J. S. (1996) 'Folk psychology and folk pedagogy'. In D. R. Olson and N. Torrance (eds) *The Handbook of Education and Human Development: new models of Learning, teaching and schooling.* London: Blackwell.

Papert, S. (1993) *The Children's Machine: rethinking school in the age of the computer.* Hemel Hempstead: Harvester Wheatsheaf.

Perkins, D. N., Jay, E. and Tishman, S. (1993) 'Beyond abilities: a dispositional theory of thinking'. *Merril-Parker Quarterly* **39**, 1 January, 1–21.

Resnick, L. B. (1987) *Education and Learning to Think.* Washington, DC: National Academy Press.

Rogoff, B. (1997) 'Evaluating development in the process of participation: theory, methods, and practice building on each other'. In E. Amsel and K. Ann Renninger (eds) *Change and Development: issues of theory, method and application.* Mahwah, NJ and London: Erlbaum.

Rogoff, B. (1998) 'Cognition as a collaborative process'. In William Damon (ed.) *Handbook of Child Psychology.* 5th edn. Vol. 2. Cognition, Perception and Language. (Volume Editors: Deanna Kuhn and Robert S. Siegler.) New York: John Wiley, 679–744.

Salomon, G. (1993) 'Editor's introduction'. In G. Salomon (ed.) *Distributed Cognitions: psychological and educational considerations.* Cambridge: Cambridge University Press.

Shepard, L. A. (1991) 'Psychometricians' beliefs about learning'. *Educational Researcher* **20** (6), 2–16.

Sylva, K. (1994) 'School influences on children's development'. *Journal of Child Psychology and Psychiatry* **34** (1), 135–70.

Torrance, H. and Pryor, J. (1998) *Investigating Formative Assessment: teaching, learning and assessment in the classroom.* Buckingham: Open University Press.

Turkle, S. and Papert, S. (1992) 'Epistemological pluralism and the revaluation of the concrete', *Journal of Mathematical Behavior* **11**, 3–33.

Vygotsky, L. S. (1978) *Mind in Society: the development of higher psychological processes.* Edited by M. Cole, V. John-Steiner, S. Scribner and E. Souberman. Translated by A. R. Luria, M. Lopez-Morillas, M. Cole and J. Wertsch. Cambridge, Mass.: Harvard University Press.

Wertsch, J. V. (1991) *Voices of the Mind: a sociocultural approach to mediated action.* Cambridge, Mass.: Harvard University Press.

Chapter 7

Listening to children

Alison Clark

The study was funded by the Joseph Rowntree Foundation in collaboration with Coram Family. This chapter is based on a paper presented at the Parent Child Conference, 2000. In this paper I will focus on a framework for listening: the Mosaic approach which I have developed during this study.

The Mosaic approach

The Mosaic approach provides a flexible set of methods which provide a platform for consulting children. It is a multi-method approach which aims to open up many different ways for young children to convey their views and experiences. Malaguzzi refers to the 'hundred languages of children' (Edwards *et al.* 1998). This framework seeks to maximise this rich potential for children to communicate and for adults to listen. The value of talking to young children is not overlooked. However, tools are suggested which also enable young children to communicate their ideas and feelings to adults in other ways, for example through photographs, drawing and walking. These methods may in turn serve as a springboard for more talking, listening and reflecting.

The Mosaic approach is about gaining young children's perspectives of their everyday lives. The focus is not on 'learning' but about the routines and patterns of each day. It is just as likely to reveal what children think about the toilets as their experiences of learning to write. The tools described here have been influenced by the participatory methods developed in participatory rural appraisal or PRA. These methods were drawn together in the 1980s and 1990s to enable non-literate adults in the majority world to play an active part in decision-making at a local level. Now non-governmental organisations (NGOs) and researchers are exploring the use of these tools with young people and children. Tools include the use of mapping and modelling, diagrams, drawing and collage, child to child interviewing and drama and puppetry. These participatory methods are about attitudes and behaviour as well as about techniques. PRA is designed to empower those who take part by enabling people to represent their *own* situations, to reflect on their experiences and to influence change.

I will briefly outline five of the tools used in the Mosaic approach; observing, child conferencing, cameras, tours and mapping. These examples are taken from my work with young children, mainly under 5s who attend the Thomas Coram Early Childhood Centre (TCECC), part of the Coram Community Campus.

Observation

Observation has been the starting point for this study, across each age group. However, for the youngest children who are pre-verbal or with limited speech, observation is of particular importance. We are able to build on a strong tradition of using observation in early childhood research and practice. Several models have influenced the framework of observation. Selleck (2001) has devised a detailed method of observation during her three year study of under threes in day care. This is based on the gathering of 'Nursery Stories'. We adapted this qualitative approach to focus on individual children within the TCECC.

We also drew on the 'Children's Questions' devised to evaluate the innovative early years curriculum in New Zealand: *Te Whaariki* (Ministry of Education 1996). These questions are drawn from each of the five strands of the curriculum: belonging, wellbeing, exploration, communication and contribution. The questions are: Do you know me? Can I trust you? Do you let me fly? Do you hear me? and Is this place fair?

We have used the question, 'Do you listen to me?' as the basis for our observations with children under two. This question has also provided an interesting starting point for dialogue with staff.

Child conferencing

Talking to young children is an important part of the Mosaic approach. What framework could be used for enabling children with differing personalities, verbal skills and backgrounds to tell us what they thought about the setting? In order to achieve this goal, there is the need to include both formal and informal conversations with children. Child conferencing provided one structured way of doing so. This is a short interview schedule devised by Bernadette Duffy, Head of TCECC for use as an evaluation tool with preschool children. The questions, (14 in total) ask children about why they come to nursery, who are their favourite people and who do they like being with, and about their favourite activities. There are also questions about how children see the adults' role in the nursery. The interview ends with an open-ended question to provide the opportunity for children to add any further information they think is important. Some children chose to add a drawing at this point or to sign their name.

Is this a useful tool for consulting young children? Child conferencing has possibilities, especially if used flexibly and in conjunction with other methods. The choice of setting for the interview is critical. The 'interview' may need to be conducted on the move, for example a three- and four-year-old began the interview inside and then proceeded to show the researcher their favourite outdoor spaces. The interview then continued outside. Child conferencing was carried out with one key group in the kindergarten of TCECC in July 1999 and repeated with those children who were still a member in November 1999. This provided opportunities for the children to reflect on their previous responses and to assess what had changed and how they now felt about life in the nursery.

The use of cameras

Visual methods are an essential element of the Mosaic approach. There was the possibility of using photographs taken by the researcher to form the basis of the interviews with young children. This tool has been used with success in research involving children under five (e.g. Candappa 1999).

However, we wanted to go a stage further in this research, particularly as we were also interested in exploring participatory methods. The use of cameras by children had great potential. Cameras provide the opportunity for children to express 'voices' without the need for the spoken or written word. Walker (1993) describes this as 'the silent voice of the camera' . This seems to have particular relevance when working with young children. Photography offers a way of communicating their ideas and feelings which allows young children to be in charge. Children can take control of the camera, choose what to make an image of and produce a final product of which they can be proud. A group of three- and four-year-olds were given a short instruction on how to use a single use camera, including how to operate the flash.

Children were asked to take photographs of things that were important to them about the nursery. Issues of importance to the children emerged during discussions whilst taking the photographs and also looking together at the finished results. These included the use of outside space, changing friendships and relationships with key workers.

Tours and mapping

There was also the opportunity to include other participatory methods in the Mosaic approach. Chambers (1997: 117) explains the use of transect walks as a method of gathering detailed information about an environment from the people who live there. He describes this process as 'systematically walking with local guides and analysts through an area, observing, asking, listening, discussing, learning . . .'. The physical nature of this process appeared to offer possibilities for exploring children's 'local knowledge' of their own environment. Langsted (1994) adopted a similar approach in a Scandinavian study of children's lives. He describes what can be seen as a 'walking interview' with five-year-olds. Children walked the interviewer through their day explaining what happens where.

The Mosaic approach was adapted to include a process of tours and mapping. The children directed a tour of the site, working individually, or in twos or threes. The children also took photographs, produced drawings and notes and made audio-tape recordings as the tour progressed. This initial exercise was followed by a map-making activity using the images produced.

This approach enables young children to be the experts in this stage of.the research or evaluation process. The researcher did not know the building as well as the children, nor the staff who the children met on the tour. The use of the children's own photographs was also a significant part of the process. Children seemed to relate more easily to images they had made themselves and were more able to construct them into a map.

Listening about living

We have described the Mosaic approach as a way of gaining young children's perspectives of their daily lives. Johnson and Ivan-Smith describe such participatory tools as enabling adults to 'view the world through the lens of children and young people' (Johnson *et al.* 1998: 8) What potential does this have for work with young children in particular settings? One advantage is moving towards a child agenda for change. The use of tools such as the camera and tours can demonstrate children's priorities which might otherwise have become lost. The issue of the use of outside space was raised by the children in the study. Several of the children recorded the importance of the 'empty' spaces, such as by the shed and beside the fence. This information could then be included in discussion when plans for reordering the outdoor area took place.

The Mosaic approach in use in an educational setting also extends consultation beyond a learning discourse. Exchanges between key workers and parents can have a focus which is not necessarily dominated by academic progress. In the study, the researcher met individually with a number of parents to discuss life in the nursery for their child. In one case, the four-year-old also joined in this discussion. The focus was provided by the documentation gathered using the Mosaic approach. A parent could discuss their child's responses to the child conferencing, see photographs taken by their child and maps made from the photographs. Descriptions of observation accounts were also fed into this discussion. Important issues for both children and parents emerged from this reflection. For example, during a tour of the building, one child had expressed her desire to be old enough to have lunch with the four-year-olds in the special room. This was a new routine, introduced to allow the older children to eat lunch together, in preparation for their moving on to school. Her mother was aware from conversations at home that this child was preoccupied by the idea of going to school and talked everyday about wanting to be old enough to go there. This piece of information provided a new insight for the key worker into this child's wishes and also her feelings about her current status within the nursery.

'Experts in their own lives'

The Mosaic approach can also be used as a reflexive tool for helping young children to reflect on their own lives. This way of working is an attempt to move children's evaluation beyond a 'like/dislike' model to one which allows children and adults to reflect on children's everyday experiences. There is firstly the initial value gained from treating children as 'experts in their own lives' (Langsted 1994: 35) By asking children what they think about being in a place, what they do there, their perceptions of what it is all about, we are beginning to take children seriously. This confidence may enable children to develop new skills and competencies, which in turn can increase their abilities to communicate with adults. Experiences recorded in this way can then be used as a reference point for children and adults to assess change over time. The use of child conferencing twice in a six-month period demonstrated this point. Children were interested in what they had said before, sometimes giggled at what they had said and used their past responses as a springboard for reflecting on what had changed.

Conclusion

We have looked at different tools within the Mosaic approach for listening to young children. This is a portfolio of tools which can be used and adapted for working in particular settings. However, the portfolio is an open one. There is, for example, the possibility of using drama, puppets, drawing, modelling and music. The range is endless. The important ingredients are firstly the methods: the combined use of tools which enable young children to express their ideas and feelings with confidence. Secondly, it is the attitude towards children which this approach represents: children as experts in their own lives. There is a value in each piece of the Mosaic. However, the value is increased by combining with other pieces or perspectives, including those of parents and key workers. The Mosaic approach is not designed to produce facts but will provide a platform for discussion, with children, staff and parents. It is in the interpretation of the information gathered that the possibility for greater understanding of young children's lives will emerge.

Alison Clark and Peter Moss subsequently published the following book: Clark, A. and Moss, P. (2001) *Listening to young children: the Mosaic approach.* London: National Children's Bureau.

References

Candappa, M. (1999) *Growing Up in the City: a consultation exercise with children and young people*. Report to the Corporation of London. London: Coram Family/Thomas Coram Research Unit.

Chambers, R. (1997) *Whose reality counts? Putting the first last*. London: Intermediate Technology.

Edwards, C., Gandini, L. and Foreman, G. (eds) (1998) *The Hundred Languages of Children. the Reggio Emilia approach to early childhood education*, 2nd edn. New Jersey: Ablex Publishing Corporation.

Johnson, V. *et al.* (eds) (1998) *Stepping Forward. Children and young people's participation in the development process*. London: Intermediate Technology.

Langsted, O. (1994) 'Looking at quality from the child's perspective' in Moss, P. and Pence, A. (eds) *Valuing Quality in Early Childhood Services: new approaches to defining quality*. London: Paul Chapman Publishing.

Ministry of Education (1996) *Te Whaariki: early childhood curriculum*. Wellington: New Zealand Ministry of Education.

Selleck, D. (2001) 'Being under three years of age: enhancing quality experiences' in Pugh, G. (ed.) *Contemporary Issues in the Early Years – Working Collaboratively for Children*, 3rd edn. London: Paul Chapman Publishing.

Walker, R. (1993) 'Finding a silent voice for the researcher: using photographs in evaluation and research' in Schratz, Michael (ed.) *Qualitative Voices in Educational Research*. London: Falmer Press.

Part 2
Early years curriculum

Jane Devereux

Introduction

> The educator working with the under fives must pay careful attention not just to the content of the child's learning, but also to the way in which that learning is offered to and experienced by the child.
>
> (DES 1990: 9)

The chapters in this section are about the curriculum and different curriculum frameworks devised and developed for children in a variety of early years settings across the four countries of the United Kingdom. Being responsible for supporting children's learning and providing meaningful contexts for children necessitates practitioners being knowledgeable about areas of learning and being able to provide experiences and contexts for children's learning that are holistic, real and which enable them to understand, make links, and make sense of the world and people around them. Each chapter explores a different area of learning and highlights particular approaches or dilemmas within that area. As practitioners develop their provision in a wide range of settings there is a need for them to be able to identify the key areas of learning being developed in their setting to ensure curriculum breadth and depth in order to ensure that children progress.

Early years curriculum

In her chapter 'Being under three years of age: enhancing quality experiences' Dorothy Selleck explores ways in which practitioners in different settings can support, 'complement, and enhance, the care, play and learning of babies and toddlers that are happening with families at home.' (p. 76). She discusses providing developmentally appropriate experiences and a curriculum informed by research. She also discusses different approaches to working with the youngest children and stresses how important it is for practitioners to follow a child's inclinations, embracing them into the community and being energetic and responsive to their needs and abilities.

Young children are always on the move. In fact practitioners often comment on children's capacity to keep going. Helen Bilton's chapter 'Movement as a vehicle for learning' explores how each curriculum area featured in this section provides a vehicle for learning about movement and physical development. She explores children's physical development and the ways in which it supports children's thinking and she raises important issues about an inclusive environment for movement. In 'Creativity: working in partnership with parents' Bernadette Duffy and Jan Stillaway describe, through the use of case studies, some of the experiences they have had at the Thomas Coram Centre, in involving parents in their attempts in supporting the development of their children's creativity. They identify respect and trust as important components of any partnerships and emphasise how important it is to take time to discuss different values and traditions with both staff and families. They explore different ways of sharing ideas with parents in the centre. The authors highlight the power of performance for the children but also the need to understand parents' perspectives and concerns.

The title of Anna Craft and Bob Jeffrey's chapter 'Creative practice and practice which fosters creativity' provides a clear indication of what this chapter is about. Through the use of vignettes and an exploration of current thinking they examine the different nature of creative practice and those practices that foster creativity, and consider whether both ideas always occur together. The conclusion suggests that they do not, but that each could lead to the other if practitioners are aware of their potential.

Robin Campbell's chapter 'Young children becoming literate' includes the story of Alice learning to write her name in a way that is driven by Alice and supported by sensitive adults. Learning to write their own name is seen as an indicator of children's subsequent success in becoming literate. Campbell shows that the way in which children are supported in this process can be as significant as being able to do the task. He argues that children should lead and drive process within contexts that make sense to them and for purposes that have meaning for them. Linda Miller and Alice Paige-Smith's chapter 'Literacy in four early years settings' explores the different kinds of literacy experiences children have in four diverse settings in England and provides a context for practitioners to reflect on their beliefs and practices in relation to the literacy curriculum. They make a plea for training and support for practitioners as they struggle with the demands of a changing environment. Linda Pound's two chapters about young children's early mathematical development and experiences are titled 'Born mathematical?' and 'A curriculum for supporting mathematical thinking'. The first of these chapters explores recent research into how competent children from 0–3 are mathematically. Using addition and subtraction as one example, she shows how very young babies can notice difference. The second chapter explores the content and processes of a mathematical curriculum for children aged 0–5 and pays particular attention within the content to measurement, number, shape and space, and patterns and relationships. Within the processes she explores, briefly, not the nature of problem solving and other ideas such as reflection, but more the nature of the kind of thinking and confidence that comes from such processes. Her approach should encourage practitioners to provide more stimulating and supportive experiences for children.

Information and communication technology as part of a curriculum for young children may raise practitioner's feelings both for and against its place in any early years setting. But Deirdre Cook in her chapter entitled 'ICT and curriculum provision in the early years' argues for a developmentally appropriate curriculum and practices based on clearly expounded values and principles, that see ICT as part of the whole curriculum experience for young children.

Jane Devereux and Ann Bridges in their chapter 'Knowledge and understanding of the world developed through a garden project' describe a project undertaken in a nursery school where the children are involved in the real life task of developing their garden. Through the use of small episodes from the project they show how a theme or project can provide the holistic context for children to experience several areas of learning in an appropriate way. They show how the children can be the instigators of meaningful learning experiences for both themselves and the staff. Ways of using artefacts, stories and play to help children to investigate and reconstruct the past are described by Rosie Turner-Bisset in her chapter entitled 'Meaningful history with young children'. She shows how by using all kinds of stories and artefacts, both old and new, it is possible to help children gain an understanding of such concepts as time, change and cause and effect, which are cornerstones of history. The approach she takes will enable practitioners to replicate her ideas and think more deeply about the nature of history and its place in our lives.

All these chapters argue, either explicitly or implicitly, that children need to experience the curriculum in ways that make sense to them. They also claim that practitioners, through careful observation and through listening to children, come to know their interests, abilities and ways of learning so that they can provide the best possible experiences for children.

References

Department of Education and Science (1990) *Starting with Quality*, The Rumbold Report. London: HMSO.

Chapter 8

Being under 3 years of age: enhancing quality experiences

Dorothy Selleck

Children are born into different kinds of families where they work out how to be themselves. They are people under 3 years of age with feelings to communicate and ideas of their own. Parents have many demands on their time, not only for child-rearing, but also to progress their own life-long learning, leisure and earning opportunities. In this chapter I present how practices in early years settings with professional staff may complement, and enhance, the care, play and learning of babies and toddlers that are happening with families at home.

Attachment

> Pauline...'Work is OK...I was off for a year after he was born, but I didn't want to go back even then. I wanted to be with my baby. I was enjoying it. But I knew I had to, financially...I can't even think about it, my not being with him. It would give me a nervous breakdown!' Pauline was not sad but her story was sad...we deny these feelings at our peril...
>
> (Benn 1998)

> [In] the beginning every child is an only child. The child is not possessive of the mother because he already possesses her...Everyone begins their life belonging to someone else...being separate, or having to share leaves one in shock...as everyone who is in love (or in mourning) knows, what is politely referred to as separation is mutilation...
>
> (Phillips 1998)

These two quotations, one from a mother and one from a psychotherapist advocating for a child's feelings, hint at a body of literature on the attachment, or bonding together, of babies and the main people who care for them, play with them and take up their cues for attention. The significance of this special relationship in developing healthy relationships later on, and in becoming confident learners, is well documented (Rutter 1995; Elfer 1997).

There is a growing body of literature that emphasises the importance of a continuing attachment relationship between key persons/key practitioners who care for, play with and educate children in settings outside their homes in close association with children's significant attachment figures from home. I return to this below.

There is also growing documentation on the consequences of damaged lives when children are not supported to form secure attachments in infancy. Parents, and later, nursery staff, by attending to infants' psychological, and biological and learning needs, can provide children with a secure attachment that will enable them to develop fruitful long-term relationships and a sense of being valued and loveable. Unfortunately, according to some, the reverse is also true. By failing to respond in a consistent and sensitive way, psychological damage or trauma may be inflicted on a child's attachment system, wounding his or her self-esteem and his or her capacity to tune into others later on (de Zulueta 1993; Robertson and Robertson 1989; Balbernie 2000; Bruner 2000).

Continuity, reciprocity, identity

In the beginning, only the presence of a parent (or committed regular key person in the nursery) can provide the continuity, attention and sensuous pleasure the baby needs to make sense of all his or her experiences and set in motion the processes of mental development. Familiarity, pattern and predictability give older babies a sense of being themselves. Continuity of attention from key people who know children well, who are interpreting and responding to their gestures and cues, enable children to attend to their inclinations and to play freely. From the sustained continuity of regular contact with a few familiar people, toddlers may enjoy an increasing range of relationships and activities (Shuttleworth in Rustin *et al.* 1997; Elfer *et al.* 2003).

By the time babies are a few months old they may instigate as well as follow quite complex games with their familiar people. There is synchrony of pitch and voice, a communicative musicality in their narratives. Expressive melodramas not unlike the improvisation of jazz performers may be 'conversations' that pass to and from little children. When there are opportunities to be in continuous relationships with adults, sustained over time, babies seem to be absorbed and involved in another's mind (Trevarthen 1999).

Children start to become aware they belong to a culture as well as to a family. Children growing up in multicultural and multilingual environments can learn many languages and pick up the cues of engagement appropriate to their own and other children's families. We know that children of a few weeks old can be engrossed in mutual interactions with another baby, and that toddlers develop close and interdependent relationships when there are regular opportunities for them to be together (Whaley and Rubenstein 1994; Goldschmied and Selleck 1996). Research shows that children may learn to treat everyone differently but with equal concern or they may, at an early age, learn negative attitudes of discrimination, prejudice or racism (Lane 1999).

The messages from this research seem clear. Children above all else need continuity of experiences with significant close adults who stay alongside children and engage with them in these three years. Adults who have the capacities and support for attachments, intimacy and involvement with children, their families and their friends, will support their wellbeing and learning best (Goldschmied and Jackson 1994; Elfer 1996). Quality services must be planned to enable such continuity for the under-3s.

Practice development

Introduction to the processes and practices for evolving quality practice

Early years managers lead teams with varying degrees of commitment and with a broad spectrum of capacities and potential. Working with babies is a vocation for some, a considered career choice, a decision to engage with a stage of a child's learning that is powerful, significant and enjoyable. For others it may be the best fit with their lack of formal qualifications and, for others, an alternative in their locality for other low-paid work. So team leaders of services to babies and toddlers have to take account of this uneven mixture of qualities of the personnel in each group.

Three areas of professional practice are of particular significance to baby/toddler practitioners.

Professional involvement

Work with babies and toddlers is physically demanding, emotionally draining, as well as intellectually challenging. It needs very observant and astute people to tune into babies from other people's families. If this work goes unsupported, unsupervised, undervalued and lowly in pay and status, it may inevitably result in practitioners offering 'burn-out, automatic-pilot performance'. They may be pleasant and benign...but is this adequate?

Intellectual curiosity. a culture of ongoing professional development

Work with babies may be seen by some as needing a nurturing motherliness that precludes intellectual curiosity and ongoing study. While the first quality is undoubtedly an asset, for practitioners to sustain vitality and a capacity for reflection, analysis and creativity in their work with children and families, an ongoing involvement in training, reading and professional team talk is essential.

Harmonious, interactive teamwork

People who work with under-3s are part of a team. Their work with parents is just as important as their responses to children. Many workers are in organisations where there are shifts and rotas for leave and training, as well as liaison with other professionals. It is inappropriate in work with the youngest children to have an attitude of 'keeping your head down and doing your own thing as best as you can'. Quality experiences for babies are best planned in a culture of equal concern and attention for each and every practitioner's thoughts and feelings in an atmosphere of challenge, trust and co-construction.

So what really makes a difference to quality for babies and toddlers? How best are staff kept up to date with research and the implications for practice? How do they work harmoniously together to observe children, develop a key practitioner approach and design their curriculum for babies?

There are many initiatives developed in Early Years Development and Childcare Partnerships (EYDCPs). These may include a good resource library, a running programme of courses and visits matched to a training needs analysis, regular in-house staff team sessions for planning and evaluation, localised home-grown and -owned curricula and networks and cluster groups of support and professional discourse.

Paramount is attention to the following *processes* and *practices* of quality: a journey of change, over time, observation, a key person approach and curriculum. I will take these in turn.

Observation: tuning into children

> [To] be a good observer...This requires a space in the mind where thoughts can begin to take shape and where confused experiences can be held in an inchoate form until their meaning becomes clearer. This kind of mental functioning requires a capacity to tolerate anxiety, uncertainty, discomfort, helplessness, a sense of bombardment.
>
> (Rustin 1997)

Observation is taking time to hear and see what a child seems to be doing, feeling or thinking. A practitioner observes, then 'documents' (Dahlberg *et al.* 1999) the experience of being alongside the child, in the child's shoes. The observation...spoken or written...is communicated through personal expressions as distinctive as any thumb print. This subjective expression reflects what each practitioner knows from studying, and then how she or he relates that knowledge to his or her own experiences in an effort to understand what may be going on for a child. Observation opens up possibilities of empathy.

Rigorous, reflective observation of babies and toddlers involves psychological and pedagogical states of uncertainty. That is, a capacity to hold back on first thoughts, resisting projecting personal ideas or feelings of our own on to the baby so as to leave time for supposing, time to imagine what other feelings might be in a child's heart and mind. That is a psychological state of uncertainty.

It is also important to reflect on a child's meanings or intentions before taking action, before planning an activity, or deciding on a method, or an approach to supporting the child's learning. That is a state of pedagogical uncertainty.

Tuning into children through observation involves the adult's capacity to tolerate the anxiety associated with uncertainty about the meaning or implication of what the adult takes in – in his or her mind and eye. That means not rushing into a response to a child without careful listening and thoughtfulness. This thinking process, rather than an instant 'common sense' response, is important if we are to enhance the quality of our interactions with a child who is learning to manage his or her own feelings, or moving on at his or her own pace to the next zone of his or her own thinking (Berk and Winser 1995; Rustin *et al.* 1997; Elfer and Selleck 1999).

These processes are exemplified from documented case study material from the London Borough of Hammersmith and Fulham (LBH&F) EYDCP. These examples come from an area of London that provides services for families from diverse economic, social and cultural communities (LBH&F EYDCP, Annex 5 of the plan, 1999). In the following excerpts practitioners have used their preferred methodology. Some observations are scribed from conversations, some are excerpts from a diary between a pair of key workers/practitioners, and others are small pieces from the 'learning stories' written by a key worker practitioner to be shared with the child's parents and the staff team. (There were also video observations that are not accessible here.) These examples are part of the documentation of a project with two staff teams over many weeks of observations in their own settings. The significance of the qualities of the observer and his or her potential for recognising as well as enhancing the quality of children's experiences is dynamic.

Ibrahim, 26 months: a spoken observation in a staff team

'Ibrahim grabbed at the fruit, I told him he had to share, the last piece was for Rose-May. I wondered how Ibrahim felt when he had to share the fruit? Was he being greedy? Was he hungry and should he have the right to help himself? Is it socially acceptable to take food in a group? If Ibrahim had helped himself there would not be enough pieces for everyone to have some, but he was hungry . . .'

'Are we preparing children to belong in the group in nursery . . . should we also be supporting them to belong to their own families and communities? Can we do both? Are manners different in groups? Maybe at home you can help yourself when you are hungry, at nursery you have to take one piece only. Are we denying children's home cultures at a formative time in their identities?'

'Ibrahim threw a piece of jigsaw at my forehead, it really hurt me when I was helping the children with the pieces. I felt upset with all the children scrabbling and pulling. Ibrahim was upset too.'

Different responses were offered as possibilities/opinions of working with Ibrahim. They included the following suggestions of how a practitioner should respond when he hurt Rose-May. Say:

'Stop crying, it's all right.'

or

'I am not cross with you, but with what you have done.'

or

'I am cross with you, that hurt me.'

or

'No! Don't do that. It is wrong.'

Managing a child's behaviour that is difficult for adults or other children

The group then explored the different values and attitudes to children and child-rearing raised by this issue and how they perceived their role in supporting and responding to Ibrahim's learning:

- As educators?
- As social trainers in acceptable etiquette?
- As carers matching their responses to children's needs, e.g. hunger; love; to be powerful and in control...?
- As adults who set limits on children's behaviour to teach them right from wrong?
- Or what?

The group said:
Responding to children depends on their age, what is going on in their life...it must be an individual response to a unique child. Ibrahim is having a hard time at the moment, you know your key children...that makes a difference. He does need telling off sometimes, he can hurt other children. As his key practitioner I can tell him off in a way that really affects him, he looks really sad, we sort of understand each other.

'Settling in'

Jack, 18 months: a spoken observation

He just wants to go to you, to be on you, to suck his thumb. He is a baby, he wants to be held, to have his finger in your ear. If you were at home he would be on your hip while you did the hoovering! Jack was over the moon to see his granny when she returned after a shorter session.

Oumou, 20 months: six-week review form and spoken observation to the team

She used to cling on to me, I used to carry her around a lot, she knew how I was special for her...but now she doesn't need me in that way she is confident and goes off with others. It was good when I had done that work well so that she was ready to move on.

Omara, 17 months: learning story (narrative observation)

Day 1: Joe (father) brought Omara in for a visit. She appeared happy and stayed close to him at all times, she made no other contact with other children in the nursery.

1st week: At the beginning she clung to her father and held her drinking bottle very tight. When I approached her she seemed to become unhappy.

2nd week: Omara cried, I picked her up and carried her round with me, I comforted her and provided her with company, I took her with me as I went about my duties in the nursery.

2nd key practitioner (job share): Omara cried all day. I carried her round and gave her water in her bottle, this did not help much. She cried for most of the day. I let her have her drinking bottle and she walked around with it to comfort her. She did not eat lunch or pudding but was able to sleep with her bottle.

3rd week: She began talking more, she ate well at lunchtime and played with the dough and the sand.

4th week: Omara came with me for a trip on the tube train. She pointed to trains at the station, laughing and shouting. She seemed very relaxed and was chasing the squirrels. She rolled on the grass with the other children and seemed to be having fun. She is able to say goodbye and wave to her father and sometimes watches him go. She will then return to her activity.

This team included staff with a range of expertise. Some are highly qualified academically and practically, whereas others were newer to work with children, or to this age-group, or recently and minimally qualified. Some staff were keen to work to preset professional guidelines – a professional job engaged in with pride and predictability. Other staff were able to approach their work in a more fluid style of involvement, open to pedagogical and psychological states of uncertainty (see above).

The quality of these observations of Jack, Ibrahim, Oumou and Omara opens up issues for practitioners, trainers and managers that are distinctive to services to children under 3 and their families, and these may be generalised to other settings.

In many pages of documentation in this project, it was possible to find many rich and significant reflective discussions about children's learning. However, comparatively few of these discussions focused on a child rather than the group; on the unique particulars of an individual child's experiences in the play spaces rather than the planned play environment for all the children, or on the received rather than the planned curriculum. It is a tribute to the sophisticated work of the team in this early years centre that there were processes and structures in place to attend to observations of children's learning (reviews, diaries, notebooks, written and video 'learning stories'). In other settings where there are no such structures there are even fewer examples of observations of individual children and their learning. What are the possible reasons for this and does it matter in the development of quality practice for babies and toddlers?

First, it seems it is hard really to look, to be in a child' shoes. It may also be painful to imagine how it might be to tune in to the parents' feelings while containing the child's desolation at separation and 'settling in' times (Omara weeping pitifully all day long, refusing food and clinging on to her new carer for comfort). It can be uncomfortable to empathise with a child who is feeling thwarted or vengeful so that his or her impulse is to hit and hurt (Ibrahim throwing the jigsaw). Yet it was because the team were able to bear it that they were capable of containing rather than denying Ibrahim's anger. They were able to bear with Omara the painful transition of settling in rather than jollying her out of it, or denying the sadness and tension of those early days in the nursery for everyone. By being able to come alongside each child's feelings in attuned observations, this team was able to evolve responsive criteria of good practice.

Secondly, our national training for practitioners working with babies and toddlers has focused on 'developmental milestones' and competency-based assessment. This culture of tidy quality rather than the complexity and diversity of babies' experiences makes it difficult to match up to each child's own interests. Practitioners have, in the past, been under pressure to 'teach' rather than to look at learning. There has been more emphasis on the 'preparation of the room' rather than on observing the learning of the children in it. This has sometimes resulted in a mismatch of curriculum for babies and toddlers. Observation of what children are really interested in and an emphasis on the *received* curriculum (through observation) rather than the planned curriculum (based on developmental stages) do seem to make a difference to children's enjoyment and involvement in their play.

For instance, Ibrahim left his repetitive play in the pushchair – pacing round the garden when Joan observed his interest in a patch of soil. She fetched a selection of spades so he could 'dig for worms'. Ibrahim initiated this new but unplanned garden activity.

Oumou chose to press the buttons of the photocopier as Sita copied letters to the parents, rather than to play in the activity set up for the group. Oumou chose to be alongside Sita. If Joan and Sita had stuck with the planned curriculum, rather than been influenced by the toddlers' preoccupations, the quality of the child's play and learning is likely to have been 'lower level' (DfEE 2001)'

Watching and listening to a child make a difference. Each child is likely to be more involved in meaningful activities when the curriculum is matched to his or her interests and when he or she is engaged in a shared purpose with others. Ibrahim didn't find a worm but pocketed his own buried coin; Oumou was delighted with the clean printed sheets she produced for Sita!

Thirdly, talking together about a child's learning needs detail, not generalities. Key practitioners who know a baby and his or her family well need to relate their curriculum to particular episodes of observed children's behaviour and play. Monica could plan for and follow up Omara's interest in the squirrels in the park. Only Monica's shared experience with Omara and her shared observations with the other staff could match Omara's personal and particular squirrel-roly-poly-grass pleasures to the team's plans and choices for play materials, songs and books to match her zone of thinking. If Monica's observation had been general ('the children had a good time in the park') rather than specific and from Omara's point of view ('Omara was relaxed and chased the squirrels, rolling on the grass'), the potential for meaningful and responsive curriculum planning might have been diminished.

More emphasis on training and professional development of observation methodology, and time to practise observation skills, is urgently needed. This is crucial if little children are not just to 'settle in' and morph into no-protest institutionalised babes where there are largely adult-led plans out of synch with an infant's moods and meanings. If babies and toddlers are to be innovators and instigators in the social synchrony of learning, the child must come before the chart, observation before responding and planning (Elfer and Selleck 1999; Trevarthen 1999; Bruner 2000).

Adults learn in a social context too. Staff teams need time to think together about their observations, to work together on the *task* of developing their practice, as well as to engage in the *process* of reflecting on the impact of their own part and contribution to their staff team.

The key person approach for children, families, staff and the nursery as a whole

Studies have helped us to understand that babies are born with a built-in readiness to make a special relationship with first one and then a small circle of adults who will protect them and meet their physical needs. Such a relationship is an 'attachment' (Rutter 1995). Babies and young children show attachment behaviour when they make sure their special adult remains nearby, crying for them, smiling when close, moving towards them when anxious and moving away and exploring when they feel safe and connected into the people who support their thinking and feelings.

Young children rely on their special adults to meet their emotional needs as well as their physical needs. Most adults most of the time are not overwhelmed by anxiety or terror or loneliness when they are away from people with whom they have close emotional ties. However, babies are easily overwhelmed by intense feelings, especially of separation from the people who have become attached: 'Ultimately the child needs to abrogate his omnipotence – abjure his magic – and learn to wait' (Phillips 1998a).

This is an elegant description of developing separateness, or independence, using the language of psychoanalysis. One- and two-year-olds begin to be able to wait a little longer than a baby can and are not so completely dependent, but they may still easily become overwhelmed. Babies and young children need a special adult on whom they can rely, someone who will meet their emotional needs as well as their physical needs. Such adults will keep them 'in mind', helping them to feel safe, understanding their expressions of love and attachment, and responding with appropriate holding, touch, movement and talk.

At home it is parents who act as these key adults and with whom the baby or young child has his or her main attachments. Key practitioners in nursery settings must take on that aspect of the parents' role during the hours they are apart. This is offering an attachment relationship, the purpose of which is to ensure the emotional and physcial needs of the baby or young child are met senstively and reliably by mainly one or two adults.

In other respects, though, relationships within the nursery are not like those at home. There is a community of people in the nursery, with a rich diversity of cultural and ethnic backgrounds, that is quite different from the family group and that offers the baby or young child special opportunities for relationships, exploration and learning not available at home. This rich network of relationships is very valuable but it complements and is dependent on the baby or young child having an attachment relationship with mainly one or two members of staff and is not an alternative to this. Very young children have not reached sufficient emotional independence to cope for other than short amounts of time without someone reliable to think about them and comfort them. With the security of this special attachment relationship, they can draw on the other relationships available in nursery settings. Without this attachment relationship, other relationships will feel bewildering and overwhelming (Shropshire and Telford EYDCP 2000; Elfer *et al.* 2001).

The diary of Omara's first few weeks recorded by her key practitioners (see above) signifies the crucial role of key practitioners in supporting children under 3 years of age and their families. In the context of carefully devised 'criteria for good practice' for 'settling in', children may have a healthy emotional start with someone in particular. In the new and stimulating nursery setting a child may then go on to learn to belong to, and become part of, the nursery community group.

An approach where practitioners may develop a pattern of trust and continuity of care with their key children and their families is crucial to a child's security. It will be necessary to manage changes in settings where children have been passed from room to room, and from key worker to key worker over their 36 months of development in one or more settings. 'Hiring teachers with a style that favours forming relationships and committing to two or three year' is a model developed in some settings (Raikes 1996). In some innovative early years centres it is now possible for children to stay with their key practitioner and to remain with their key group of peers as they progress from babyhood into the 'foundation stage' (Pascal *et al.* 1999; West 2000).

This commitment to constancy and continuity in relationships within settings is likely to be the most significant factor in the quality experiences for children under 3 years of age.

Developmentally distinctive curriculum

The following three observations of different children in different settings are picked out in order to consider what may be a distinctive curriculum for the under-3s. In the stages from birth and on to connect into the Foundation stage, these three children are making their own choices, following their own schema, using the spaces, materials and resources available to them. They are making sense of what is of interest to them.

Samir, 20 months, with Tyrese, 18 months

After a tearful and tense start to the morning, Samir settles with a group at the water trough. He selects two plastic cars from the boxes of toys. He places them at opposite corners on the rim of the water trough and then drives them together and crashes them with accompanying crash noises. He selects another car and offers it to Tyrese in a gesture that invites him to join in. Tyrese copies Samir and runs the car across the opposite side of the trough. 'I got car,' calls Samir as he follows the rim of the trough. Samir drives the cars round the corners and finally crashes again. 'I got car,' he calls each time to Tyrese as he seems to celebrate the drive round the edge and the crashing crescendo.

Ibrahim, 26 months

He wakes from his afternoon nap, gathers his bedding, and hands it to an adult. Then while he is waiting for help with his shoes, he takes a small toy truck and wheels it round the perimeter of the rug. He carefully follows the border of the rug and precisely 'drives' it round each of the corners. As soon as he is dressed he chooses a trike from the garden and drives it round the perimeter path.

Hermione, 30 months, and Jayanthi, 26 months, with Mandy (practitioner)

Hermione sucks on her bottle lying in the home corner after her nanny leaves her in her playgroup. Mandy offers pillows, occasionally passing, sometimes talking with her in an unhurried manner over 25 minutes.

Hermione is sucking and rocking dreamily. Once or twice she stands up and looks about the room, adjusts the enclosure she has made for herself, pushing the home corner furniture closer together, creating a set of boundaries for the space she was in alone.

After the bottle was finished she stood and watched all the activities in turn, sand, clay, an adult making Christmas chains, the climbing frame, the sand. Hermione inspected each activity, looking at what was on offer, talking to the children and adults briefly and briefly connecting with each group, making a circuit of the room.

Then she rushed out to the garden and the trikes as the outside doors were opened. Hermione called to Jayanthi and they made a number of circuits of the whole garden rushing from one side to the other and back again. Then Hermione instigated a number of stops, the fences, the bump in the grass, the pillar. Each time stopping to talk to Jayanthi, to call her to stop too, and to plan with her where to cycle next, and where they would stop next, she called to Jayanthi: 'Turn at the fence; stop by Mandy; over the bumbbety bump . . .'

These three children are learning in so many ways but, for the purposes of this chapter, we will think about just one area of learning . . . mathematical development. These three children are learning the foundations for mathematics. Hermione (with Jayanthi) and Samir (with Tyrese) are being active mathematicians, expressing mathematical ideas and making mathematical discoveries with a companion. The children call to one another as they trace the boundaries. Ibrahim and Hermione are exploring the garden space on the tricycle, feeling the extremities of the pathways. Each child is repeatedly 'measuring' the length of the path, and mapping the route and its landmarks, the pillar, the bump over the grass, the end at the fence, turning corners. Three toddlers expressing with their active bodies their thinking, imagining and understanding of mathematical concepts and ideas (ECEF 1998).

Hermione, at 30 months, has progressed to developing her own mathematical ideas and methods to solve practical problems. She is able to play at, as well as talk about, position, direction and movement in her trike riding. She was able to give instructions to other children about movement and direction: '*round* the pillar, *over* the bump, *turn* at the fence, and *stop* at the bench by Mandy.' All these calculations and transactions are accomplishments that match the end-of-year outcomes for reception class children set out in the National Numeracy Strategy and in the curriculum for the Foundation stage (QCA 2000). Samir and Ibrahim sustained an interest for a length of time on a construction they each decided to work on (driving round the boundary of the rug and the water trough). They describe the simple journey with their own imaginative vocalisations about force and direction, 'stepping stones' of progress as detailed in the curriculum guidelines (QCA 2000: 80).

What is distinctive about the learning powers of this age-group and the practitioners who need to develop their practice to support that learning? Pedagogues from different cultures and theoretical perspectives have documented the significance of children in the spaces of their environment. Athey (1990) and Nutbrown (1994: 10–15) assert it is not sufficient simply to identify a child's interest or his or her pattern of repeatable behaviour into which experiences are assimilated and gradually co-ordinated. If observation seems to indicate that Samir, Ibrahim and Hermione are preoccupied with the early action 'schema' of 'going round a boundary' then each child needs to be provided with a range of interesting and stimulating experiences (including but not exclusively mathematical ones) which extend thinking along that particular path.

We may match our observations to our chosen frameworks or theories (e.g. Montessori, High/Scope, national guidelines for day care or an approach of observing children's schema). We may also be bound by our own constructions and cultures of childhood. (A powerful child or an obedient child? An innocent child or a little terror? A child growing towards independence and omnipotence or dependent and democratic?) These debates must be the backdrop to each setting's own preferred curriculum.

So there should be no certainty or absolute in advocating curriculum for, or with, this age-group. What seem most important, bearing in mind contemporary research and diverse family and community contexts, are the following:

- *Following a child's inclinations*, curiosities, schema and then as adults we may wonder, reflect and enjoy the children's capacities, imaginations and creations, found by themselves, and engaged in for themselves.
- *Being energetic and responsive* in turn to offer the most aesthetically pleasing, multi-sensory spaces, places and objects to engage with a child's powers to think, to express and explore, to represent, construct and reconstruct according to each child's own logic, pace and pattern.
- *Embracing each baby into a community* of conviviality, passionate and compassionate feelings, lively reciprocity of conversation-like exchanges within the shared cultural values of each of our multifaceted communities, a social culture that may be modified and flexible in the interests of the people in it – people under 3 years of age too!

References

Athey, C. (1990) *Extending Thought in Young Children: a parent-teacher partnership*. London: Paul Chapman Publishing.

Balbernie, R. (2000) 'Violent behaviour: tracing its roots'. *Young Minds Newsletter*, no. 46.

Benn, M. (1998) *Madonna and Child: towards a new politics of Motherhood*. London: Jonathan Cape.

Berk, L. and Winser, A. (1995) *Scaffolding Children's Learning: Vygotsky and early childhood education.* Washington, DC: NAEYC.

Bruner, J. (2000) 'Tot thought'. *New York Review,* 9 March.

Dahlberg, G., Moss, P. and Pence, A. (1999) *Beyond Quality in Early Childhood Education and Care: postmodern perspectives.* London: Falmer Press.

de Zulueta, F. (1993) *From Pain to Violence: the traumatic roots of destructiveness.* London: Whurr Publishers.

DfEE (2001) *National Standards for Under Eights. Day Care and Childminding.* DfEE 0488/2001.

Early Childhood Education Forum (1998) *Quality in Diversity.* London: National Children's Bureau.

Elfer, P. (1996) 'Building intimacy in relationships with young children in nurseries'. *Early Years* **16**.

Elfer, P. (1997) *Attachment Theory and Day Care for Young Children. Highlight* **155**. London: National Children's Bureau.

Elfer, P. and Selleck, D. (1999) 'Children under three in nurseries: uncertainty as a creative factor in child observations'. *European Early Childhood Education Research Journal* **7**.

Elfer, P., Goldschmied, E. and Selleck, D. (2001) *Working with Children under Three: The key person relationship.* Available from Peter Elfer at the University of Surrey.

Elfer, P., Selleck, D. and Goldschmied, E. (2003) *Key Persons in the Nursery.* London: David Fulton Publishers.

Goldschmied, E. and Jackson, S. (1994) *People Under Three: young children in day care.* London: Routledge.

Goldschmied, E. and Selleck, D. (1996) *Communication between Babies in their First Year.* London: National Children's Bureau.

Lane, J. (1999) *Action for Racial Equality in the Early Years.* London: National Early Years Network.

Nutbrown, C. (1994) *Threads of Thinking.* London: Paul Chapman.

Pascal, C. *et al.* (1999) *Research to Inform the Evaluation of the Early Excellence Centres Pilot Programme.* Worcester: Centre for Research in Early Childhood, University College Worcester.

Phillips, A. (1998) *Monogamy.* London: Faber & Faber.

QCA (2000) *Curriculum Guidance for the Foundation Stage.* London: QCA/DfEE.

Raikes, H. (1996) 'A secure base for babies: applying attachment concepts to the infant care setting'. *Young Children* **51**, 59–67.

Robertson, J. and Robertson, J. (1989) *Separation in the very young.* Free Association Books.

Rustin, M. (1997) in Miller, L., Rustin, M. and Shuttleworth, J. (eds) *Closely Observed Infants.* London: Duckworth.

Rutter, M. (1995) 'Clinical implications of attachment concepts, retrospect and prospect.' *Journal of Child Psychology and Psychiatry* **36**, 549–71.

Shropshire and Telford & Wreakin EYDCP joint training initiative (2000) *Staff Development for Baby and Toddler: observations in group care.*

Trevarthen, C. (1999) An interview recorded and scribed for BBC Radio 4 by Angie Mason in the BBC Radio series *Tuning into Children*. Extracts in Purves and Selleck (1999).

West, M. (2000) 'A case study of the key person approach'. Available from Dorothy Selleck.

Whaley, K. L. and Rubenstein, T. S. (1994) 'How toddlers do friendship'. *Journal of Social and Personal Relationships* **11** (3), 383–400.

Chapter 9

Movement as a vehicle for learning

Helen Bilton

Introduction

Wells (1987) describes children as 'meaning makers'. In many respects we are all meaning makers, trying to make sense of the world around us. By adulthood we have found many of the answers but children constantly have to make sense of everything that is happening around them and to them. To understand why things happen as they do, to understand what is safe, what is not, what is right, what is wrong, what is interesting, what is not, why an object works as it does, why our family or community behaves as it does are all questions that puzzle children. There are various ways to help children explore and make sense of their experiences and it is important to find the easiest and most accessible mode that engages the child. For young children the most effective vehicles by which to teach and help them learn are play, movement, talk and sensory experience. Young children are naturally drawn to play, are constantly on the move, have a strong desire to talk and want to examine, feel and explore anything they come into contact with. So as adults we need to tap into these modes and teach through them. Interestingly not only are play, movement and sensory experience vehicles for learning, they act as learning in themselves. Children learn *through* play, movement, talk and sensory experience, they also learn how *to* play, move, talk and experience. So as an adult plays with a child, or helps a child to stack bricks, the child learns how to play or move and learns about how to behave in a certain situation or how the exact placing of the bricks creates a high stack. Movement and moving to learn helps the child to think and socialise, and supports their physical development.

Movement is bound up with the whole development of a child, with their physical, intellectual, emotional and social development, and all that they do, think and feel can be helped through movement and examined in movement terms. Mind and body need to develop together and support each other. It needs to be appreciated, however, that there is movement and there is physical development; the former is a mode through which children can learn and the latter is one aspect of child development. Movement is walking, playing with another child, pulling a truck, building with bricks, painting a picture, or walking along a balancing beam. It can be physical, constructive or creative play and is therefore more than just physical development. Physical development is about 'change in organisation and structure' (Stainthorpe 1989: 12). It is about the change in size of the body, how the various parts of the body work together, about the strengthening of the body and all its parts and a more and more refined use of the body and its parts. It is about developing more control, coordination and balance and is about the refinement of gross and fine motor skills such as the development of walking and pencil control. Physical development and movement need to be seen as different but not mutually exclusive. Both are equally important to a child.

Movement and settings

Davies (1995) argues that 'Movement is so much a fundamental part of our lives that, understandably, those concerned with child care and education may not necessarily see the need to classify what must, after all, seem obvious' (p.1). This problem has been compounded with the listing of development in statutory curricula and guidance and the importance placed on seven-year-olds passing tests. Mathematical and linguistic development can be seen as more important than many other areas of development, particularly physical and creative development. As physical development and movement are often confused, this has resulted in the unfortunate consequence of movement being demoted as a mode of learning. However, it needs to be appreciated that movement is central to young children's learning and can be described, promoted, supported, enriched and recorded.

Movement from birth

The centrality of movement to growth and learning can be seen from the very start of life. From birth, children discover through moving themselves about and manipulating materials about them. The prime concerns for a baby are interaction with others and to be in a position to explore, hence the strong drive to reach, sit up, crawl and walk. The Sure Start guidance on children from birth to three, *Birth to three matters* (Sure Start Unit 2002), describes, very clearly, four development stages:

   0–8 months – heads up, lookers and communicators

   8–18 months – sitters, standers and explorers

   18–24 months – movers, shakers and players

   24–36 months – walkers, talkers and pretenders.

   (p.14)

This list demonstrates that 0–3 year olds are concerned with moving, communicating and playing. A baby loves to play the disappear/reappear game where they drop an object and someone else picks it up and returns it. Through this game the baby is moving the object about, so they are learning to grasp, pick up and let go but they are also learning about the fact that something gone does not go for ever and that an object can return to their sight and is still the same. And so this discovery continues until the three- and four-year-old wants to understand such concepts as 'near and far', 'heavy and light', 'lines and curves' and similar principles. Children need to explore these for themselves, to find out by looking and feeling for themselves. Their own movement and the manipulation of the world around them is their way of finding out about such concepts. For example, 'heavy and light' can be explored through pulling a truck with and without a child in. 'Lines and curves' can be discovered by making these with bricks, blocks or stones.

Three year old Roothfada spent ten minutes collecting milk crates, one at a time and placing them thoughtfully in a long line. When she had finished she beckoned the teacher over and said, standing at one end, 'Isn't that long?'

For this child using real equipment and making a long object best achieved the understanding of the concept long and its opposite short. This would not have been achieved if the child had been told to draw a long and a short line on a piece of paper. She had to really feel 'long' to understand and appreciate it (see Figure 9.1).

Figure 9.1
Building a long line.

Having learnt to crawl, walk and run, children continue to refine these skills and learn through these skills. Infant children enjoy playing chase games. Through these games they are learning the physical skills of moving fast, stopping quickly, turning and reacting quickly. But they will also be experiencing feelings such as excitement through being chased, the thrill of not being caught and learning to cope when they are caught. So although 'catch' can look like nothing much – just a bit of running about – it involves activity, feeling and thinking.

Movement and thinking

Bruner (1981) argues that the modes of learning for young children are the enactive (action), the iconic (graphic or visual), and the symbolic (abstract). The enactive mode, based on action is about learning by doing it oneself. Athey (1990) identifies schemas that are patterns of behaviour that are significant in helping children make sense of their world and learning. What is important about schemas is that they involve repetition. For example a toddler may get off and on a box 15 or more times. The child is mastering and refining the technique of moving up and down. A child may use scissors to cut anything and everything in order to discover the full range of possibilities with scissors. Athey argues that through physical activity children can secure information about themselves, the environment and the topological properties of objects, and understand shape, form and movement. Through movement children can find out about space, direction, laterality, dominance. All of these are important with regard to, for example, coping with writing, manipulating tools or crossing the road. Maude (2001) argues that children who have to overcome problems of delayed movement development, such as dyspraxia, need more opportunities to improve and master their actions. Movement is about enabling children to get to grips with things so that they can eventually get to grips with ideas.

Four-year-old Mario had a truck stacked with crates, which were badly arranged, and in danger of toppling over. In fact this was exactly what happened when another child crashed into the truck. Mario set to work and tried to stack them in a more orderly fashion but with the addition of the tenth crate they all fell down. Mario decided to take all the crates out of the truck and start from the beginning. He tried the crates so that the maximum surface area of the truck was covered. He eventually worked out that two flat, and one on its side, used the space most effectively. He then very carefully stacked the crates one on top of the other, ensuring they all fitted properly. The stacks got too high and Mario was confused as to what to do to be able to continue stacking. He then decided to use a chair to stand on. Having finally got the thirteen crates into the truck, Mario, *without* moving the truck, realised that the crates balanced on their sides would fall out unless he secured them in some way. He asked the teacher for a rope, and spent some time attaching the rope to the crates on their side and then feeding the rope through and attaching it to the securely standing crates. Mario moved off with the truck and the crates stayed in place. The whole process had taken thirty minutes (Bilton 1989).

Apart from a brief functional conversation, Mario had not spoken, but this did not mean he had not been thinking. He had solved a number of problems and had foreseen another. Mario could not have solved the puzzle of fitting 13 crates into a truck if he had been asked to work it out on paper, but through this activity this is what he did.

Movement social interaction

Children want and need to talk and be with other children and adults. Babies will seek out others to converse and play with; if they do not get the contact they will cry out for it. The strong drive to actually get moving has a dual purpose – to enable the child to discover more of the world and to have control over who they interact with. Babies are naturally drawn to play, whether it be 'peepo' or playing with a rattle. As the baby moves into toddler-hood this interest in play continues and they want to be the actual character, whether it be the mother, mechanic or fast-food assistant. Role-play by its very nature involves movement, activity and talk; you cannot be a mum or dog unless you are allowed to move around and communicate.

Two-year-old Rachel filled a bucket with sand using a small spade. She gave the bucket to her mother. 'Ta' said her mother and pretended to eat the 'food'. The mother then asked, 'Could I have some more food?' Rachel took the bucket back to the sand pit, emptied and refilled it. When the mother had finished 'eating' this sand, she said, 'Would you like some?' offering her the bucket. Rachel said, 'No'. However, she went back to the sand pit, filled another bucket and returned to sit next to her mother and 'eat'.

Through this play scene the child was acting out the procedures of making and serving food – a daily family activity. If the mother had said she wanted Rachel to talk about how we prepare and serve food, the child would have found this a difficult and meaningless task, but by her actions she was showing her knowledge. The child demonstrated the significant nature of the play, by not wishing to share her mother's food with her, because in their home each person has their own plate of food.

Movement and feelings

Movement is clearly linked to emotional development. The way a person or child moves says something about the way they feel. If a child walks with their head down, plodding along lethargically, it may mean they are not feeling too happy. However, if a child is striding along, swinging their arms, it suggests that they have a purpose and want to achieve it. Through movement children can express their feelings, whether by skipping for joy, running to win, stamping to let out anger, shaking with excitement or walking to get rid of tension. Movement and activity can reflect inner thoughts and feelings. The 'terrible twos' is described as such because two-year-olds can often display what might be described as quite difficult behaviour. They behave like this in part because they are at a stage where they understand far more than they can actually do and explain and so become frustrated. Throwing a toy, which they cannot fit together, is often simply a sign of frustration, not naughtiness, a way of expressing their feelings through action.

Success in movement can improve self-image. Children who are successful in movement terms, whether it be running or using a pencil or simply getting into a car, will feel more confident in all other areas. Success in movement reinforces children's self-image; how they feel about their body will affect how they feel about themselves (Gallahue 1989). The opposite must, therefore, also hold: that lack of success in movement can lower the self-image. A study by a physical education teacher (Stewart 1989) into children with coordination problems found that these problems caused other difficulties, namely, lack of confidence and self-esteem, poor behaviour, restlessness, poor handwriting and introversion. By offering these children a structured PE programme he found that not only did the children's motor skills improve but so too did their self-esteem, both in physical education and in general class activities. Where teachers make children take some exercise before the sedentary work, they find children are more able to settle as their bodies have been exercised and are ready for the rest. Exercise can raise the mood of a person, lessen anxiety and raise self-esteem. Many people go to gyms; they come away, albeit tired, but usually with a raised state of emotion, wellbeing, satisfaction and achievement.

An environment for movement

If children need to move and learn through the actual movement, then it follows they need an environment that will promote this type of behaviour. Practitioners need to make the environment safe but one that can be used to its full potential. It is therefore important to let children experiment and discover rather than stop them doing something. For example it is much more effective for the child's development to sit on the stairs with them and let them experiment going up and down rather than never allowing them to touch the stairs. Likewise it is more effective to remove the fragile ornament than having to constantly stop a child touching it. Better to put something in their reach that is safe. An effective and safe environment is one where children can move objects around by themselves, be it a box of bricks or cushions from the sofa or soil in the ground. Young children need resources they can use, with adults about keeping a watchful eye. As children get older they do not need to be watched quite as closely but still need the resources to experiment with. An environment for the promotion of movement does not require lots of expensive equipment but simply the imaginative use of most household items, for example sofa cushions on the floor to represent a boat, or an old curtain draped over two chairs to represent a den. A cardboard box can create endless opportunities for finding out and learning through movement. Movement as a mode of learning can occur anywhere, in both the indoor and the outdoor environments. What the outdoor environment can offer, which indoors cannot, is the space for children to move freely, to move so that they can use their whole bodies in imaginative and fantasy play situations, to grapple with concepts which can more easily be understood and appreciated on a large scale, such as space and shape (see Figure 9.1).

Some children may need adaptations made to the environment so they can learn through movement. DJ, who had sickle cell anaemia and partial sight, started nursery just after he was four. His mother was very concerned about how he would cope with the hustle and bustle of a busy classroom and could be overprotective. DJ was seen as another member of the class and the environment was adapted to suit his needs. Initially this adaptation came in the form of constant adult support, but DJ did not want things done for him. He needed adults to give helpful information as to where things were and if he was about to bump into something. His favourite area was outside and the staff initially adapted this by trying to keep equipment in a similar place each day. Once DJ had settled in nursery he did not need the helpful information and the children became 'DJ aware'. They would tell him if he was about to crash and learnt not to run directly at him. With these small adaptations DJ was able to gain more from his nursery experience.

In conclusion: movement is a natural part of any child's life. Through movement children can express their ideas and thoughts, make connections in their understanding and show how they feel about something. The study of children through their movements is central to understanding them.

References

Athey, C. (1990) *Extending Thought in Young Children: a parent–teacher partnership*. London: Paul Chapman Publishing.

Bilton, H. (1989) *The Development and Significance of the Nursery Garden and Outdoor Play*, unpublished MA dissertation, University of Surrey.

Bruner, J. (1981) 'What is representation?', in Roberts, M. and Tamburrini, J. (eds) *Child Development 0–5*. Edinburgh: Holmes McDougall.

Davies, M. (1995) *Helping Children Learn through a Movement Perspective*. London: Hodder and Stoughton.

Gallahue, D.L. (1989) *Motor Development. Infants, Children, Adolescents*, 2nd edn. Indianapolis: Benchmark Press.

Maude, P. (2001) *Physical Children, Active Teaching*. Buckingham: Open University Press.

Stainthorp, R. (1989) *Practical Psychology for Primary Teachers. Putting theory into practice in the classroom*. London: Falmer Press.

Stewart, D. (1989) 'Forward role', *The Times Educational Supplement*, 21 April, B2.

Sure Start Unit (2002) *Birth to Three Matters: A framework to support children in their earliest years.* London: DfES.

Wells, G. (1987) *The Meaning Makers: children learning language and using language to learn.* London: Hodder and Stoughton.

Chapter 10

Creativity: working in partnership with parents

Bernadette Duffy and Jan Stillaway

Introduction

At Thomas Coram Early Childhood Centre, we see creativity as part of all areas of learning and as much a part of literacy and mathematics as of music and painting. Learning through the visual and performing arts is viewed as beneficial in its own right and is seen as contributing to all aspects of a child's development (Duffy 1998). This view is shared by many early years practitioners and is endorsed by Qualifications and Curriculum Authority Foundation Stage Guidance: 'Creativity is fundamental to successful learning. Being creative enables children to make connections between one area of learning and another and to extend their understanding' (QCA 2000: 116). It is also reflected in the DfES guidance for the very youngest children *Birth to Three Matters*, where one strand of the component 'A Competent Learner' is 'Being Creative' (Sure Start Unit 2002). The Foundation Stage Guidance and *Birth to Three Matters* also stress the importance of working with parents and carers as partners and this raises a number of questions. How do parents feel about creativity? Do all parents feel the same? Or are there differences based perhaps on age, culture, gender, class and faith? Do all parents see creativity as an essential life skill? In this chapter we will look at these, and other questions, based on our experience at Thomas Coram, where we are fortunate to work with parents in a linguistically, religiously, culturally, ethnically and economically diverse community.

Thomas Coram Early Childhood Centre

In order to make sense of the case studies below it may be helpful to give a little background information. Thomas Coram Early Childhood Centre is part of Coram Community Campus, which is situated in south Camden, London. The campus is home to a number of providers from the maintained and voluntary sectors who share a common aim of supporting children and their families. The early childhood centre is open from 8.00 each morning until 5.30/6.00 in the evening for 48 weeks of the year and has places for 108 children from six months to five years. The centre is staffed by a multidisciplinary staff team, which includes a music teacher funded by the National Foundation for Youth Music who runs the 'Finding our Voices' project. There are strong links with community arts organisations such as the October Gallery and Camden Dance Festival. Parents and carers are actively involved in all aspects of the centre's work (Draper and Duffy 2001). They are particularly involved in supporting creativity and the case studies below explore some dimensions of this partnership.

Case study one. The importance of relationships, respect and trust

Often early years practitioners express concern, or even, occasionally, annoyance, at some parents' unwillingness to allow their child to freely explore materials such as paint, clay or water. Heidi was one such parent. She and her partner expressed their views vocally during the initial parent conference. They did not want their son Brendan messing about with paint because it ruined his clothes and was a waste of time. Staff spent some time explaining the centre's philosophy and, while Heidi and her partner accepted that Brendan would have access to paint while he was at the centre, they remained unconvinced that this would benefit their son in any way. While Heidi was settling Brendan into the centre his key worker used the time to build a relationship with Heidi as well as Brendan. As the key worker got to know Heidi, she came to understand that for Heidi and her partner, Brendan's physical appearance was a reflection of their care and concern for him, so if he looked messy this meant that he was uncared for. Heidi's own experiences of school art had not been positive: there had been little opportunity to explore and create, and a strong emphasis on things looking 'right'. The key worker encouraged Heidi to observe Brendan's exploration of paint and to see how carefully he chose and mixed the colours he wanted. She also encouraged Brendan to wear the aprons provided and to roll up his sleeves to minimise the amount of paint he got on his clothes. Heidi was especially impressed by how long Brendan spent concentrating on his creations and the pleasure and satisfaction he showed in his work. Over time Heidi became much more confident in the centre's approach and started to get involved in some of the sessions the staff run to look at different aspects of the curriculum. When her second son was born she brought him along to the painting workshops and encouraged him to get fully involved as soon as he could crawl!

Case study two. Taking time to discuss different values and traditions

Values and traditions differ between communities and it is important that practitioners respect this and give parents opportunities to discuss and share their views. Thomas Coram adopts a developmental approach to writing: we encourage children to explore mark making from babyhood onwards and, over time, help children develop their understanding and use of conventional scripts. For some parents this is a very different approach from the one they are used to, and such an approach seems less effective to them than formal teaching and an emphasis on copying letters. During a curriculum workshop Miriam, a parent from Palestine, explained that she was used to a much more formal approach and was concerned that her three-year-old daughter was missing out: 'It's much quicker to show her what to do and get her to copy until she gets it right.' Another parent from India joined in the discussion. He explained that he used to share that view and initially had been concerned that compared with her cousins in India his daughter, Aysha, was making slow progress; however, he had now changed his view. While it had taken Aysha longer to form letters correctly, the developmental approach had enabled her to make sense of the process and at five she was a fluent writer who loved to write whenever she got the opportunity. As her father commented, at this point: 'It's not the way we were taught but I can see it works for Aysha.'

Case study three. Finding different ways of sharing

As a staff team we see music as part of what makes us human (Trevarthen 1995) so we began the music project 'Finding our Voices' with great enthusiasm. We spent time discussing how the music maker would work with children and staff, how children would be grouped, the content of the sessions and how we would evaluate the project. However, during the early stages of the project staff grew frustrated that, despite repeated requests, parents continued to send their children to nursery in tights (often under trousers) on music days. As the children needed to be barefoot in sessions this tended to greatly increase the time and support children needed before and after their group times, as well as sometimes seeming to cause the children some embarrassment. After making enquiries of parents, staff concluded that the tights were only rarely worn in line with particular cultural beliefs, so why were parents not co-operating and supporting the music project? It occurred to us that while we had spent time discussing the project among ourselves, we had not given equal time to discussion with parents, but had assumed they shared our views and understandings. Staff decided to address this by videoing some music sessions and showing the footage of the music sessions at a parent workshop. As this was also the beginning of the workshop programme, staff were expecting perhaps five or six parents to attend. However, on the day that the music session video was shown, staff watched with some amazement as the workshop room quickly filled to capacity and as, once all the seats were taken, more parents continued to arrive and had to stand at the back or sit on the floor. What had seemed to the stressed staff team to be a lack of interest from parents was, more accurately, a lack of any real understanding of what the project was trying to achieve. During the meeting parents explained that they had dressed their children in tights and trousers to ensure that they kept warm especially during the long periods they spent outside exploring the nursery garden. Following the workshop, and of course the occasional reminder, tights did begin to disappear on 'dance days'. Parents also began to give staff much more feedback about their children's responses to the sessions and to discuss the project with much more confidence. This experience reminded us of the importance of continually discussing our work with parents. We also discovered that making a video showing children participating in something was much more meaningful than all our attempts to describe what the dance and music sessions involved. No amount of explaining was equal to being able to see and hear the children actually performing, and being given the opportunity to discuss what the children were getting from the sessions.

Case study four. The power of performance and the importance of sensitivity

A group of older children and some staff participated in Camden's annual dance festival for schools, which culminated in the children performing a dance on stage at the Bloomsbury Theatre. While generally positive about the experience, staff expressed a range of anxieties about the project. Not least was the concern that the notion of 'rehearsals' was not developmentally appropriate for such young children. In keeping with their characteristic creativity the children often preferred to invent their own variations on the theme! When we finally danced on stage, however, almost every parent, many of whom work full time, managed to come and see their child perform. Staff were overwhelmed with thanks from parents and inundated with requests for video footage and photographs. The video was shown repeatedly at nursery to an appreciative audience of parents and children. As a staff team we have come to recognise the importance of sharing the children's work through performances. Initially we were concerned that such occasions would put the children under too much pressure and stunt their creativity. Instead we have found that the warm and positive feedback the children receive from parents and the wider community enhances their self-esteem, and parents take real pride and pleasure in their children's achievements. This sharing of the children's creativity leads to shared understanding and sense of community.

However, we always have to be sensitive to the needs of particular families. When staff asked permission from parents for their children to perform at the theatre, they noticed that one set of parents failed to return the form. Their daughter had thoroughly enjoyed the practice dance sessions and was an unusually imaginative and graceful dancer. When pressed, her father seemed somewhat reluctant but duly returned the form giving permission for her to participate. On the day of the performance she simply didn't come to nursery. She reappeared several days later with a vague explanation from her parents that she had been unwell. She was obviously disappointed that she had missed the visit to the theatre. We had failed to find a way to listen to these parents' initial concerns about the dance performance with the respect and seriousness they deserved. Perhaps if we had, we might have found a way either to allay their fears or to at least ensure that their child didn't expect to perform. This would have shown her that we respected her family's viewpoint. The family might also then have been able to make a decision about how much she would be involved in preparations for the performance. It is also possible that practitioners underestimate how difficult it might be for parents to explain their views when they challenge our own. This is particularly true if parents fear hurting the feelings of people they otherwise respect or fear seeming 'ungrateful' in face of the obvious enthusiasm and commitment of staff.

Conclusion

There is no such thing as a typical parent! From our experience at Thomas Coram we have learned that we need to actively seek the views of all the parents we are working with and not assume that the views of some are representative of all. We have to offer parents different ways of sharing their views – some parents enjoy group discussion, while for others individual approaches are far more productive. It is also essential that staff are clear about the importance of creativity and the arts in early childhood, and throughout life, and use a variety of ways of sharing this with parents and carers. Actually seeing their child's enjoyment and satisfaction, for example as part of a dance performance, has been key for a number of parents, and the use of video footage and digital photography has been a way of preserving these experiences. Giving parents an opportunity to explore the thrill of creation for themselves has been important for many parents. Finally, it is important to see discussion as ongoing and developmental. Shared understandings take time to evolve and are well worth the investment when it comes to supporting and developing children's creativity.

References

Draper, L. and Duffy, B. (2001) 'Working with parents' in Pugh, G. (ed.) (2001) *Contemporary Issues in the Early Years*. London: Paul Chapman Publishing.

Duffy, B. (1998) *Supporting Creativity and Imagination in the Early Years*. Buckingham: Open University Press.

Qualifications and Curriculum Authority (2000) *Curriculum Guidance for the Foundation Stage*. London: HMSO.

Sure Start Unit (2002) *Birth to Three Matters – a framework to support children in their earliest years*. London: DfES.

Trevarthen, C. (1995) 'The child's need to learn a culture' *Children and Society* **9** (1), 5–19.

Chapter 11

Creative practice and practice which fosters creativity

Anna Craft and Bob Jeffrey

Introduction

In this chapter, we discuss some distinctions between creative practice and practice which fosters creativity. In doing so we draw on case study data from empirical work carried out in English nursery and first schools since the mid-1990s. Throughout the chapter we use the term 'practice' to encompass all early years activity. It is suggested that these terms may be relevant across all early years settings, although in this reading the research we draw on was done with teachers in school and nursery settings.

What do *you* think of, when you imagine creativity in early years practice? The following event took place near the start of the school year, in a class of five-to six-year-olds, where one of the authors was working as a researcher, alongside the teacher.

Possibilities and thinking thumbs

A small group of five-year-olds are working with a disparate selection of materials that their teacher has introduced to them. The materials include bread, glue, tissue paper, scissors, water and card. During the discussion, before they start on their own individual projects, their teacher encourages them to explore the properties of each resource, showing that they are thinking by waggling their 'thinking thumbs'. She talks gently but purposively with the children, trying to maintain a relationship with each as an individual. As the children come up with ideas of how the materials could be used, she uses language carefully to hint that each person will make up their own mind about how to use these materials. '*You* might be going to do that,' she mentions several times in response to ideas.

Is this acting creatively to embrace effective learning or is it a practice which fosters creativity? Or is it both? And what do we mean by these?

If we look at policy on education, we find a distinction made in 1999 by the report of the National Advisory Committee on Creative and Cultural Education (NACCCE 1999). It defined creative teaching as 'teaching creatively' (using imaginative approaches to make learning more interesting and effective) and 'teaching for creativity' (forms of teaching that are intended to develop children's own creative thinking or behaviour).

In this chapter, we use the terms 'creative practice' and 'practice which fosters creativity' to encompass the same ground as that intended by the NACCCE report, but in a way which is relevant for all early years practitioners, not simply those who are teachers or teaching assistants in classrooms. The whole chapter explores ways in which children can be offered access to decision making, control over some of their activities and acknowledgement for their ideas.

Creative practice

What does creative practice mean for practitioners? Studies of practice have established that practitioners feel creative when they control and take ownership of their practice, are innovative and ensure that learning is relevant to learners.

Woods and Jeffrey (1996: 13) suggest that creative practitioners are flexible about how they apply their philosophies and methodologies to the varied and highly complex situations they meet in the classroom. They find inventive ways into children's learning.

In the example given at the start of this chapter, the teacher invited the children to take control and ownership of what they hoped to do with the materials she had provided them with. She emphasised the need for them to make their own meaning and to develop their own personal plans, by acknowledging that each of them may do it differently. In this way she aimed to make the learning experience relevant to each child. She was, we suggest, inviting them to be innovative in their constructions, by emphasising the individuality of each person's suggestion. She was, of course, the teacher; however, there will be equivalent situations for other early years practitioners, in which children can be encouraged, through task and language, to take on control and ownership.

Creative practitioners, suggests Jeffrey (1997), are skilled at drawing on a repertoire of approaches to enable children's learning:

> they devise, organize, vary, mix whatever teaching methods and strategies they feel will most effectively advance their aims.
>
> (Jeffrey 1997: 74)

The creative practitioner can envisage possibilities and differences, and see these through. The teacher at the start of this chapter had decided to initiate a series of creative thinking activities. She embedded these activities into the curriculum plans made with the parallel class teacher. But in order to be creative in her practice, she needed the opportunity to do so. Teaching assistants and others in support roles in the classroom, as well as practitioners in other early years settings, are not always in the position to initiate in the same way. The proposals suggest that support staff carry out the plans of the teacher rather than initiate their own. However, teachers are experienced at creatively appropriating programmes of study (Woods 1995) and there is no reason to suppose that non-teacher practitioners cannot be as creative.

Where a practitioner is carrying out the ideas of someone else, there is always room for interpretation, and for using professional discretion where appropriate, as shown in the following case study, from a Foundation Stage classroom (which incorporated both nursery and reception), in a primary school.

> Beverley, a classroom assistant, is leading a cake-making activity with six children, aged three and four. The activity has been suggested by the teacher and Beverley has taken the group to work in an area just outside the classroom, near to the portable oven. Instead of passing around one big bowl with the children taking it in turns to mix its contents, she has decided to give each child their own bowl. Each child experiences the whole process from measuring out the ingredients to mixing them up and putting their mixture into a paper case.
>
> (Field note, Hertfordshire primary school, November 2002)

In this example it seemed to us that Beverley took ownership of the planned work and adapted it to suit the situation. She was creative by taking control and transforming the context into an effective learning experience. She encouraged children's creativity by offering them each the opportunity to engage more actively with, and to explore for themselves more fully, each part of the learning activity. What she is doing is more than 'starting with where the child is', which is sometimes described as another feature of 'good teaching'. It is offering children an opportunity to engage individually and in parallel with others, with more of the process of cake mixing, from start to finish, thus giving each child more space to ask their own questions and make their own discoveries. It is also exemplifying how, even where the framework of a practitioner's work is defined by someone else (in this case Beverly was asked to make cakes with the children), it is possible to act creatively within this.

Practice which fosters creativity

The NACCCE Report emphasises, as do others (Craft 2000; Beetlestone 1998) that creativity is relevant across the curriculum and not purely in the creative and performing arts. Children can be encouraged to be inventive, to generate possibilities, to ask 'what if?' and to suggest approaches to problems and opportunities in any aspect of their learning. Indeed, it could be argued that we are all 'naturally' creative in this way, to some degree.

But what exactly does 'practice which fosters creativity' involve? Recent research work in English nursery and Key Stage 1 classrooms has highlighted an important approach in practices which foster creativity. This approach has been named 'learner inclusive' (i.e. involving the children and trying to 'hear' their perspectives on the learning, to the extent they have some control over it) (Jeffrey and Craft 2003). This can be seen as a 'child-in-context' practice, in other words an approach to supporting learning in which practitioners observe, reflect and support the individual children's learning, as well as giving children many choices and a great deal of control over what they explore and how. Some might even argue that it is simply 'good teaching' to adopt a learner inclusive approach. But over time, the dominant view of what has been seen to be 'good teaching' has shifted. The child-centred movement came under much criticism in the 1980s and 1990s for many reasons, one central one being that too much control by children led to a lack of overview and direction by the adult in charge. In schools in particular, the child-centred approach has been continuously threatened at policy level since that time. We would suggest that, given the current curriculum frameworks for young children, and our obligations to provide learning opportunities within these, it is possible and, in the case of creativity in particular, necessary, to re-introduce and reconstruct child-centred education (Sugrue 1997).

The learner inclusive environment

Writing in the late 1990s, Duffy (1998) discusses the creation of conditions which inspire children, and ways of intervening with sensitivity to enable children's thinking to be valued. Based on recent empirical work, we suggest (Jeffrey and Craft 2003) that practices which foster learner creativity involve the construction of a learning environment appropriate to the children in it. In this approach, the learner is, as the term suggests, often included in the process of what knowledge is investigated, discovered and valued. As discussed earlier, it could be argued that this is what lies at the heart of 'good teaching'. This contrasts with a more outcomes-based definition of good teaching, where the quality of teaching is judged by the outcomes, often achievement-based. The two approaches are not incompatible; it is possible for children to achieve highly within a learning environment where they have a strong input into the process and content of their learning (Jeffrey and Woods 2003). We prefer not to draw a distinction, therefore, between the construction of an inclusive learning environment, and the notion of 'good teaching'. We suggest that in an inclusive learning environment, the children's creativity is nurtured and developed through the use of 'possibility thinking' and co-participation in particular.

Possibility thinking can be seen as being a major feature of an inclusive environment (Craft 2001, 2002) and involves posing questions such as 'what if?' Possibility thinking includes problem solving as in a puzzle, finding alternative routes round a barrier, the posing of questions and the identification of problems and issues. It thus involves imagination and speculation. Co-participation, referred to in the Reggio Emilia preschools in northern Italy (Edwards *et al.* 1995), is one way in which learners can be included in the sharing of and creation of knowledge (Woods and Jeffrey 1996; Jeffrey and Woods 2003), countering negative feelings of being individually tested and having to compete with peers (Pollard and Triggs 2000; Jeffrey 2003). In another sense, all creative thinking involves engagement with the thinking of others – or some form of dialogue, as Wegerif (2003) has argued. In these ways, creativity can be seen as always involving some sort of collaboration or thinking together.

Being learner-inclusive is important because as the child contributes to the uncovering of knowledge they take ownership of it and if control over the investigation of knowledge is handed back to the learner (Jeffrey and Craft 2003) they have the opportunity and authority to be innovative.

Inclusive learning case study of fostering creativity

Sarah introduces work on the body from two big books to her Year 2 learners. She invites them to tell the group about stories of personal accidents and then she asks the children to imagine what would happen if their bones did or did not grow in relation to the rest of their body. The children used their imagination to create a fuller understanding of their knowledge of the body (Jeffrey and Woods 2003):

I'd be all floppy if my bones didn't grow.

My skin would be hanging down off the end of my fingers.

My nose would be dangling down there.

My earrings will be down touching the floor.

If my bones grew when my body didn't I would be all skinny.

I would have extra lumps all over me.

My bones would be stretching my body so I would be very thin.

I'd be like a skinny soldier and bones would be sticking out of my skin.

My brain would be getting squashed.

Young children like experimenting and problem solving, 'I look forward to doing experiments like the lights and batteries. It is like testing things. I don't care if it goes wrong. If I was a witch and I had to make a new potion in my cauldron I would experiment' (Craig, Year 2).

Being encouraged to pose questions, identify problems and issues together with the opportunity to debate and discuss their 'thinking' brings the learner into the process of possibility thinking as a co-participant (Edwards *et al.* 1995). Sarah wanted to engage her mixed 5–7-year-old children in a discussion about learning. She started with an investigation of how babies learn by asking them how they would fill up an alien's empty brain and the children not only used their imagination but they confronted each other's contributions:

I would do it in a laboratory.

I would do it by telling.

You can't. Because it hasn't got anything in its brain to think with.

He wouldn't be able to remember anything.

You could make him go to sleep and then open his head a little to put the right information on his brain.

The process of discussion opened up avenues for learning, which included a philosophical debate:

The following question came out of the blue and was taken on by the others. 'This question is a hard one because how did the first person in the world know all the things about the world?' 'God taught them.' 'But he was a little baby.' 'How did the world get made?' 'How did the first person get made?' 'How did the whole universe get made?' 'How did life grow?' There followed lots of chatter permeated with questions and assertions and answers.

(Field note 1999)

These knowledge discussions and investigations open the possibility of an analysis of the processes of learning:

The answers not only contribute to knowledge but the contributory climate encourages them to share their knowledge. 'I listen and you teach us.' 'You need to use your ears to listen, your nose to smell and your eyes to see.' 'You need to listen most of the time and to be quiet.' 'It is like you have dots in your brain and they are all joined up.' 'You think about it and stuff like that as well.' 'Your brain is telling you how to use your eyes.' 'The college tells you what to tell us and you tell us and we get the answer.'

(Field note 1999)

A learner-inclusive approach includes learners in the subjects to be investigated, values their experiences, imagination and their evaluation of the learning experience (Jeffrey 2001).

We have found that practitioners who at first intend only to use creative practice to enhance their effectiveness respond creatively to the potential in situations they meet.

Justine, the teacher, commented on how the topic had taken off, having fired the children's imaginations:

I have been caught up in this. It has encompassed the children's imaginations and sustained the interest of all the children from five to seven, from new children to experienced ones. It has been more successful than I had ever dreamt it was going to be. They ran with it. Children were sneaking off behind me to start instead of waiting for me to say, 'Come on, now let's sit, and let me talk you through it.' I would turn round and there would be children behind me doing it, and doing it correctly. It was a project where children didn't need stimulating. One of the things that I enjoyed about it was sitting with the children and talking about what they were doing, and listening to them enjoying this session. It is very relaxing and I also think they genuinely had a very strong sense of achievement.

So – here Justine provided an environment which led unintentionally to learner creativity, as children came up with their own ideas and put them into practice; for children naturally experiment with imaginative constructions and play with ideas (Craft 2002).

It became learner inclusive, as the children became more interested and involved in the project. For example, this is an extract from an interview with Abigail, who is six years old and who has been involved in a topic in her classroom on the art and craft of William Morris. This project had originally been a light touch look at designs in materials but developed into a major project with children constructing their own designs from materials in the environment. In discussion with the researcher, Abigail said:

> We did our own designs on a piece of paper. They were photocopied at lunchtime to make lots of copies. In the afternoon we stuck them on to a piece of paper how we wanted them. This is the design I chose. I have repeated it. We need to do each section the same colour to make it look like a design. If I did them all different colours it would not look much like a design. It is all the leaves and flowers on a theme. We brought these things in from outside. There is a fir cone, this is a catkin. I often see this sort of design being done on a computer. You can see designs on walls, cushions, bedclothes, wrapping paper, jars, and clothes.

So – Abigail shows us how included she felt in this theme of work; her teacher had provided her with an experience of practice which fostered creativity, and a learner inclusive environment. But to return to the ideas of creative practice and practice which fosters creativity, how far do these occur together?

Do creative practice and practice which fosters creativity always occur together?

Creative practice does not necessarily lead to learner creativity, although it may provide suitable contexts for both teacher and learner to be creative as teachers use their own creativity and learners use the spaces provided to maintain and develop their own creative learning. It may also actually encourage children's creativity as teachers model the expression of their own ideas.

A practice which fosters creativity depends on practitioners being creative to provide the ethos for enabling children's creativity, in other words, one that is relevant to them and in which they can take ownership of the knowledge, skills and understanding to be learnt. A practice which fosters creativity goes further in actively involving the child in the determination of what knowledge is to be investigated and acquired and ensuring children a significant amount of control and opportunities to be innovative.

What does this mean for the practitioner?

Creative practice may, but does not necessarily, lead to learner creativity. Practice which fosters creativity is more likely to succeed where learners are included, i.e. where the approach is a learner-inclusive one.

References

Beetlestone, F. (1998) *Creative Children, Imaginative Teaching*. Buckingham: Open University Press.

Craft, A. (2000) *Creativity Across the Primary Curriculum*. London: Routledge.

Craft, A. (2001) 'Little c Creativity', in Craft, A., Jeffrey, B., Leibling, M. (eds), *Creativity in Education*. London: Continuum.

Craft, A. (2002) *Creativity and Early Years Education: a lifewide foundation*. London: Continuum.

Duffy, B. (1998) *Supporting Imagination and Creativity in the Early Years*. Buckingham: Open University Press.

Edwards, C., Gandini, L. and Forman, G. (eds) (1995) *The Hundred Languages of Children: the Reggio Emilia approach to early childhood education*. Norwood, NJ: Ablex Publishing Corporation.

Jeffrey, B. (1997) 'The relevance of creative teaching: pupils' views', in Pollard, A., Thiessen, D., Filer, A. (eds) *Children and their Curriculum: the perspectives of primary and elementary children*. London: Falmer, 15–33.

Jeffrey, B. (2001) 'Primary pupils perspectives and creative learning'. *Encylopaedia*, **9** (June-July), 133–52 (Italian Journal).

Jeffrey, B. (2003) 'Countering student "instrumentalism": a creative response'. *British Education Research Journal* **29** (4).

Jeffrey, B. and Craft, A. (2003) 'Creative teaching and teaching for creativity: distinctions and relationships', paper given at British Educational Research Association National Conference on Creativity in Education (meeting of Special Interest Group – Creativity in Education), Feb 3rd, 2003, at the Open Creativity Centre, The Open University.

Jeffrey, B. and Woods, P. (2003) *The Creative School*. London: RoutledgeFalmer.

NACCCE (1999) *All Our Futures*. London: DfES.

Pollard, A. and Triggs, P. (2000) *What pupils say: changing policy and practice in primary education*. London: Continuum.

Sugrue, K. (1997) *Complexities of teaching: child centred perspectives*. London: Falmer Press.

Wegerif, R. (2003) 'Creativity, thinking skills and collaborative learning', paper presented to the Open University Creativity Research Group, at the Open Creativity Centre, Milton Keynes, March 2003.

Woods, P. (1995) *Creative Teachers in Primary Schools*. Buckingham: Open University Press.

Woods, P. and Jeffrey, B. (1996) *Teachable Moments*. Buckingham: Open University Press.

Chapter 12

Young children becoming literate

Robin Campbell

Introduction

Alice was motivated to look at books on her own before her first birthday, she contributed words and phrases to story readings during her second year and wrote her own name unaided by 3 years 6 months (Campbell 1999). Alice was becoming literate, demonstrating that by her actions. Of course, there are many indicators that tell us a young child is emerging as a literacy user (Hall 1987). Showing an interest in, and enjoyment of, books are often regarded as paramount (Butler 1998) especially in Western industrialised countries. We know much literacy learning develops from engagements with books (Teale 1984). Singing and nursery rhymes, playing with, and making up their own, rhymes (Chukovsky 1963) supports the child's awareness of phonemes. Responding to environmental print (Miller 1999), and making marks that increasingly look like writing (Schickedanz 1990), demonstrates important knowledge and understanding. These are evidence of young children becoming literate. Spoken language is central to this learning process, as we discuss later in this chapter, as is the role of play as a vehicle for language and literacy learning.

Riley (1996) suggests there are two indicators, which are linked to young children's future success in reading and writing by the end of Key Stage 1 in England. These are children's ability, on entering school at five years of age, to write their own name, and their knowledge of the alphabet. It is therefore interesting to note that in the Foundation Stage Profile in England (QCA 2003) the section on communication, language and literacy includes 'writes own name...' (p. 30) and 'Links sounds to letters, naming and sounding the letters of the alphabet' (p. 24). However, focusing on the achievement of such indicators, rather than the process by which they are achieved, can lead to unwelcome changes in practice. David *et al.* (2000) noted 'early years practitioners in England have felt pressurised by government initiatives to include more literacy in the nursery school programme' (p. 120). Therefore goal setting can put pressure on how those attainments are achieved.

Tensions may appear between achieving simple literacy goals and the use of developmentally appropriate practices. Therefore, early years practitioners have important questions to consider: What is an appropriate literacy curriculum for the early years? What will working towards goals for literacy learning entail? What is involved in adults promoting literacy learning? Those questions also need to be seen in the context of earlier literacy learning before three and how literacy learning is encouraged and extended between five and eight years of age, at Key Stage 1 in England.

Learning about literacy: from birth to three

'Becoming a skilful communicator' is a key aspect in the new framework for children aged birth to three in England (Sure Start Unit 2002). Important experiences identified include the use of stories and songs in their home language, pretend play and symbolic understanding (making one thing stand for another) and play experiences linked to storybook characters. Many young children will learn about literacy and emerge as literacy users during these first three years. How do they achieve that when largely they are not taught literacy directly? As Wade and Moore (2000) noted, young children who share books with an adult at home achieve well when they go to school. They do so because they learn from books, they learn about books, and they learn literacy. That learning by three years of age often includes knowing how to use books, being familiar with the structure of stories, contributing to the story readings and knowing some letters and words (Campbell 1999). Much of this happens by being engaged in an enjoyable shared reading of worthwhile books. When Alice was two years and nine months she enjoyed sharing with an adult *Good-Night Owl* (Hutchins 1972):

Grandfather:	*Owl tried to sleep.*
	The owl's sleeping in the tree isn't it?
Alice:	Yes.
	Owl's got his eyes closed.
Grandfather:	*The bees buzzed,*
	buzz, buzz,
	and owl tried to
Alice:	*sleep.*
	There's the buzzy bees.

(Campbell 1999: 58)

In this short extract the child's involvement, and learning, is evident. Alice indicated her close attention to the pictures, she noted that owl's eyes were closed and she pointed to the bees. She also took part in the reading providing 'sleep' at the end of the sentence. Many books that are read to young children provide support that enables them to take part in shared story readings. Therefore two- and three-year-old children are enabled to act like readers and begin to be readers (Minns 1997).

Of course, as noted above, there are other literacy activities that support that development. For example, opportunities to respond to environmental print and mark making are activities that a child can enjoy with an adult, to support literacy learning. So, children who are provided with such experiences and opportunities come to early years settings knowing about literacy.

What is an appropriate literacy curriculum for the early years?

Those activities that children enjoy at home begin to suggest an early years curriculum. Being able to write one's own name and recognise the letters of the alphabet by shape and sound are important. Supporting children to work towards those goals in developmentally appropriate ways before entering school seems sensible. Therefore, early years practitioners will want to help children acquire that knowledge in early years settings or in the reception year of school. However, those two features of literacy development are insufficient if that is all that the child acquires. They need more than the tip of the iceberg in a literacy curriculum. The children need the whole iceberg which suggests a very wide range of literacy knowledge and experience to underpin the surface knowledge. That raises issues about the content and process of the early years curriculum.

Marian Whitehead (1999) suggested four essential strategies for literacy that could provide a broad framework for the literacy curriculum. Those were talk, play and representation; rhyme, rhythm and language patterns; stories and narrative; and environmental print and messages.

Talk, play and representation

Corden (2000) argued the case 'for the centrality of spoken language in the learning process' (p. 12). Much of children's initial learning is based on talk with oneself, with other children and adults. During that talk comments are made, questions asked, responses provided, and conversations occur. Often the talk is linked to play as young children explore their world imaginatively and verbalise as they do so. Part of that play includes representation as the child creates a farm with bricks, with a hat becomes a fire-fighter, and creates representations of objects and people with marks that become increasingly recognisable as drawings. In time those representations begin to include letter-like marks as the child explores writing.

When play corners are organised as a vet's surgery, a post office, or supermarket, literacy materials are an integral part of the provision (Hall and Abbott 1991). Commonly adults provide print materials such as message pads by the telephone, writing paper and envelopes with pencils or other writing tools; telephone directories, magazines, brochures and catalogues; possibly too a keyboard, typewriter, or computer.

The presence of adults to model writing and talk about it with the children is important. A writing centre encourages children to write, to think about words and letters (so learning about the alphabet) and to develop as literacy users. Frequently that writing will be linked to drawing and painting as the children represent the world symbolically in different ways.

Rhyme, rhythm and language patterns

Rhyme, rhythm and language patterns are found in nursery rhymes, songs, poems and many stories. Young children get great enjoyment from playing with language and learn much about literacy as they do so. Meek (1990) suggested that when children have frequent opportunities to engage with and enjoy nursery rhymes and songs they also learn and extend their phonological awareness. Children enjoy the rhythm of nursery rhymes such as:

> Mary, Mary, quite contrary,
> How does your garden grow?
> With silver bells and cockle shells
> And pretty maids all in a row.

They are also developing an awareness of the '-ow' rime unit and 'gr' and 'r' onset units, even though that awareness need not be made explicit at this point. Although the enjoyment, and transfer, of a cultural heritage are reason enough to engage in these activities they also teach about letters and sounds (Meek 1990).

Stories and narrative

Stories and narrative are important to young children: as Bruner (1968) indicated, narrative is one way of thinking. Children, and adults, make sense of their world by creating a narrative of events that they experience. Children also learn from the stories that they hear told and read by adults. In many of these stories there are rhyme, repetition and rhythm, which Wade (1990) refers to as 'the three r's' of language and stories that support young children's learning. Many books that young children hear include rhyme. In *Slinky Malinki* (Dodd 1990) we read that:

> He was cheeky and cheerful,
> friendly and fun,
> he'd chase after leaves
> and he'd roll in the sun.

The rhyme of 'fun' and 'sun' appeals to young children and informs the children incidentally about onset and rime. Later that will help children to read and write by analogy words such as 'bun' and 'run' (Goswami 1999). Then the repetition of phrases and sentences, rather than of single words, creates a story interest for young children and helps the children to join in as readers and become readers. In *Good-Night Owl* (Hutchins 1972) the repetition of 'Owl tried to sleep' draws children into the reading and supports their literacy development. Often it is the use of rhyme and repetition that creates a rhythm to the story as in *Green Eggs and Ham* (Seuss 1960). Yet story does even more: very young children comment upon words known because they saw them in particular books (Baghban 1984; Campbell 1999).

A starting point for early years literacy are frequent story readings (Campbell 2001a) and the benefits are well documented (Teale 1984). Children develop a love of books and an interest in reading, they acquire characters as imaginary friends, learn words and sentences, begin to understand story structure, and appreciate the rhyme features of many books. In addition the use of repeated readings enables children to gain 'ownership' of the story. For very young children adults make the story readings interactive and provide opportunities for responses. The children can draw, paint, make models, create puppets (to be used during subsequent rereadings of the book) mark make and write. So they represent the story in a variety of formats. Gregory (1996), discussing children learning English as a second language, refers to the 'Outside-In' approach to literacy that uses story as a means of providing the experiences that lead to literacy. That is balanced by the 'Inside-Out' approach that uses the knowledge, experiences and language that children bring to school from their own communities as a basis for becoming literate in an additional language.

Shared reading with big print that all the children in the class can see is another useful literacy activity for similar reasons (Holdaway 1979). However, when used as part of the literacy hour in England (DfEE 1998) it has been changed to emphasise attention to print features – looking at words, considering letters and sounds, noting punctuation and spelling patterns. The format is used to teach directly aspects of literacy and there is a real danger that instead of exciting children about reading it diminishes an interest in books. But shared reading can be used more appropriately for a wider purpose (Whitehead 1999). 'Listening to stories with interest' (QCA 2003: 26), feeling good about the stories, and wanting to engage with other stories will be key at the Foundation stage.

Environmental print and messages

In our society a great deal of environmental print is experienced and young children demonstrate that they are inquisitive to find out about it. This inevitably leads to discussions about letters of the alphabet. Currently the yellow *M* is among the first letters to create a response from young children when they spot a McDonald's logo.

Environmental print is brought into the setting and talked about (Miller 1999) and, as Kenner (2000) demonstrated, linked to the languages of home for bilingual children. Logo displays, creating alphabet environmental print books and having a print party are all suggested. Labelling resources and encouraging children to use labels to guide them provide a real purpose for literacy. Classroom print for a purpose that is talked about adds to the children's literacy learning in a meaningful context.

Learning about letters is developed further when children have the opportunity to mark make and send messages. Sending greeting cards is an activity that children may have witnessed, e.g. Christmas and Chinese New Year. Alice sent a card at 3 years 3 months (Figure 12.1), although at that stage the card included just two words, 'To' and ' Gd' (Grandad) (Campbell 1999: 76).

Figure 12.1

Nevertheless, there was evidence of involvement with the letters of the alphabet and an attempt at her own name as she wrote 'Alloo' on the back of the card. Already she recognised the need for five letters: an initial capital 'A' and then an 'l' followed by three other letters – which were not yet accurate. Achievement of the two key learning goals was being attained without any direct attention to those features. They were occurring within the context of children as active literacy learners.

When children have the opportunity to engage with language and literacy within this broad framework, then the writing of their own name, and knowledge of the alphabet, can be learned easily because it develops as part of wider experiences. Early years practitioners support children by providing learning opportunities that complement activities at home or provide new experiences for some children who have not had these literacy activities.

Working towards goals for literacy learning?

Because the writing of own name and knowledge of the letters and sounds of the alphabet appear to be two easily contained items there is a temptation to think of those being taught directly to the children. The practitioner might even be tempted to use adult-led and adult-directed activities including worksheets, activity cards and reading schemes. Worksheets are seldom, if ever, the best way of teaching literacy. David *et al.* (2000) suggested 'systematic and explicit "instruction" is inappropriate during the early years' (p. 46). Indeed, if own name and the alphabet are taught directly it appears that the children have an insufficient background to support their literacy development. Children who have the opportunity to play, sing and use language creatively have a basis for making much more rapid development with literacy (Mills and Mills 1998). It is encouraging children who want to read that is important, and as a Northern Ireland curriculum document indicated 'The disposition to read is encouraged by reading rather than by instruction in how to read' (CCEA 1999: 9).

The broad range of literacy experiences suggested above as a means of supporting the writing of own name and knowledge of the letters and sounds of the alphabet is needed. Fortunately young children appear to be naturally interested in writing their own forename. In many of the studies of young children developing as literacy users before attending school we read of the attempts of Giti (Baghban 1984), Cecilia (Payton 1984), Adam (Schickedanz 1990) and Alice (Campbell 1999) to write their own name at about three years of age. Writing materials, support for children's own attempts to write and responses to questions were provided by the adults. Early years settings provide a wide range of opportunities for young children to recognise and write their forename. These include names on coat pegs for recognition, name cards collected at the beginning of the day and at other times, a class birthday chart, an alphabet book of class names, and tapping out the syllables of own name. The children are also encouraged to write their name by signing a register list, writing their own name on paintings, drawings and notes, and creating their own name with different media (Campbell 2001b). Children are encouraged and supported to write their own name rather than being directly taught to do so.

Similarly when considering the alphabet Strickland (1998) suggested that 'the best practice is to help children identify letters in an enjoyable way as they acquire the broader concepts about print and books' (p. 56–7). She then provided a list of activities that started with a 'focus on letters that have special meaning for children, such as the letters in their own names. This is more effective than simply teaching one arbitrary letter per week' (p. 57). Own name and alphabet are linked as the letters of the children's names provide a focus and context for considering the alphabet.

Of course children learn about the alphabet as they explore the writing of their own name. Singing the alphabet song helps children to learn the names of English letters and the alphabet sequence (Campbell 2002). Making an alphabet book of the environmental print supports a developing knowledge of the alphabet. There are additionally many attractive alphabet books, e.g. *Animalia* (Base 1986), that can be shared with the children. So the children write their own name and gain knowledge of the alphabet as part of a wider based literacy provision. They specifically experience those two literacy activities supported by the teacher and other adults not by direct teaching, although the adults do have an important role.

Adults promoting literacy learning?

If the practitioner is not directly teaching, because that is not the most developmentally appropriate practice for young children, then what will be their role? We have noted that the adult will read, model, demonstrate, interact, scaffold and support, sing, talk and inform children (Campbell 1996). Those roles have to be performed with skill and thought. When a story is read the adult has to know the book, read at an appropriate pace and read with expression. During shared reading there is a demonstration of reading including how the print is used. When words are written on to a word wall it is writing that is demonstrated. The adult interacts with the children so that there is an opportunity for the children to comment, question and respond.

All of that is made evident when we look at how Adam (Schickedanz 1990) and Alice (Campbell 1999) attained the goal of writing own name. They both did so before attending school because they were surrounded by literacy, with books read to them and familiar books repeated. They had adults who talked with them about what they were trying to achieve. And they had numerous opportunities provided for writing whenever they wanted. When they began to write their own name the adults supported them but accepted a learning process that lasted some months. The adult was there to scaffold, support and inform but did not feel it necessary to dictate what should occur. The outcome was a secure knowledge of writing their own name by three and a half years of age. It is a replication of that provision, support and encouragement in early years settings that helps other children to achieve those goals.

Extending literacy learning?

In England the National Literacy Strategy (DfEE 1998) indicates the use of a literacy hour at Key Stage 1, from 6 to 8 years of age. The requirement is for the teacher to provide four elements of shared reading/writing; focused word work; independent reading/writing and review. For many teachers that format is seen as a 'straitjacket' that ultimately bores the children (Anderson *et al.* 2000). However, teachers often divert from the narrow confines of the literacy hour in order to create more interesting, meaningful and appropriate literacy activities.

A Year 1 class teacher read the story *Hairy Maclary from Donaldson's Dairy* (Dodd 1983). Briefly some children acted the story as the teacher reread the book. Then she invited the children to tell about other dogs during shared writing. Eventually the children wrote their own verses into small origami books (Johnson 1995). They captured the nature of the rhyming writing verses such as:

> Billy the Bulldog
> Eats like a hog
> Jumping around
> Just like a frog

Some of the children read their books to the class and the books were placed in the class library for others to read. The activity lasted more than an hour and the structure did not follow sequentially the literacy hour guidelines. Nevertheless the children listened to a story, acted the story, took part in a shared writing, engaged with word level work that emphasised onset and rime, produced some independent writing, read their books aloud as part of a review and established some texts for independent reading. The teacher had extended the literacy hour and there was more of a natural flow to the literacy events based on an enjoyable story. The children were interested and involved as they participated in developmentally appropriate literacy activities. Literacy goals were being achieved.

Conclusion

Adults need to support literacy learning but to do so without concentrating on teaching literacy goals directly. Many early years practitioners in England feel pressure being exerted from various government initiatives towards more direct teaching (David *et al.* 2000). Yet the *Curriculum guidance for the Foundation Stage* (QCA 2000) indicates for literacy learning that the practitioner needs to 'provide opportunities, encourage, talk about, play games, model, and sing, etc.' (p. 61). It is developmentally appropriate to utilise strategies linked to the children's interests and needs rather than attempting to teach directly particular learning goals. Learning needs to be the product of a wide range of activities and opportunities. Attention given to simple literacy goals is just a part of that much wider provision. So specific learning goals are not neglected but rather they become part of far more broad-based literacy foundations. It is a base for children's whole literacy development.

[This chapter is adapted from an earlier work, 'Exploring key literacy learning: own name and alphabet' (Campbell 2002) in Miller, L., Drury, R. and Campbell, R. (eds) (2002) *Exploring Early Years Education and Care*. London: David Fulton Publishers].

References

Anderson, H., Digings, M. and Urquhart, I. (2000) 'Hourwatch: monitoring the inception of the National Literacy Strategy'. *Reading* **34** (3), 113–18.

Baghban, M. (1984) *Our Daughter Learns to Read and Write*. Newark, DE: International Reading Association.

Bruner, J. (1968) 'Two modes of thought', In Mercer, J. (ed.) *Language and Literacy from an Educational Perspective. Volume 1: Language Studies*. Milton Keynes: Open University Press.

Butler, D. (1998) *Babies Need Books: sharing the joy of books with children from birth to six*, rev. edn. Portsmouth, NH: Heinemann.

Campbell, R. (1996) *Literacy in Nursery Education*. Stoke-on-Trent: Trentham Books.

Campbell, R. (1999) *Literacy from Home to School: reading with Alice*. Stoke-on-Trent: Trentham Books.

Campbell, R. (2001a) *Read-Alouds with Young Children*. Newark, DE: International Reading Association.

Campbell, R. (2001b) '"I can write my name I can": The importance of the writing of own name'. *Education 3–13* **29** (1), 9–14.

Campbell, R. (2002) *Reading in the Early Years Handbook*, 2nd edn. Buckingham: Open University Press.

CCEA (1999) *Key Messages from The Curriculum 21 Conferences and The Curriculum Monitoring Programme 1998*. Belfast: Northern Ireland Council for the Curriculum, Examinations and Assessment.

Chukovsky, K. (1963) *From Two to Five*. Berkeley: University of California Press.

Corden, R. (2000) *Literacy and learning through talk: strategies for the primary classroom*. Buckingham: Open University Press.

David, T., Raban, B., Ure, C., Gouch, K., Jago, M., Barriere, I. and Lambirth, A. (2000) *Making Sense of Early Literacy: a practitioner's perspective*. Stoke-on-Trent: Trentham Books.

DfEE (1998) *The National Literacy Strategy: Framework for teaching*. London: Department for Education and Employment.

Goswami, U. (1999) 'Causal connections in beginning reading: the importance of rhyme', *Journal of Research in Reading* **22** (3), 217–40.

Gregory, E. (1996) *Making Sense of a New World: learning to read in a second language*. London: Paul Chapman.

Hall, N. (1987) *The Emergence of Literacy*. Sevenoaks, Kent: Hodder and Stoughton.

Hall, N. and Abbott, L. (eds) (1991) *Play in the Primary Curriculum*. London: Hodder & Stoughton.

Holdaway, D. (1979) *The Foundations of Literacy*. London: Ashton Scholastic.

Johnson, P. (1995) *Children Making Books*. Reading: Reading and Language Information Centre, University of Reading.

Kenner, C. (2000) *Home Pages Literacy Links for Bilingual Children*. Stoke-on-Trent: Trentham Books.

Meek, M. (1990) 'What do we know about reading that helps us to teach?' In Carter, R. (ed) *Knowledge about Language and the Curriculum*. London: Hodder & Stoughton.

Miller, L. (1999) *Moving Towards Literacy with Environmental Print*. Royston, Herts: United Kingdom Reading Association.

Mills, C. and Mills, D. (1998) *Dispatches: The Early Years*. London: Channel 4 Television.

Minns, H. (1997) *Read it to me now! Learning at home and at school*. Buckingham: Open University Press.

Payton, S. (1984) *Developing Awareness of Print: a young child's first steps towards literacy*. Birmingham: Educational Review, University of Birmingham.

Qualifications and Curriculum Authority (2000) *Curriculum Guidance for the Foundation Stage*. London: Qualifications and Curriculum Authority.

Qualifications and Curriculum Authority (2003) *Foundation Stage Profile*. London: Qualifications and Curriculum Authority.

Riley, J. (1996) 'The ability to label the letters of the alphabet at school entry: a discussion on its value', *Journal of Research in Reading* **19** (2), 87–101.

Schickedanz, J. A. (1990) *Adam's Righting Revolutions*. Portsmouth, NH: Heinemann.

Strickland, D. S. (1998) *Teaching Phonics Today: a primer for educators*. Newark, DE: International Reading Association.

Sure Start Unit (2002) *Birth to three matters: a framework to support children in their earliest years*. London: DfES.

Teale, W. (1984) 'Reading to Young Children: Its significance for literacy development', in Goelman, H., Oberg, A. and Smith, F. (eds) *Awakening to Literacy*. London: Heinemann.

Wade, B. (1990) (ed.) *Reading for Real*. Buckingham: Open University Press.

Wade, B. and Moore, M. (2000) *Baby Power*. Handforth, Cheshire: Egmont World Ltd.

Whitehead, M. (1999) *Supporting Language and Literacy Development in the Early Years*. Buckingham: Open University Press.

Children's books

Base, G. (1986) *Animalia*. New York: Harry Abrams.

Dodd, L. (1983) *Hairy Maclary from Donaldson's Dairy*. Harmondsworth: Puffin Books.

Dodd, L. (1990) *Slinky Malinki*. Harmondsworth: Puffin Books.

Hutchins, P. (1972) *Good-Night Owl*. London: The Bodley Head.

Seuss, Dr. (1960) *Green Eggs and Ham*. New York: Beginner Books, Random House.

Chapter 13

Literacy in four early years settings

Linda Miller and Alice Paige-Smith

The literacy curriculum in the early years

This chapter considers practitioners' concerns, beliefs and attitudes towards literacy in the early years curriculum in four early years settings in England and the ways in which these impact on children's experiences of literacy.

The *Curriculum Guidance for the Foundation Stage* (QCA/DfEE 2000), which covers the age range three to the end of reception year, was introduced in England in 2000. It was developed in consultation with practitioners and authorities from the field of early childhood. The guidance built on an earlier document *Early Learning Goals* (QCA/DfEE 1999) following concerns that this document emphasised the achievement of learning goals rather than the process of learning. The guidance was also linked to the National Curriculum in primary schools. David *et al.* (2000) have noted that the more formal approach to teaching literacy, which begins at the end of reception year in England, may have a 'top-down' negative effect on literacy in the early years. The (QCA 2000) guidance broadened language and literacy to include communication and emphasised 'opportunities' and 'experiences' rather than the achievement of outcomes (pp. 44–5) although goals for learning were retained. It referred to the importance of speaking and listening and of providing a play environment rich with print. Support for this view of literacy learning is offered in a report from the Education and Employment Committee (EEC 2000), which advocates play and exploration as a basis for literacy learning in the early years.

Practitioner beliefs and literacy practices

Appropriate literacy practice has been subject to different interpretations according to different views of how children become literate (Barratt-Pugh 2001; Fisher 2000). Anning and Edwards (1999) found practitioners had different views about how young children learn to be literate, which were influenced by their backgrounds in 'care' or 'education' and by their respective training.

Practitioners working in care settings prioritised language development rather than the 'school' view of language and literacy found in teachers' views. David *et al.* (2000) found that practitioners in England had differing views about what children's literacy activities should involve. Some practitioners thought that children should not be involved in literacy activities until age five and should learn through play, whereas others believed that children are immersed in and are learning about literacy from birth. The research also revealed interesting contradictions between beliefs and practices. Despite an expressed belief in developing literacy through play, in some settings children were removed from their play to carry out adult-directed tasks, whereas in other settings a play-based philosophy was in evidence. The reasons given for formal literacy practices were practitioners' expectations of inspection requirements in relation to curriculum guidance (see also Miller 2000). Browne (1998) found links between the training and experience of staff and developmentally appropriate interpretations of curriculum guidance. Some settings had adopted a formal literacy curriculum based on reading schemes, phonic programmes and worksheets in order to achieve the outcomes for learning.

The project

One of the authors of this chapter (Miller 1996) has advocated a literacy curriculum which builds on children's literacy experiences in the home and community and which is embedded in enjoyable and playful experiences. Our research aimed to explore practitioners' beliefs about how literacy should be taught and their views on the *Curriculum Guidance for the Foundation Stage* (QCA/DfEE 2000), and also to look at children's experiences of literacy. Four settings were chosen to represent a range of early years provision and included: a reception class in a primary school on an inner-city council estate, a private nursery in suburban north London, a local education authority (LEA) nursery in a London suburb and a playgroup in a semi-rural shire county. We spent one week (5 sessions) in each of the settings and carried out observations on 20 'target' children, and key adults in the settings were interviewed. We observed if, and how, literacy play was resourced and noted 'literacy events' as described below. David *et al.* (2000) describe literacy events as occurring through social interaction with another literate person and through planned activity, and are created by adults as they take advantage of children's natural curiosity about reading and writing. For example, 'What does that say?' as children point to a printed word or sign. We also refer to 'fixed literacy events', which are those that take place on a regular basis such as group story times or completing the weather chart.

The research reported below is part of a wider scale project (Miller *et al.* 2002). In this chapter we describe the four settings and offer 'vignettes' of the children's literacy experience in each setting on the days we visited and 'snapshots' of the views and beliefs of key adults in the settings.

We posed some key questions:

1. What were key adults' beliefs about how literacy is learnt and taught?
2. What were their views about the curriculum guidance for literacy?
3. How did adults initiate or support literacy?
4. What were the children's experiences of literacy?
5. What were the main literacy events in each setting?
6. How was literacy play resourced and encouraged?

Literacy in four settings

The nursery class

The nursery class is in a primary school in a large Victorian building. It is in an open plan room with a reception area used for story telling. The 52 children on roll are aged three-and-a-half to rising fives and attend for both full- and part-time sessions. They include children of asylum seekers from Somalia and there is an Ethnic Minority Achievement (EMA) teacher who supports children who have English as an additional language. There is one qualified teacher, a teaching assistant and a nursery nurse. The setting was well resourced for literacy play, which included an office area, a puppet theatre and a designated language and literacy area that was in constant use by the children. The nursery was full of print and notices written by both children and adults in a range of languages. Storybook activities were linked to the project theme of 'animals underground'. The nursery nurse was sited in the book corner to share stories with the children from a range of books, including 'big' books and those made by the children. Mark making was a key literacy event and paint, chalks and pencils were readily available. Literacy permeated the day and was planned into the children's play and ongoing project work.

The teacher viewed the introduction of the Foundation Stage guidance as supporting play-based literacy and felt its guidance endorsed her views:

> It reiterates what I have always believed in. It mustn't be too structured in the early years. You have to make it flexible and balanced. Curriculum areas are interrelated and interact with each other. A few years ago it was becoming too formal in reception. I think it's really nice that it's gone back to teaching literacy through play.

However, she acknowledged constraints on the curriculum, for example that testing in the primary school influenced parental expectations about the literacy achievements of children in the early years:

> I think there's a tendency for parents to become very over anxious now. With the introduction of SATS in year 2, they think that work books are the answer.

The following example shows how staff planned play scenarios, in this case an office area. It also illustrates how the adult initiated a literacy event that influenced the children's literacy play.

Sabrina and Yohannah

With support from the teaching assistant, Sabrina was writing a wiggly line inside a snake using a pencil; she then tried to write her name:

Sabrina: 'I'm doing it, it's going to be very nice, do you know how to spell my name? S A B R I N A' (she spells her name).
Teaching Assistant: 'Can you write your name on it?'
Sabrina: 'No'.
   The teaching assistant wrote Sabrina's name on the back of the sheet, saying 'Sabrina' as she wrote it out.
   Sabrina went over to the office play area to join a child who was mark making. She used a ruler to draw lines, showed her work to the teacher and re-joined her friend.
Sabrina: 'I'm going to do some writing today – not reading, I'll get your name and you have to write it down, not now. Come with me.'
   She led the other child to the cloakroom where there was a table with magnetic names and a magnetic board.
Sabrina: 'Here are the letters, can you find your name – can you find Yohannah? 'Here's my name S A B R I N A (she spells it out), can you spell your name?'.
Yohannah: 'Yes.' Yohannah pretends to write her name with her finger on the table.
   They then went back to the office area:
Sabrina. 'You need a felt tip, I'll write your name 'O' and down like that?'
Yohannah: 'Yeh, Yeh, Yeh, add the E like that'.
Sabrina: 'Don't use my book I need to do my counting today.' She takes the hole punch and makes a hole in the paper. 'OK what do you want to write then?' She scribbles SSSS shapes – 'There you go,' and gives it to Yohannah.

The teaching assistant had shown Sabrina how to write her name. Sabrina then joined her friend in the office area and transferred what she had learnt to a play situation, supported by literacy props, in this case the magnetic name labels. In this setting support for literacy was offered through play scenarios, resources for literacy play and through adult support.

The private day nursery

The day nursery is housed in a large house in an affluent suburb. The 11 children are aged 3–4 years and can attend from 8 am until 6 pm and can have their meals there. Vanessa, the group leader, was studying for an early years qualification and was assisted by Helen, an experienced practitioner.
   The home-like atmosphere of this setting was reflected in the most frequently observed literacy events, which included book sharing between individual children and among small groups of children and adults. Adults supported literacy events far more than they initiated them. The children engaged in

considerable mark making in their play, which often led to emergent writing. Observations showed that the children linked their play to books and stories they had shared. For example, Emma, who arrived dressed as a fairy, was linked into a story about a bad fairy. The bad fairy was then incorporated into the hospital play, which had been set up by the staff. This emphasis suggests that staff understood the value of reading stories to children and of children listening to those stories. The most frequently occurring events were: book sharing between adults and children, mark making during play, and imaginative play.

Vanessa, the group leader, was new to the setting and was developing her awareness of the Foundation Stage guidance. She talked about how her course was influencing her practice and the experiences she offered to the children:

> I've been getting out activities and thinking 'why'? What are the children going to gain from that and that each child has different individual needs. Giving children things to colour in – it's limiting their motivation.

Her training was changing her understanding about literacy learning. For example, she had previously thought that children should write their names by following dot to dot but she now creates play scenarios such as a shop or hospital:

> You can see they are all doing mock writing. I ask them to write by themselves.

In the following example the home corner had been turned into a fire engine; it was the week of bonfire night, which had been discussed earlier that day. Two children were writing notes and mark making while they used the telephones; they exchanged notes and discussed their writing.

Emma and Alex

Alex: 'Emma, in the fire engine, quickly, NE NAH NE NAH.'
Emma: 'Let's do this OK?' She writes with a pencil on the notebook next to the phone.
   They both pick up the phones.
Emma: 'Hullo, Yes.'
Emma and Alex: 'Hullo, Hullo,' while talking on the phones and laughing.
Emma: 'Look.' She shows her writing to Alex and folds it up and then concentrates on the phone.
Helen (practitioner): 'I think we'll postpone our reading activity because you are all playing so well.' She turns towards Alex and Emma: 'If anybody rings can you leave a message?'
Alex: 'I phoned.'
Emma: 'Look.' She shows her writing to Helen.
Helen: 'What does it say?'
Emma: 'Hairy hat man.' (She has written a row of Hs amongst other mark making.)
Emma goes back to the phone. She holds the note she's written and puts it in her drawer and runs over to give Alex a rag doll.

In this setting the group leader was changing her practice as she became more informed about developing literacy through well resourced play. The adults were flexible in their approach and did not disrupt the play when it was time for a planned activity.

The reception class

The reception class was housed in a primary school in a Victorian building. In the class of 25 4- to 5-years-olds there were four English-speaking children; the remaining children had English as an additional language. The families were mainly Turkish and Somalian refugees or asylum seekers. For the first term there were two qualified teachers until a second reception class opened, where one of the teachers then taught. A classroom assistant and an EMA teacher supported individual pupils. The children are able to have breakfast in school. The class teacher, Anna, has a Master's Degree in Education from the USA, and Jane, the second teacher, is newly qualified.

Most key literacy events were initiated and led by adults. These included daily phonics activities and a focus on print, symbols and formal writing. There were whole-class literacy activities: using an alphabet mat to learn the letters and sounds of the alphabet; book making; a class newspaper; worksheets and formal writing. Every day the children carried out a mark making, worksheet or colouring activity. The children listened to stories, shared books regularly and used literacy props such as white-boards and felt pens. Adults initiated fixed literacy events through whole-class activities such as: a weather and date chart; using alphabet books; engaging in alphabet-based activities; book making and worksheets. After completing planned activities the children could choose what to do such as mark making on the white-boards. Friday afternoon was a designated time for play, for example with the puppet show. The only literacy play observed was when one child chose to play with a box of word labels. Opportunities for free play or free choice activities were constrained by the time needed for other literacy-related activities.

Despite the more directive approach to teaching observed, when interviewed the teachers expressed the belief that play was important and described some play activities:

> It's very important and we use it every day at some point in the day. Whether it's in the home corner and they're re-enacting a story or playing with letters and what sounds they make. We use the computer games as well.

However, a typical morning consisted of structured activities:

> In the morning they come in and read, then we do the calendar and the days of the week. Then they do a piece of work which is usually literacy based and then sometimes they play games as a group, sometimes they do individual work, sometimes they work with a teacher or an older child.

This more directive approach to literacy teaching is illustrated in the example of David below. The approach also links to one teacher's views on the Foundation Stage curriculum:

They're (the children) expected to do a lot more in year 1. But now they've gone back to the Foundation Stage how can they expect us just to change? There's no change in year 1.

The teacher seemed concerned about meeting the demands of the year 1 curriculum. This view contrasts with that of the nursery teacher cited earlier in this chapter, who expressed concerns about formal practices in reception year and regarded the new guidance as offering the freedom to follow a less directive curriculum.

David

Anna (the teacher): 'Yesterday we looked at 'a' and 'b' (she makes the phonic sound of 'a') what sound does the letter b make?'
David: 'Makes a 'b' sound'
Anna then goes through the 'a' words in the large alphabet book on the easel. She points to the name of the author and explains that he is the 'author' of the book.
David: 'Author.'
Anna: 'Today we're going to do the "c" sound, castle, cake, cat, car, I can't hear you.'
    The children chant after her.
    David has his hands in his mouth and does not join in.
Anna: 'How do you spell cat in your work, what sound does 'c' make?'
    The children then chant the 'c' words while Anna points to the pictures. David sits and looks.
Anna: 'What letter comes after 'c'?
    A child in the class puts his hand up and says 'd'.
    Anna asks the whole class and then asks David: 'Who can think of a word beginning with "d"? David? Dolphin?'
David: 'David.'
Anna: 'Lets say together "d".'
    David says 'd' – but doesn't join in with the reciting of the words.
Anna: 'Raise your hand if you know what letter dog starts with.'
    David sits and looks.
Anna: 'Who can think of a word that begins with c?'
    Anna then tells the children that they will be colouring in a c and d worksheet and that: 'Eventually we'll have a whole book of words.'

Anna then directs the children to follow-up activities, which include: putting the alphabet in order, making a book of letters, sponge painting with alphabet letters and making a hanging mobile with the letters of their name.
    Anna stands next to David who is at the table with the 'd' worksheet and tells him to: 'Colour in the letter 'D'. He colours in the letter.

The practitioners in this reception class were attempting to rise to the challenge of the demands of the National Curriculum at Key Stage 1 and were very aware of the good results achieved by the school in national assessment targets in literacy at age seven. The downward pressure of the primary school curriculum on the early literacy curriculum described by David *et al.* (2000) seemed to be driving aspects of the teaching in this setting.

The playgroup

The playgroup is housed in a portacabin adjacent to the village primary school. The premises consist of two large rooms plus a kitchen and office area. One room is used for creative activities and sand and water play and there is a well equipped outdoor play area. There are 30 places for children aged two to five, who attend part time. Not all attend on the same days.

The expressed belief of the playgroup leader, who had a Diploma in Pre-School Practice, was that children should learn about literacy through play. This was reflected in much of the practice observed, for example in the wide choice of manipulative activities offered to the children. These included using writing tools, paint bushes, scissors and jigsaw puzzles, which were seen as important informal preparation for later writing skills. Fixed literacy events included a weather chart, day-of-the-week chart, story time on the mat and being invited to recognise name cards at snack time. The literacy play observed was incidental rather than planned, for example children taking basket loads of books to look at in the play bus sited near the home corner. In contrast, in some afternoon sessions more formal activities were planned, which were seen as helpful preparation for school.

The leader spoke about the type of literacy curriculum she thought was appropriate for young children:

> I think they should learn through play and their literacy should be no more than conversation and being able to name things and being able to explain and talk about things. I don't think they should be expected to do anything more than make marks with writing tools. I don't think this child should be able to write their name before they leave here, because some of them are just 4 when they go to school. I know most of them can because we've been under pressure.

About the Foundation Stage guidance she said:

> We do feel under pressure...because you will get parents that will come in and say 'well my friend's child can write their name, why can't mine?' But I think the parents are under pressure as well. I think too much importance is put on the three Rs and the rest of it gets forgotten. The hardest part is just trying to make them understand that you are teaching, although you're not sitting them down and saying you've got to do this.

When asked about more formal literacy practices she replied:

> With the older ones in the afternoon we do have the more formal sit down letter formation type thing. Again it's a thing we have to do, it's not something I would do by choice.

The example below shows one child's experience of such a session.

Josh

The room layout in one afternoon session provided a contrast to the free-flowing activities of the morning. The creative area was closed off and the main activities cleared away. Small tables were set out each with four chairs around them. There were writing implements, name cards and worksheets on the table. The eight children were asked to stop playing and to sit at the tables.

Josh is sitting at the table. The adult says, 'Can I have some of your letters on there' (pointing to his blank sheet of paper). He attempts to write his name by copying from his name card. Worksheets involving drawing along dotted lines are introduced and Josh says 'I can't do it.' He flicks his pencil away saying 'Go Away.' The adult helps him to trace the line. She talks to him about writing his name, 'Yes – a huge J.' The children are then given a shapes worksheet and Josh says, 'Go away I don't want a pencil' – he pushes away the pencil and paper. He says, 'I don't need mine any more he can have it' (referring to a child who is unwell and is lying on the cushions in the book area). Josh tries to leave the table but the adult persuades him to stay and colour in a blue circle. He colours it in very quickly. She asks him to do a 'J' for his name but he says he can't do it. She says next time she will do dots for him so he can do a 'J'. He says, 'Yes – dots.' He goes off to lie on the floor saying, 'I'm tired.'

This conflict between expressed belief and what happened in practice in the playgroup (and also in the reception class) seemed to be related to how the curriculum guidance was being interpreted, the demands of the primary school curriculum and parental pressure for their children to achieve literacy goals, which they saw as indicators of success in literacy.

Literacy beliefs and literacy practices

Our findings suggest that the practitioners viewed and interpreted the guidance for the Foundation Stage in different ways, despite working towards the same learning goals. Both the reception class teachers and the playgroup leader expressed the view that children learn about literacy through play. In the playgroup this belief was seen in much of the practice observed. However, the leader did bow to perceived pressures and sometimes engaged in more directive teaching. In the reception class the view that children with diverse language needs had to be prepared for Key Stage 1 resulted in more directive and formal approaches to teaching literacy. The belief that children require formal adult-led teaching in order to meet literacy outcomes seems to persist in some settings, despite evidence that such teaching is not advantageous for young children (EEC 2000).

In the private day nursery the group leader was influenced more by her training than by curriculum guidance. Her developing beliefs about literacy were translated into practice as illustrated in the fire engine play. In the LEA nursery the teacher felt the guidance endorsed her belief that literacy teaching should not be too structured in the early years. She saw it as liberating reception classes from more formal practices; however she recognised that external pressures such as tests in the primary school may lead to downward pressures on the early years curriculum. In her own setting this teacher's beliefs were reflected in her play-based approach to literacy.

Literacy beliefs and children with English as their second language

> Notices and labels printed in different scripts, dual language texts in the book corner, and recordings of songs and rhymes on audio cassettes can offer a meaningful context for bilingual children in school.
>
> (Jago 1999: 161)

Inclusion is central to the Curriculum Guidance for the Foundation Stage (QCA/DfEE 2000), which says that no child should be excluded because of culture or home language. Although not a specific focus of this project, the bilingual children in the reception class and the nursery class were supported by some common practices described by Jago (1999) above as offering a meaningful context for literacy. These included enriching the language of the children through play experiences (although few of these were observed in the reception class) and through dual language books, print, stories, signs and labels. In both settings there were signs and labels in several languages – Turkish, English, Arabic and Bengali. In both classes children were given opportunities to take home books in their home language so their parents could read to them. Both classes offered support from EMA teachers.

However, there were also some differences in teaching approaches, particularly in relation to the direct teaching of the English alphabet and phonics. The nursery teacher's view was that:

> They are not ready for phonics. They should be playing with letters, making letters in the sand and with play dough.

In contrast, one reception class teacher expressed the belief that:

> Without the alphabet you can't learn to read. They're relying on us to teach that to them.

In the nursery class practitioners mainly saw their role as enriching the language of the children through playful experiences and through project work and linked visits in the local community, for example to look at shop and street signs. In the reception class a focus on print and knowledge of the English alphabet was considered to be important because the children would be familiar with a different alphabet at home, such as the Arabic alphabet.

In both settings the children were offered literacy experience that acknowledged their language and culture. However, the emphasis in the reception class on the direct teaching of the English alphabet and phonics conflicts with ideas about a developmentally appropriate curriculum for young bilingual children (Jago 1999; Whitehead 2000). It is interesting to note that the EMA teachers in both settings and the reception class teacher, Anna, wanted more training on how to teach bilingual children:

> How to help and support them and what activities are good for them, just basic understanding of their language.
>
> (Anna)

Implications for practice

The Education and Employment Committee report (2000) drew on studies of brain development in young children to conclude that a rich, stimulating early years environment is important for early development. It concluded that many skills such as walking and talking develop naturally through play and exploration, whereas others such as reading, writing and maths require teaching. However there is no convincing evidence to suggest that teaching these skills too early (i.e. before the age of six) is advantageous. It advocates well resourced preschools where children can learn through play and exploration and so learn about how to learn.

Practitioners need to understand that fast-tracking children along a route to literacy in order to achieve designated goals can damage children's disposition to learn. There is no evidence to suggest that 'sooner is better'. Developing 'positive attitudes and dispositions towards their learning' is a stated aim for children in the Foundation Stage (QCA/DfEE 1999: 90). Children need time to learn through active exploration, discovery and through the provision of appropriate resources and support from skilled and knowledgeable adults. By putting pressure on children to demonstrate their learning through 'write and tell' activities, as in the case of Josh described earlier in this chapter, puts them in danger of failing and may put them off literacy for life.

The differences in approaches to the teaching of literacy and the subsequent impact on the children's experiences of literacy in the four settings appeared to be linked to the following factors: practitioners' beliefs about the teaching of literacy; different interpretations of the Foundation Stage curriculum; external pressure from the demands of the primary school curriculum and parental pressure. It is now over a decade since the Rumbold Report (DES 1990) reported on the quality of education for children under 5 and highlighted the tension between the process and the outcomes of learning and it seems that the debate continues (EEC 2000). Anning and Edwards (1999) have described how practitioners gained confidence in articulating their beliefs and understandings about literacy and in managing children's literacy learning, when they were supported in their own learning. Our findings highlight the need for practitioners who believe in offering a holistic curriculum based on play and active learning to be confident in interpreting the curriculum guidance in creative ways. They also highlight the need to support some practitioners in developing appropriate practices and holistic approaches in order to enable children to become lifelong literacy learners.

References

Anning, A. and Edwards, E. (1999) *Promoting Children's Learning from Birth to Five.* Buckingham: Open University Press.

Barratt-Pugh, C. (2001) 'The socio-cultural context of literacy learning', in Barratt-Pugh, C. and Rohl, M. (eds) *Literacy in the Early Years.* Buckingham: Open University Press.

Browne, A. (1998) 'Provision for reading for four year old children', *Reading* **32** (1), 9–13.

David, T., Raban, B., Ure, C., Goouch, K., Jago, M., Barriere, I. and Lambirth, A. (2000) *Making Sense of Early Literacy: a practitioner's perspective.* Stoke-on-Trent: Trentham Books.

DES (1990) *Starting with Quality.* The Rumbold Report of the Committee of Inquiry into the Quality of Educational Experience offered to 3-4-year-olds. London: HMSO.

Education and Employment Committee (EEC) (2000) *Early Years* (online), The Report and the Proceedings of the Committee of the Education Sub-Committee Relating to the Report. London: The Stationery Office. Available at: http://www.publications.parliament.uk/pa/cm200001/cmselect/cmeduemp/33/3302.htm (accessed 7 May 2003).

Fisher, R. (2000) 'Developmentally Appropriate Practice and a National Literacy Strategy', *British Journal of Educational Studies* **48** (1), 58–69.

Jago, M. (1999) 'Bilingual children in a monolingual society', in David, T. (ed.) (1999) *Young Children Learning.* London: Paul Chapman Publishing.

Miller, L. Soler, J., Foote, L. and Smith, J. (2002) 'Literacy in early childhood settings in two countries', in Miller, L., Drury, R and Campbell, R. (eds) *Exploring Early Years Education and Care.* London: David Fulton Publishers.

Miller, L. (1996) *Towards Reading: Literacy Development in the Pre-School Years.* Buckingham: Open University Press.

Miller, L. (2000) 'Play as a foundation for learning', in Drury, R., Miller, L. and Campbell, R. (eds) *Looking at Early Years Education and Care.* London: David Fulton Publishers.

Qualifications and Curriculum Authority (QCA) and the Department for Education and Employment (DfEE) (1999) *Early Learning Goals.* London: QCA/DfEE.

Qualifications and Curriculum Authority (QCA) and the Department for Education and Employment (DfEE) (2000) *Curriculum Guidance for the Foundation Stage*. London: QCA/DfEE.

Whitehead, M. (2000) *Developing Language and Literacy with Young Children*, 2nd edn. London: Paul Chapman Publishing.

Chapter 14

Born mathematical?

Linda Pound

Most adults will readily agree that young children are competent learners but few realise just how competent. Current research techniques (Karmiloff and Karmiloff-Smith 2001) have given us new and exciting insights into very young children's thinking. These techniques have enabled researchers and psychologists to determine babies' interests or preferences, to understand what causes anxiety. Perhaps most startling of all, they have also revealed that babies have a range of surprising, inborn mathematical abilities (Devlin 2000). As Devlin reminds us, mathematics is not only about number but 'about life' (2000: 76) and involves thinking and learning processes such as the identification of pattern, handling information in abstract forms; and a wide range of problem-solving strategies. This chapter also considers the abilities of babies and toddlers to understand something of shape and space, measures and, most strikingly, of number and computation.

Mathematical processes

From birth, humans are programmed to seek out pattern. Our brains are good at recognising pattern, a strategy which we use to identify the thousands of faces with which we come into contact. We enjoy stories because we see in them patterns – 'real or imagined, visual or mental, static or dynamic, qualitative or quantitative, utilitarian or recreational' (Devlin 2000: 11). From their earliest days babies prefer 'complex patterns of high contrast' such as 'checkerboards and bull's-eyes' (Gopnik *et al.* 1999: 64). Pattern is also an integral part of the musical interaction that permeates babies' lives (Pound and Harrison 2003). In the first year of life babies show a remarkable ability not merely to identify but to anticipate patterns in songs and rhymes (Trevarthen 1998). The young child's giggling sense of anticipation that precedes the final 'tickling under there' in *Walking Round the Garden* develops because he or she is aware that we are deviating from the rhythmic pattern of the rhyme.

The ability to think about things that are not present or do not exist at all is 'one characteristic feature of the human brain that no other species seems to possess (Devlin 2000: 117). This ability is at the heart of mathematics. The ability to categorise according to shape, colour or sound – one manifestation of abstract thought – is present at birth (Butterworth 1999). Language is itself a symbolic system and as language use is extended, young children's ability to deal with abstract information develops. Use of language also accompanies young children's increasing ability to categorise – which reflects their desire to deal with abstract information. At around 15 to 18 months of age they ask the names of objects obsessively. The words heard during this 'naming explosion' (Gopnik *et al.* 1999: 115) in response to the oft-repeated question *'what's that, what's that?'* are learnt very rapidly because at this stage the baby is interested in categorising (Karmiloff-Smith 1994). New words can be linked together as a group or category and thus remembered or recalled more readily – a process known as 'fast-mapping' (Gopnik *et al.* 1999). Many young men have been embarrassed by a baby pointing persistently at them and shouting *'dada'* – this familiar scene is simply evidence of fast-mapping. The unknown young man is being placed in the same category as the child's familiar father.

Humans also make use of a wide range of problem-solving strategies. Logic is commonly thought of as central to mathematical thinking. However, it is clear that logic is not the only means of reasoning at our disposal (Claxton 1997). Even the youngest baby hypothesises, reasons, predicts, experiments and guesses in just the way that scientists do (Gopnik *et al.* 1999; Devlin 2000), using these skills to make sense of the world. Gopnik *et al.* (1999) describe experiments where young babies learn to move a mobile when a ribbon is tied from it to their ankle. Several days later they will repeat the movement if the same mobile is used – but not if the mobile has been changed. This suggests that the baby's hypothesis is that the movement has something to do with the mobile itself.

Infants learn early that nappy changing and clattering crockery precede mealtimes. Learning to reach out, clutch an object, pull it towards the mouth and let go is a series of motor actions which require careful sequencing – pulling something towards you before you have grasped it is unrewarding. As children develop, their play includes sequences of action of increasing complexity. Despite their physical dependency, young babies are increasingly seen to be highly competent learners. One of the forces which appears to drive their actions is the desire to seek control of both their social world (Dunn 1988; Trevarthen 1998) and the physical world (Gopnik *et al.* 1999). They learn early that particular actions cause or produce specific effects and responses. Indeed babies' survival depends on being able to capture and hold the attention of another person and make known to them their needs. This ability to act with intent is reflected in the development of language. Babies and toddlers demonstrate through their early use of *there!* or *oh dear!* that they have a plan or intention in mind. This occurs for example where they have succeeded or failed in building a tower of blocks.

Shape, space and measures

Just as these processes permeate our lives, so the more explicitly mathematical aspects of shape, space and measures are fundamental to everyday activity. Awareness of shape is linked to both our enjoyment of pattern and to our interest in abstract thought, as we exercise 'the human brain's ability to reason about the environment' (Devlin 2000: 246).

Spatial awareness is part of our evolutionary heritage. Survival in trees and life on the savannah required understanding of both two- and three-dimensional space (Devlin 2000). This is reflected in infancy as babies reach out towards a stimulating object, explore their own bodies, the bodies of others and the world around them. Exploratory play reflects children's interest in shape and space as they push paper into cardboard tubes, squash tissues into boxes and use their fingers to probe all manner of objects, including the mouths and ears of others! On a larger scale, dropping objects from a height, throwing them high and steering wheeled toys through a tight space are all part of this learning process, which infants seem driven to seek out in their search for control and problems to solve.

Physical action is used to explore and think about shape and space. Spinning round, running up and down a slope, wriggling through a play-tunnel and hiding inside a blanket tent are a vital part of this process. Language is linked to the young child's growing understanding. Early use of *up* or *down* to signify something to do with direction is commonplace. Either might serve to mean *'pick me up'*, *'put me down'* or *'I want the things on that high shelf'*. This is illustrated in two-year-old Xav's afternoon of activity. He placed some circular place mats on the floor – walking round them, repositioning them and walking on them like stepping stones, while maintaining the circular pattern. He ran out to the back garden and walked around and around the tree seat; then started running while balancing on the circle of bricks which edged the flower bed. He then ran in increasingly large circles around the tree. Later that afternoon he repeated similar movements in the front garden – taking a circular path around the flower bed, the tree and the whole garden. Throughout this frenetic activity, so characteristic of this age group, he recited to himself *'round and round, round and round'*.

Language also reflects children's understanding of measures. *Big*, *little* and *more* are similarly brought into action to denote height, weight or volume. Here too physical action remains important. In describing or drawing attention to something that is moving very fast, young children typically move their arms horizontally at speed, often accompanying these actions with running movement and appropriate sounds. Very large or very tall objects are depicted with sweeping gestures in the appropriate direction, arms and legs outstretched.

Understanding number

This is where our new found understanding of what appears to be happening inside babies' heads becomes awe-inspiring. There is a wealth of studies (some of which are described in Dehaene 1997; Butterworth 1999; Devlin 2000) which make it clear that from the first day of life babies have some knowledge of number, or numerosity. (The ages shown below are indicative – the findings of studies should not be taken as representing the age at which some things can or cannot be done. Much depends on the context, the skill of the researcher and the personality of the baby involved. Some of the findings will relate simply to the age of the babies available when the researcher wished to carry out his or her experiments.)

There are studies which indicate that babies as young as a day old can differentiate between cards with two or three dots (Antell and Keating, cited in Butterworth 1999); that babies of four days of age can differentiate between words with two or three syllables (Bijecjac-Babic *et al.*, cited in Dehaene 1997). Studies looking at slightly older babies from five or six months generate responses which indicate that infants of this age can apply their awareness of number in a range of situations – recognising changes to a set of three or four moving objects on a computer screen; discriminating between the number of jumps made by a puppet; and, when shown sets of pictures and objects, preferring to link pictures and groups of objects which display the same number rather than depicting the same object (Butterworth 1999; Dehaene 1997). That is to say that, for example, babies of this age are likely to be more interested in the fact that a picture of buses is similar to a set of teddy bears because there are three of each in each case, than that there are three toy buses and a picture of three buses – numerosity is more important to them than other similarities (Starkey *et al.*, cited in Butterworth 1999).

Psychologists have been particularly interested in a link made by babies which appears to make their awareness of number even more surprising. The studies described above involve linking pictures and objects and demonstrate babies' visual awareness. It is clear however from other studies that, in addition, babies have an innate oral awareness of number. When, for example, they are played a series of words with the same number of syllables, babies notice when the number of syllables changes. Perhaps even more interesting is the fact that they also make links between visual and oral information. Presented with sets of two or three objects, they will when played a number of drum beats choose to look at the set of objects which matches the number of drum beats heard (Starkey *et al.*, cited in Dehaene 1997). So not only are babies interested in the numbers of things they can see but they are also able to make links between the number of things they can see and the number of sounds they can hear.

Counting or guessing?

Clearly, in none of these studies were the babies involved able to articulate the number of objects in any group or set – they were making connections or comparisons between the numbers within groups. The numbers involved in the studies outlined above were small – usually up to three or four. This ability is not the same process as counting – counting involves (Gelman and Gallistel 1978) being able to:

- use one number name for one object (one-to-one principle)
- remember to use the number names in the same order (stable-order principle)
- understand that the last number name used gives the size of the group (cardinal principle)
- recognise that anything can be counted – you can count a set of similar objects such as dolls, or a set of dissimilar objects which might include knives, forks, plates, cups and oranges (abstraction principle)
- accept that no matter what order you count things in the answer will always be the same – so long as you apply the one-to-one and stable-order principles (order-irrelevance principle).

What the babies in the studies cited by Butterworth and Dehaene were doing was not applying these principles and therefore counting but recognising a group of objects at a glance – a process known as subitising. Over time it appears that young children come to be able to recognise larger groups of objects – alongside, but different from, the development of the abilities that contribute to counting.

Macnamara (1996) has studied this ability and has shown that children in nurseries are sometimes able to recognise groups of objects of five, six or seven in this way. Her studies also show that many children on entering formal schooling lose this ability and, rather than simply being confident that there are enough sweets for the group, begin to count everything. Macnamara (1996: 124) gives the example of a boy who had been a very confident 'subitiser' in the nursery. When asked to repeat the same test in the reception class he became distressed because his teacher had told him he must count everything.

There are some important lessons to be learnt from Macnamara's work. Any failure to support and build on young children's abilities may cause them to lose confidence. A very important aspect of mathematics is the ability to estimate. Indeed, much of the mathematics that we use in our day-to-day lives requires approximate answers – in instances like buying paint, deciding how much money to take on holiday or planning a journey we are not trying to come up with accurate answers – merely good enough estimates. We do this alongside the important job of learning to recite number names and count groups of objects using Gelman and Gallistel's five principles.

Macnamara gives further examples of children in the reception class who remained good at recognising groups – to the point where some could identify groups of nine or ten objects at a glance. When questioned it appeared that these children achieved success by a combination of subitising and counting on. One child commented *'I remember some and then I count the rest'*, by which he meant that while looking at the group of dots or objects he was able to identify (by subitising) a group of six or seven objects and then to count on mentally the three or four additional objects which had not been part of the first group. Given that much time is often taken up early in formal schooling helping children to learn to count on – being able to hold one number in mind while adding a second set or number to the first – it may be that our failure to recognise children's ability to make use of both sets of skills is contributing to their later difficulties. Both guessing (or subitising) and counting have a part to play in children's mathematical development and practitioners need to support both.

Adding and subtracting

As if all of this were not surprising enough, it seems that in the first half of the first year of life babies seem able to predict what ought to happen when objects are added to or taken away from an existing set of objects. A mother's naturalistic observation of her five-month-old daughter (cited by Karmiloff-Smith 1994: 173) perfectly reflects the phenomenon unveiled in complex experiments:

> Sometimes we play games after she's finished eating in the high chair. She loves one where I take a few of her toys, hide them under the table top shouting 'all gone' and then making them pop up again just after. She squeals with delight. I once dropped one of the three toys we were playing with by mistake, and I could swear she looked a bit puzzled when I put only two toys back on her table.

These studies of addition and subtraction underline what was found in the studies of recognition of groups. The baby is more interested in number than in the objects themselves. The toys used could be exchanged – cuddly toys being replaced by coloured balls – but so long as the number of objects was correct the baby was not concerned (Butterworth 1999).

Counting on our fingers

Human understanding of number appears to be linked to our use of fingers for counting and computation. This is because the two functions are governed by closely related areas of the brain (Ramachandran and Blakeslee 1999). Understanding of number is from the earliest stages of learning linked to the use of the hands, the control of which takes up a larger proportion of the brain than any other part of the body (Greenfield 1997). The relationship between this part of the body and numbers can be seen in babies and toddlers, as they take up one, then two objects in their hands. They may signal a number of objects by using their fingers, holding up all ten fingers fully spread to signify a large number – sometimes accompanied by language – *'I want this many'*.

At this stage the ability to recognise a group of objects is not linked to an ability to count. A group of two objects is recognised as a group of two, without any link to language or any facility to compare one group with another. Learning to recite number names in order – although a vital skill at a later stage – is a separate part of a highly complex learning process. Here too the human mind has, in addition, two important advantages. One is the use of fingers and the other is the role of music in infant development (Pound and Harrison 2003). Cultures around the world use songs and action rhymes, which combine the use of fingers, the role of rhythm and the pleasure of physical and playful contact to make number memorable.

So what should practitioners do?

Many of these exciting findings related to the mathematical abilities of young children demand only what practitioners working with young children have thought of as common sense. Providing a rich range of experiences and materials for problem-solving and exploration enables children to develop connections in the brain which will support future thinking, including mathematical thinking. Counting songs – especially those which include the use of fingers and movement – also reinforce learning, enabling children to memorise, represent and recall numbers.

The findings should also encourage practitioners to look for evidence of these apparently innate abilities. Being able to communicate mathematical ideas enables children to think mathematically since communication and thought are mutually supportive (Goldschmied and Selleck 1996; Siegel 1999). In order to help young children to communicate their ideas we should learn to enjoy their problem-solving abilities; notice when they are identifying or creating patterns – whether musical, based in their movements, talk or in other aspects of their play.

We should also encourage imagination, as it contributes to abstract thought – imagining things which are not actually present. This occurs through play and stories, and by talking about things that we are going to do and have already done. Where this can be supported by photographs and relevant objects this will support children in visualising abstract ideas.

Above all, adults can support children's considerable abilities by respecting and trying to identify their mathematical intentions. We do this very readily with spoken language – we are delighted when children use a single word and work hard to support them in making their meaning clear. We accept that milk might mean water or orange – what they want is a drink. We also accept their imaginative ideas – taking delight in their ability to pretend that a block is a banana or a mobile phone. Let's work equally hard to ensure that we don't get too caught up in feeling that their mathematical ideas must always be wholly accurate. Let's encourage mathematical play and guessing!

References

Butterworth, B. (1999) *The Mathematical Brain*. London: Macmillan.

Claxton, G. (1997) *Hare Brain and Tortoise Mind*. London: Fourth Estate.

Dehaene, S. (1997) *The Number Sense – how the mind creates mathematics*. London: Penguin Books.

Devlin, K. (2000) *The Maths Gene*. London: Weidenfeld & Nicolson.

Dunn, J. (1988) *The Beginnings of Social Understanding*. Oxford: Blackwell.

Gelman, R. and Gallistel, C. R. (1978) *The Child's Understanding of Number*. Cambridge, Mass.: Harvard University Press.

Goldschmied, E. and Selleck, D. (1996) *Communication between Babies in their First Year*. London: National Children's Bureau.

Gopnik, A. *et al.* (1999) *How Babies Think*. London: Weidenfeld & Nicolson.

Greenfield, S. (1997) *The Human Brain – a guided tour*. London: Weidenfeld & Nicolson.

Karmiloff, K. and Karmiloff-Smith, A. (2001) *Pathways to language: from fetus to adolescent*. London: Harvard University Press.

Karmiloff-Smith, A. (1994) *Baby It's You!* London: Ebury Press.

Macnamara, A. (1996) 'From home to school – do children preserve their counting skills?' In Broadhead P. (ed.) (1996) *Researching the Early Years Continuum*, 118–27. Clevedon: Multilingual Matters.

Pound, L. and Harrison, C. (2003) *Supporting Musical Development in the Early Years*. Buckingham: Open University Press.

Ramachandran, V. S. and Blakeslee, S. (1999) *Phantoms in the Brain*. London: Fourth Estate.

Siegel, D. (1999) *The Developing Mind*. New York: Guilford Press.

Trevarthen, C. (1998) 'The child's need to learn a culture', in Woodhead, M. *et al.* (eds) *Cultural Worlds of Early Childhood*. London: Routledge.

Chapter 15

A curriculum for supporting mathematical thinking

Linda Pound

Mathematics is an essential element of young children's learning and it is sometimes assumed that teaching basic skills is simply a question of ensuring that children learn the basics – counting, number bonds and so on. Unfortunately this approach has led to a situation where generations of adults lack confidence in their own abilities and regard themselves as simply not being mathematical. Learning mathematics involves not only the required content – generally thought of as measurement, number, shape and space – but also a focus on a range of learning processes. If children are to become confident, lifelong mathematical thinkers, the mathematics curriculum must also take into account aspects of thinking and learning such as problem-solving, reflection, playful exploration and relevance. This chapter considers the elements of both the content and the learning curriculum, identifying key aspects of provision which will support children's mathematical development.

A continuum of learning throughout the early years

Birth to three

It is no accident that the authors of *Birth to Three Matters* (Sure Start Unit 2002) have chosen, not a subject based curriculum, but one which emphasises young children's competence in learning and communication. Children at this earliest stage of development require 'not scaled-down versions of a good program for preschool children' (Bredekamp 1987: 17) but a curriculum which helps them to focus on making sense of their world, including their mathematical world. The distinct curriculum offered to young children in these crucial years will promote:

• social interaction and communication, because this is the basis of all thinking
• children's interests as the starting point for learning
• imaginative and exploratory play, which allows children to practise, rehearse and represent things that they have seen, heard and experienced.

Learning at this stage must be supported by adults who are willing to interpret children's intentions and who understand how to use aspects of children's daily lives to develop mathematical thinking. Skilful adults can nurture this process by playing *with* children in order to model the process of making one thing stand for another, pretending, sequencing and exploring. The importance of building on the child's own interests is recognised because this sustains children's interest. How often have you seen a toddler slide away from something he or she had been happily engaged in when an adult moves in and asks questions? The most effective support is watchful and sensitive to what the young child wants to do, building on rather than diverting or distracting children from their purpose.

From three to five

Because much of the formal guidance offered to practitioners at this stage refers to mathematics as a subject in its own right, adults sometimes feel that their teaching must reflect this. This has sometimes led practitioners to introduce formally structured mathematics sessions. When combined with a formally structured session for literacy this is inappropriate for children of this age. Young children do not learn most effectively in large groups, nor is it comfortable or healthy for them to sit still in relatively passive roles for extended periods of time. Some practitioners (particularly those who lack confidence in their own mathematical ability) turn to worksheets. There is no place in early years settings for worksheets. They get in the way of children's reflective thought; they do not give an accurate view of what children can do; and they stifle independence and self-initiated activity (Fisher 1996).

Since mathematics is a vital means of making sense of the world it is important to ensure that it is presented as something that affects all aspects of children's experience – maths in the sand tray, maths on the bus, maths in stories, songs and rhymes. Communication, a curriculum built on children's interests and the value of play remain important elements of supporting mathematical development and thought. At a time when practitioners may begin to feel pressured, it is vital to ensure that children see mathematics as fun. In addition, curriculum approaches for this age group emphasise the importance of encouraging children to:

- develop problem-solving strategies and approaches
- talk about or describe the strategies they have developed in order to clarify mathematical thinking
- explore informal recording and representations before being introduced to formal methods of recording.

The following examples of everyday activities help children to integrate mathematical thinking and learning into all other aspects of learning:

- guessing how high the aeroplane is
- building a wall that the wolf can't blow down
- making a tent big enough for all my friends
- sorting and putting away my toys
- wondering why the tall thin bottle holds less than the short fat bottle
- noting whose sunflower has grown the tallest.

(based on Leeds Under Eights Service 1996: 40)

Key Stage 1

Traditionally it has been at this stage that pressures to place an emphasis primarily on the content aspects of the curriculum emerge. This has sometimes led to an approach where children are required to work through workbooks or worksheets slavishly. Where classes are large and staffing ratios unfavourable such devices may offer busy teachers valuable respite – but they do not support mathematical thinking.

More recently the National Numeracy Strategy (DfEE 1999) and the revised requirements of the National Curriculum (QCA 1999) have had a broader focus. These frameworks support an emphasis on oral approaches, by delaying the introduction of formal written methods and by supporting the development of children's own preferred mathematical strategies and methods of recording.

Learning to think mathematically continues to be supported by maintaining an emphasis on communication, individual approaches and interests. It must also be supported by continued opportunities for play and stimulating real-life experiences, emphasising the way in which mathematics permeates life. All of these aspects need to be reflected in both content and learning aspects of the curriculum.

The content curriculum

Measurement, number, and shape and space are generally considered to be the main elements of mathematics. However, mathematics has been described as 'the science of patterns' (Devlin 2000: 11) and the use, identification and creation of patterns deserves a firmer place in a curriculum designed to promote mathematical thinking in young children than is generally planned. The importance of pattern is therefore considered in this section.

Measurement

Measurement is the area of mathematics on which children perhaps draw most heavily on their everyday experiences. Comparisons of length, mass, volume, capacity, and even time, are part of many day-to-day conversations. Children's understanding of different measures develops at different rates but is closely related to their experience. Things which are important within the child's family and broader culture will be most readily learnt. Complex measures such as area and speed are not generally seen as essential elements of a curriculum for young children. However, in homes where they hear adults talking about which cars go fastest, how much carpet or curtain fabric will be needed, children will develop understanding.

Number

In their dealings with young children, most adults place considerable stress on numbers. Learning numbers by heart is vital – counting has been described as a special kind of song without end (Ginsburg 1977). If you have ever tried to recite every other word of a poem or song (counting in twos), or beginning somewhere in the middle (counting on), it soon becomes clear why it is so vital to know the order of the counting words inside out!

Reciting number names in the correct order is, of course, not enough. Number goes well beyond counting and involves a wide range of operations, many of which are familiar to children in their everyday lives – one more, only three more, fair shares, none left, doubling, halving and estimating. Money has particular significance and clear characteristics, with the possibility of exploring the principles of exchange. Children who have not yet understood this are often delighted to receive five or ten brown coins in exchange for just one small silver one.

Shape and space

In the early years of schooling, an emphasis is frequently placed on learning the names of two-dimensional shapes but this may not be the easiest starting point for young children. With more experiences of three-dimensional shapes Dean might have avoided his dilemma in the following example. Six-year-old Dean (Owen and Rousham 1997: 259) has been completing a worksheet which asks him to say how many sides and corners some two-dimensional shapes have. Corners are no problem, but for each shape he has recorded that there are two sides. His teacher questions him:

Teacher:	Dean, I'm not sure this is right, is it? Do all these different shapes have two sides?
Dean:	(Belligerently) Yes.
Teacher:	Well, can you get your shapes and show me the two sides?
Dean:	(Returning with his set of plastic shapes.) Look, (holding triangle in one hand and using his other hand to point, he places his index finger in the centre) one ... (turns shape over) ... two.

Practitioners can help children to avoid such misunderstandings by making sure that plenty of practical experience and discussion precedes any demands to work independently with pencil and paper in this way.

Large motor movement has an impact on spatial awareness, which in turn contributes to mathematical understanding. Children who have played with large blocks or crates, explored areas on wheeled toys and enjoyed climbing are likely to have greater confidence and insight into dealing with problems relating to space and shape.

Searching for patterns and relationships

The human mind is a pattern recognizer.

(Devlin 2000: 61)

We see this in our ability to recognise literally thousands of faces and in the way in which we create and relish stories – identifying the patterns and connections in what might otherwise be disconnected events and facts. We can also see this when we read to young children – just try missing parts of a well-loved story! Searching for patterns and relationships is fundamental to all mathematics. This includes sorting, matching, ordering, seeing similarities and differences, predicting, sequencing and repeating patterns. There is a danger that we may underestimate children's abilities in these aspects of mathematics by presenting them with meaningless exercises rather than with stimulating challenges.

For example, from about the age of 2 children are able to assemble the necessary components of a pattern, although they continue to have difficulty in actually reproducing the pattern right through to 4 or 5 years of age. However, their ability to identify and recreate pattern is much greater in other areas of experience. This is probably because bead patterns do not match up to the *enthusiasms* of children of this age. If we really want to know about and foster young children's understanding of patterns and relationships we should look to the patterns that excite and interest them, including musical and linguistic patterns. Children learn early to identify and repeat the patterns found in songs and rhymes.

The learning curriculum: mathematical processes

The development of mathematical thinking requires learning that is also vital in other areas of the curriculum. Confidence, independence, risk-taking (essential in estimating and approximating), learning from others and learning from exploration will support *all* learning, including mathematics. In this section, four such aspects will be explored, namely: problem-solving; reflection; relevance; and the value of playful mathematics.

Problem-solving

Problem-solving is one of the core elements of the development of mathematical thinking. Children's suggestions for solving problems tell us a great deal about their level of understanding and give us an insight into the power of their 'puzzling minds' (Tizard and Hughes 1984). When asked how best to empty the large sand pit (Pound *et al.* 1992), the children in a nursery school make a range of suggestions. Pippie comes up with the fantastic idea of putting all the sand into a chest of drawers which can then be moved along on something slippery. Her suggestion 'What about ice?' is precisely the strategy used by the Chinese to move across their country to Beijing a huge slab of marble which now forms a decorative panel in the Forbidden Palace.

Confidence is a vital element in problem-solving. In mathematics one of the difficulties is that practitioners often lack confidence. This is often unwittingly communicated to children and sometimes prevents adults giving children the time and space they need to work things out for themselves. We become afraid of being asked questions to which we may not know the answer. We worry that children will be confused by the fact that many questions or problems have more than one right answer.

Reflection

Learning to reflect is vital to the development of mathematical thought. This element of the learning curriculum for mathematics enables children to develop strategies for seeing things in their mind's eye and to represent their ideas in words or in visual forms.

Language

Words have tremendous power in shaping thinking. Children do not always need actual objects to count – with small numbers, even quite young children can imagine them. Ask a three-year-old what two and one is and you will be met with blank stares – but ask how many sweets or even elephants two and one is and they will have an answer. Words give the question a context – turning an abstract idea into something that can be imagined.

Asking children about the images they see when presented with mathematical ideas or simply saying 'How did you work that out?' can promote mathematical thinking. Even if they do not respond, the question may well trigger thinking which will make them aware of their own thinking. Giving praise for explaining methods can encourage children to develop mental strategies.

We should not forget that the specialist use of language can sometimes create unhelpful mental images. What does a five- or six-year-old conjure up when a teacher talks about 'taking away'? It is unlikely to be subtraction – more likely pizza or chow mein. Trying to see things from the child's point of view can help us anticipate likely confusions.

Mental images

The familiar guessing games played in many early childhood settings are useful in helping children to create mental images. These games often take the form of hiding something in a bag or sock and describing the object's characteristics until someone guesses correctly what is hidden. Similarly a small object may be placed inside a box and children asked to guess what might possibly be inside.

Pattern is useful in establishing mental images. The patterns on dice for example soon become instantly recognised. Numberlines (both washing lines with numbers to peg on and strips up to 10 or even 100) and hundred squares provide important images from which children can work. Fingers, abacuses and structural apparatus can all play a role in supporting the development of mental images, particularly as they provide a physical dimension to memory.

Recording ideas

Recording is useful in promoting and clarifying thinking. Role play is an excellent context for mathematical mark-making – filling in forms in the post office, recording appointment times at the hairdressers or writing out bills in the cafe enable children to draw directly on their experience. Gifford (1995) suggests encouraging children to keep scores in their games – using tallies, drawings or even entirely idiosyncratic symbols. Like children's invented writing, in the early stages these notes may seem haphazard or indecipherable but over time, given encouragement and appropriate models, children's efforts will become increasingly comprehensible.

In the long run children's mathematical understanding will benefit immensely from the use of standard number symbols. These symbols are part of a universal language, they contain a large amount of information in a very compact form and they can give children and parents a keen sense of achievement (Atkinson and Clarke 1992). Unfortunately, practitioners sometimes feel pressured into introducing standard notations too early. This often has the effect of undermining children's confidence, robbing them of any sense of relevance and causing confusion.

Relevance

Some children had been taken to the Natural History Museum to follow up a project on mammals. On returning to school, they were asked what they had liked best. 'Going upstairs on the red bus,' said Matthew! This familiar story underlines the fact that relevance is dictated by each child's personal interests and experience.

In seeking to make the mathematics curriculum relevant to each child practitioners will need to ensure that:

- planning is based on observations of children so that what children are asked to do builds on what they already know and can do
- children are given choices so that they themselves can find materials and examples which are meaningful to them
- opportunities for small group interaction and discussion are provided since this will help children to see the relevance of their peers' experiences and interests
- real-life experiences, rich in mathematical potential, are provided.

Playful mathematics

Few of us will ever attain the degree of mathematical playfulness which led Devi (1990: 9) to write:

> At three I fell in love with numbers...Numbers were toys with which I could play... there is a...richness in numbers: they come alive, cease to be symbols...and lead the reader into a world of intellectual adventure...

However, to help children move towards this playful and creative love of mathematics there are a number of things we might do. Children need a balance of teacher-directed and self-initiated activity, and time and space to engage in what Bruce (1991) has termed 'free-flow play' is essential. In many classrooms the balance is heavily tilted in the direction of teacher-initiated activities, and play is all too frequently relegated to something that happens when children have completed their work.

In addition to the mathematical learning in free-flow play, including role-play, block-building or throwing a ball, children also need to be allowed to explore other situations and experiences playfully. If a four-year-old says that there is a dinosaur under the table the chances are that we will enter into the game – pretending to be afraid or exhilarated. However if the same child suggests that there are only three sweets rather than the five we can see, the chances are that we insist on counting them laboriously. We do not generally make jokes about mathematics and in making a different response we signal that mathematics is serious and different – 'lightening up' might make maths more playful and creative.

Games are sometimes thought of as the mathematical equivalent of comics. There are any number of commercially produced games which can be chosen to meet specific learning objectives. We need to ensure that children have access to familiar games and can choose to play them over and over again – in much the same way as they choose favourite books. At home, four-year-old David played a large and rather complicated board game, which had been played by the family, on his own in every spare moment of the day for several weeks. His interest was undoubtedly connected to his determination to understand rule-based games.

Books and stories offer playful exploration of mathematical ideas. The mathematical learning offered by counting books is clear but stories have mathematical potential. Mathematical discussion, questioning and problem-solving, which may arise from familiar stories, can be playful and creative. Familiar stories such as *Rosie's Walk* promote mathematical talk and thought particularly when accompanied by plastic farm animals, which allow children to play with the ideas in the book.

Summary

The mathematics curriculum should focus on *all* the aspects that children will need in order to become confident and thoughtful mathematicians. This will include the need for practitioners to be aware of the continuity of learning which occurs from birth onwards, to ensure that all aspects of content, including pattern, are addressed, and to pay attention to the learning processes that are an essential part of learning to think mathematically.

References

Atkinson, S. and Clarke, S. (1992) 'The use of standard notation', in Atkinson, S., *Mathematics with Reason*, 30–8. London: Hodder & Stoughton.

Bredekamp, S. (ed.) (1987) *Developmentally Appropriate Practice in Early Childhood Programs Serving Children from Birth through Age 8*. Washington: NAEYC.

Bruce, T. (1991) *Time to Play in Early Childhood Education*. London: Hodder & Stoughton.

Department for Education and Employment (1999) *The National Numeracy Strategy*. London: DfEE.

Devi, S. (1990) *Figuring*. London: Penguin Books.

Devlin, K. (2000) *The Maths Gene*. London: Weidenfeld & Nicolson.

Fisher, J. (1996) *Starting from the Child?* Buckingham: Open University Press.

Gifford, S. (1995) 'Number in early childhood'. *Early Childhood Development and Care* **109**, 95–119.

Ginsburg, H. (1977) *Children's Arithmetic*. New York: Van Nostrand.

Leeds Under Eights Service (1996) *Let's Get it Right: dimensions of quality education and care*. Leeds: Leeds City Council.

Owen, A. and Rousham, L. (1997) 'Maths – is that a kind of game for grown-ups? Understanding numbers in the early years', in D. Whitebread (ed.) *Teaching and Learning in the Early Years*, 255–74. London: Routledge.

Pound, L. *et al.* (1992) *The Early Years: mathematics*. London: Harcourt Brace Jovanovich.

QCA (1999) *The National Curriculum – handbook for primary teachers in England: Key Stages 1 and 2*. London: DfEE/QCA.

Sure Start Unit (2002) *Birth to Three Matters: a framework to support children in their earliest years*. London: DfES.

Tizard, B. and Hughes, M. (1984) *Young Children Learning*. London: Fontana.

Chapter 16

ICT and curriculum provision in the early years

Deirdre Cook

Papert (1996) says that to ask how old children should be to use computers is rather like asking when they should have crayons or dolls. He is quite clear that just as computers can be well used at any age, so too can they be badly used. He states:

> I am fearful of using computers as 'baby stimulators' and 'baby-sitters' by exploiting their holding power before we understand it enough to use it wisely. I am fearful of the idea that children can be better prepared for life by doing schoolish kinds of learning at the earliest possible age. [...] To these old objections I add a new one: The computer opens opportunities for new forms of learning that are far more consistent with the nature of the young child. How absurd then to use it to impose old forms.
>
> (Papert 1996: 98–9)

Young children's learning and the curriculum

The old forms of learning Papert has in mind are not those of the great educational thinkers, who inspired generations of early childhood educators to consider the total wellbeing of the child as paramount. Papert believes in the power of self direction but is realistic enough to recognise that in an educational setting a certain amount of instruction offers some practical utility. He feels one of the greatest dangers is that computers too easily lend themselves to the practices of the 'old forms' of the curriculum, and can tip the balance too easily towards narrow notions of basic-skills and instruction.

Developmentally appropriate use of ICT in the curriculum

Computers are not intended to be a substitute for first-hand experiences but used appropriately they can offer children new ways of exploring the everyday world. Appropriate use means having opportunities for playful and creative learning that lets children 'make things happen' with computers in ways that recognise each individual's stage of development. Children need to be able to experiment, repeat activities in a variety of ways and have some control over the pace of what they are doing. They should be able to discuss what they are doing, collaborate with adults and each other and share their discoveries and triumphs. Computer activities should offer new challenges that extend or transform learning. Used in this way, ICT becomes developmentally appropriate.

The idea that resources to support learning be subject to scrutiny is not new. Even the newest parents make hundreds of rapid on-the-spot decisions about what is safe for their baby to have as playthings. They make aesthetic judgements, consider value for money and child attention, value some cultural norms, bear in mind the fitness of the item for the purpose in hand, the ease of availability, the usefulness of others' recommendations, and so on. There is nothing intrinsically different about the decisions practitioners make in early years settings except that they need to establish clear learning outcomes with children of differing abilities from diverse backgrounds.

Software

An important aspect of resource decision-making relates to software choices. Making evaluative decisions about software we intend to purchase is directly related to the learning outcomes we have in mind, to developmental appropriateness and to striking the right balance. Software for young children should be easy for them to use but not try to make learning simplistic. Children should be able to find out easily what they can get the program to do rather than have it close all options down so that only one routeway to a predetermined end is possible. Papert seized upon the term used by two kindergarten pupils about work with computers, 'hard fun', as describing well the challenge and engagement that comes with meaningful learning. He outlines objectionable features of software as:

- *giving agency to the machine and not the child*

By this he means seeing children only as 'answering machines', not recognising the strengths they bring to learning. Very young children need opportunities to explore, to point and click and see what happens. Providing just enough guidance helps build confidence that this is something they can do by themselves. Adults need to give careful thought to the nature and timing of their interventions.

- *being deceptive and proud of it*

What he has in mind here is software that promotes itself by claiming something along the lines that this is such fun your children won't realise they are learning.

As adults we need to take care we do not impose on children our perceptions that learning is difficult. Slipping mathematics or anything else subversively into children's learning programs is taking the wrong approach; rather we should find mathematics they love doing and use this as a starting point.

- *favouring quick reactions over long-term thinking*

This is a criticism, Papert says, often levelled against video games but which is also true of much question-and-answer software. Just providing immediate feedback of the right/wrong/try again variety is insufficient to promote problem solving, abstraction or conceptualisation. What video games do very well is reward success with an increased level of challenge at certain points. Children enjoy this as much as adults. Good software needs to offer challenge at a variety of levels to complement children's varying needs.

Much good software currently available does not treat the child as an answering machine, allows easy access and experimentation, encourages children to play constructively with a range of ideas, is easily navigated and has bright, colourful and uncluttered screens. Much of the creativity in curriculum applications still comes from practitioners' imaginative use of the more open-ended materials available to them and linking these to learning activities in such a way that ICT adds an extra dimension to the learning or even transforms it.

Creative, exploratory and playful applications of ICT

'Play' is a word with myriad meanings; when we use it in association with learning it has serious implications for practice and for us as practitioners. As adults we still need to play, sometimes with objects and even more often with ideas, especially when we have new learning opportunities to explore. Just as we enjoy and recognise the value of our playing with, and alongside, children in the sand or imaginative play area then so do we need to engage with, and enjoy playing around with, the computer. Such play is probably the best opportunity to get to know the resources currently available. Even when it is not possible to include children in such playful explorations personal computer use makes a significant contribution to professional understandings. Not to be able to play and explore strategies and resources makes it more difficult to see all the learning potential within the equipment available. It is also helpful occasionally to be reminded of what it feels like to be a new learner.

Personal, social and emotional development

The negative aspects associated with stereotypical views of computer use have been very pervasive. I emphasise again that it is the developmentally appropriate use of computers, integrated into a broad range of activities used in a social context in a balanced way, that is important whether the child is at home or at school or nursery. The careful evaluation of software and websites is essential as they are not neutral but contain images and messages from which children will learn much about the world. Every one of the inclusivity criteria used when selecting books, pictures and toys is just as relevant here: for example, ensuring even representation of genders and roles, representing different cultural backgrounds, family groupings, ages and abilities and taking care not to promote violence. These resource materials need to promote the positive values we wish to endorse by depicting people or characters acting co-operatively, sharing and valuing friendship and respecting the rights and feelings of others.

Many early years settings have used still and video photographs as both a record of children's activities and achievements and as the starting point for discussions. As Mavers and Lakin (2001) point out, 'going digital' has many advantages. The most obvious is the immediacy of access: images can be brought into action as quickly as required and, shown on a computer screen, can be discussed collectively. Mavers and Lakin suggest that this activity can contribute substantially to children's self-esteem and their ability to become involved in decision making about significant moments in their learning. Making images available to parents and practitioners, either electronically or as printouts has, as they point out, considerable value for home–school links and for the creation of electronic portfolios for record keeping. What does seem clear is that harnessing ICT power allows practitioners to promote communication, collaboration, positive social values and self-esteem in an exciting and dynamic way. Such activities require children and adults to work together but this the authors see as beneficial. The children learn from watching adults, hear the correct technical language and see procedures in a meaningful context as part of everyday activity.

Finding opportunities for parents and carers to play with their child and the computer is important. Creating times when grown-ups can do this helps develop understanding about the contribution ICT makes to the curriculum. The learning potential within the planned activity should be as clear as possible, especially the difference that ICT makes.

Physical development

Staff should be aware of the health and safety aspects of computer use, especially as much available equipment was not designed with small people in mind. It is important that equipment is safely positioned for users. Chairs, desks and screens should be at the correct height and of the right quality and arranged for social chat and for watchers to observe, learn and gain confidence. The activity should not be overused by any child, but this seems unlikely if it is integrated into an exciting, varied and balanced curriculum.

Much fine motor physical co-ordination is required in many ICT activities and at first it may take time for children to realise the 'cause and effect' relationship between their hand actions with fingers, mouse, keyboard or light pen and the end results. Once this has happened then 'point and click' comes about readily. The best way to acquire the fine motor skills required here is by having time to play, experiment and explore. Children need some help, and will probably frequently close programs down, but with carefully chosen software appropriate for beginners they will learn for themselves. Software with clear screens, simple instructions either with verbal support or picture icons and with 'teacher-lockability' in terms of opening or closing programs is most appropriate here. Children use all their senses to learn and multimedia support maximises opportunity.

Language and literacy development

Kress (1997) reminds us how broadly we should cast our nets when considering the ways in which children learn to be literate. He asks us to consider forms of representation as unexpected as building with bricks, arranging household objects (cushions, rugs and so on), and mark-making of various kinds including experiments with pictures, print, plans and diagrams. In becoming literate children need to understand the symbolism in all of these by 'reading', or interpreting them, and 'writing', or creating them. Reinking (1994) points out that a generation accustomed to multimedia and hypertext presentations in everyday life will have many understandings about what it means to be literate, including some that are different from those of their teachers. The path to literacy of each generation will be different from that of their predecessors. We need to offer children as many ways of making meaning with symbols as we can and not confine learning with ICT to 'drill and practice'. Computers, when correctly located and used, should foster talk and interaction between adults and children and between children and their peers and siblings when playing and experimenting together. Even 'watchers' learn about talk and should be allowed to participate quietly in this way as long as they wish. The role of adults in fostering talk about computer activities, and in 'on-screen' and 'off-screen' interactions, can challenge children's thinking as well as help them understand how to use the resources.

A wide range of child-friendly software is available to support appropriate literacy work, from open ended packages with multiple applications to specifically designed paint and word processing programs. Such software gives control to children by allowing open ended, playful explorations and experiments. Pictures can be drawn, marks of all kinds made which replicate pencils, pens and giant markers. Children can experiment with the keyboard, have fun exploring punctuation marks and other symbols, use stamps, make 'repeats' and change the colour, size and style of their creations. More recent programs allow different parts of children's work to be easily moved from one application to another.

A study by Shrader (1990) found that children's computer writing development mirrors closely that made with conventional tools. Children choose to use computers as readily as crayons, pencils and markers as well as to create signs and stories, send messages, and make notes and lists. When children's experiments with print are supported by sounds, as with talking word processors, then the possibilities increase. Finding their way around the keyboard or having the control to 'write' with the 'draw' tools, knowing which are pictures and which text, having confidence that they *can* do it, all seem good foundations to build on for the more instructional phase. Electronic 'talking books' are not intended as substitutes for all the experiences that come from a rich and loving sharing of a favourite story, but they do offer different, but equally valuable, forms of joint interaction with a trusted and loved adult. These complementary experiences offer a great deal of support for more independent engagements with texts. As with any other book experience choosing good material is the secret. If a text would not be accepted if it were a print item then it most certainly will not be worth having electronically. What is important is the quality of the text, illustrations and reading support as well as the operational simplicity. As practitioners we need to be clear about the pedagogical strategy and learning outcomes we intend to implement for those children who have moved beyond introductory explorations.

Creative and aesthetic development

ICT use offers children another tool to use in exploring ideas and creating representations. Where images of different kinds can be integrated with sounds and music then ICT transforms what children can achieve and allows them to create something not possible in any other way. Making images and music electronically offers a novel approach to learning that still allows children to create and evaluate their own products. Electronic paint doesn't work like everyday paint, the colours behave differently, images can be repeated, enlarged, multiplied and reversed or even linked to particular sounds. ICT makes it possible for children to explore and experiment with line, shape, colour and pattern. Creative activity can make a rich contribution to learning in other curriculum areas as well as the aesthetic domain, and electronic explorations should sit alongside work with other media and be one technique among many others.

Making music, listening and responding to it centres primarily around expressing feelings and emotions. Technology of all kinds has in recent years increased the range of musical experiences available to children and changes the ways in which they can interact with it. Again ICT extends the range of techniques and musical ideas (the sounds of different instruments, rhythm, pitch, volume, mood) that children can play around with in ways not possible without this support. Resources on CD-ROM or the internet allow practitioners and children to extend their repertoire of songs and traditional rhymes for enjoyment and as a support for literacy activities.

Knowledge and understanding of the world

Using ICT in imaginative role-play situations offers support to many areas of learning. One nursery I know uses a set of small robust notepads in thematic play activities such as 'the estate agents' as just another resource. Notepads are about the size of an A4 sheet of paper, light, portable and relatively inexpensive, have easily rechargeable batteries and are compatible with other computers and printers. In this nursery a notepad is also available on the writing table as another tool alongside pencils, pens and markers, paper clips, scissors and related thematic materials. Staff introduce the notepads to children by playing with them as well as finding opportunities to discuss letters, words or numbers. Learning 'about' events as well as having opportunities to re-enact them are the learning objectives: there is no expectation that children will create a printed product, though any child who wishes to go further with the notepad is encouraged to do so. Children's computer writing is included in the nursery produced books, which in turn become a further reading resource. The notepads can go home to support home–school projects also. As these machines have conventional keyboards, this exploratory play helps children begin to sort out alphabetic symbols from numerical ones. Since many children are bilingual, this type of use facilitates staff/parent dialogue about the similarities and differences amongst the many community languages.

Exploring the world scientifically through CD ROMs or the internet opens up perspectives that go beyond pictures and text and allows children to begin to understand what the world is like for other people. Complementary to the range of lenses, magnifiers and other viewers are computer microscopes. Because the magnified images are displayed on screen they are big, bright and easily seen by small (and bigger) people who have difficulty closing one eye and looking at the same time. These are really intended for older children and have many additional features, but watching a caterpillar munch is magic and not just to be kept for big kids!

Mathematics

One reception class teacher involved in an ICT project about effective teaching noted her dissatisfaction with much of the software available at the time to support the early number work she felt some of her children needed. She wanted to create meaningful and varied opportunities for children to practise aspects of counting. The report of her work (Mosley *et al.* 1999) makes fascinating reading. She describes how she used the stamping facility of certain software to help children create 'counting pictures', which then became incorporated into a wide range of classroom activities. In creating and sharing these pictures the children counted and recounted things many times because it was an important part of the process. They also created 'counting houses', which moved them on to the ideas of grouping numbers and sets of the same kind of object. Counting songs were also re-created. Once the children were familiar with operating the program they continued the creative work without adult support. Mathematics is not only about helping children understand numbers and counting but also about developing confidence and enthusiasm in using mathematical knowledge in a range of situations.

Most early years settings find creative ways of using roamers, pixies and other programmable toys. 'Customised' versions of roamer or Pip are directed by children to make visits around the group at circle time, or play a part in story re-enactments by carrying out the command sequences – for example, visiting the three little pigs' houses in turn.

Achieving and maintaining balance: construction, instruction and initiation

Inappropriately used ICT does not contribute much to learning: for example, when computers are used to keep children busy, as a reward or motivating tool or simply to practise skills. Young children should enjoy playful and exploratory ICT use in support of learning but not experience too much instruction too soon. The critical factor is getting the balance right by establishing clearly focused learning outcomes for both adult and child initiated activity. There is little to be gained if learners are frustrated by not knowing what they need to know when they need to know it. Also, those working in school settings frequently assert how impossible it is to wait for the spontaneous emergence of just the right moment for each child. As children reach the end of the Foundation stage, there is a requirement to ensure that they become familiarised with the formal demands of the teaching approaches they will experience at the next stage; instruction will be one of these. Professional judgements are not always easy to make, but to see computers as merely useful in an 'instructional' sense would be to seriously underestimate the potential of ICT as a means of transforming learning.

Roles of adults

Adults have a significant role in providing and resourcing learning environments, guiding children's interaction with the experiences offered, granting sufficient challenge to learners and carefully observing the outcome of how and with whom the children choose to learn. Such observations provide the basis for ongoing planning and assessment. We have learned much in recent years from research about the amount of early literacy and mathematical learning that takes place informally and incidentally. These studies have shown how frequently this learning goes unrecognised in educational contexts: this would seem to be equally true of computer use. Research, mostly with older pupils, suggests that computer use at school lags behind that in the home in quantity, quality and variety. It would be odd if this did not also affect the lives of younger children, especially those with older siblings. Liaison between parents, carers and practitioners is essential to ensure that early learning is used as an effective foundation. Where these home opportunities have not been available we must ensure that provision in the early years setting offers equity of experience. This may mean a directive role for the adults as such children may be reluctant to engage in ICT related activities. Adult intervention, direction and encouragement to participate are critical if we are to avoid further distance between the digital 'haves' and 'have-nots'. We need to share what we know about ICT and learning with children's parents as they know a great deal more about their own children than we will ever learn, but also they might be well placed to use our insights constructively in their homes.

Adults have several important roles in facilitating and enhancing learning with computers. Perhaps one of the most important is knowing when to intervene and when to stand back and let children take the initiative. While children will find out a great deal for themselves adult help is useful when needed. Supportive adults are one help-line for children. They understand how programs operate, can model overlooked functions, extend children's thinking by questions and prompts and discovering 'teachable moments'. They can encourage co-operation and collaboration between children and ensure the integration of computer activities into the overall curriculum. They can be 'trouble shooters' when, as is inevitable, problems arise not just with the hardware and software but with 'mouse wars' and 'arcade game clicking' (see Labbo *et al.* 2000).

Conclusion

Great claims have been made about technology and learning by both advocates and detractors. Papert talks about the gap between 'someday and Monday' that we sometimes experience, that is we believe that teaching and learning will be changed in unimaginable ways by this type of technology but in the meantime there is a need to teach in the situation we find ourselves in. His response is that to have a vision of what we would like to do will guide us towards the 'someday'.

This chapter is adapted from an earlier work by the author in Monteith, M. (2003) *ICT for Curriculum Enhancement.* Bristol: Intellect.

References

Kress, G. (1997) *Before Writing: re-thinking the path to literacy.* London: Routledge.

Labbo, L. D., Sprague, L., Montero, M. K. and Font, G. (2000) 'Connecting a computer centre to themes, literature and kindergarteners' literacy needs', *Reading Online* **4** (1), July, available at http://www.readingonline.org/electronic/labbo/

Mavers, D. and Lakin, I. (2001) 'Look what I did today', in *Beyond the School Gates.* Newman College with MAPE. Northampton, UK: Castlefield Publishers.

Mosley, D., Higgins, S. *et al.* (1999) *Ways Forward with ICT: effective pedagogy using ICT for literacy and numeracy in primary schools.* University of Newcastle, UK.

Papert, S. (1996) *The Connected Family: bridging the digital generation gap.* Atlanta, Georgia: Longstreet Press.

Reinking, D. (1994) *Electronic Literacy.* (Perspectives in Reading Research, No. 4). Athens: University of Georgia, National Reading Research Centre.

Shrader (1990) 'The word processor as a tool for young writers', in Yost, N. (circa 1999) *Emerging Literacy: crayons, markers, pencils and computer experiences,* available at http://childrenandcomputers.com/Articles/emerging_literacy.htm

Chapter 17

Knowledge and understanding of the world developed through a garden project

Jane Devereux and Ann Bridges

Introduction

In the *Curriculum Guidance for the Foundation Stage* for the implementation of the Early Learning Goals in England (QCA 2000) it states that to give all children the best opportunities for developing effectively their knowledge and understanding of the world, practitioners should provide first-hand experience, an environment with a wide variety of activities, indoor and outdoors, and appropriate adult support when needed. Knowledge and understanding of the world includes providing experiences that would help children in later years enjoy the studying of such subjects as science, design and technology, history, geography, and information and communication technology (ICT). The kind of key concepts and skills that would support this later subject study include developing children's understanding of time, space, place, forces, energy and materials from many different perspectives.

This chapter describes how one nursery school based in West London used the real experience of developing their nursery school garden to support and extend children's developing knowledge and understanding of the world. Through the short descriptions of some significant episodes it is possible to see how the practitioners and the children planned the project and how the children became engaged and proactive in constructing their own questions and solving some of the problems encountered as they developed their outside area. The examples chosen illustrate areas of the curriculum associated with knowledge and understanding of the world as well as showing how the children's ideas and skills progressed beyond the expectations of the practitioners because the children saw the relevance of what they were doing. Within the garden project children were continually revisiting some of the central concepts listed above, as they handled new materials and changed and modified their outside environment. For instance they found various artefacts and explored what they might be, how old they might be, what they were made of and why they were where they found them; thus engaging in exploring their ideas about place, time and materials, to name the more obvious concepts. Each episode provides an opportunity to examine the kind of knowledge, understanding attitudes and skills supported by such experiences.

The setting and the context

The nursery school is housed in a small corner of a West London Borough on the edge of an estate built in the early twentieth century. There are 45 full-time equivalent (FTE) children of whom 22 stay all day and the rest attend for half days only. The school has a large indoor room and a small but varied outside area that includes a tarmac area and a grass slope shaded by trees, both of which offer varied experiences to children. There is a large sandpit, an area with a climbing frame and safe landing areas. There is also a large storage shed and a small room situated in the garden that can be used for group work with the children.

In evaluating the kind of provision the nursery was making for the children in its care the staff discussed the development of the garden and it was agreed there was a need to make the garden safer and more usable for longer periods of the year. A steep grass slope was unable to be used safely for lengthy periods of time because of the effects of the weather, which made it dangerous; it frequently became totally devoid of grass and very muddy and slippery. This reduced considerably the amount of space available to the children. The slope afforded children the opportunity to view things from a different perspective so staff were reluctant to lose the height it provided, but it was important to consider its place and value in the garden. Watching what the children did on the slope and which children used it most informed the debate about its potential.

Planning the project

In this particular setting the whole curriculum is frequently planned around a 'real' project, such as developing their garden, and the children are involved in all stages of the planning and solving problems as they arise. Detailed planning stems from different aspects of the project as the work is carried out. Weekly planning is done collaboratively, with an initial evaluation of work from the previous week and children's progress during that week. From this, key generic learning intentions are formulated for the week or fortnight and activities that would help children towards understanding the learning intentions identified. This project runs alongside and with a varied array of experiences and areas normally expected in early years settings such as sand and water trays, role play, blocks, painting, craft and music, and resource areas that children can access for themselves.

The initial plan was to map out the stages and to consider how to launch the project. It was decided that the initial stage of the project was to look at the garden as it was. Children and staff discussed what they liked about the garden and what changes they would like to make. In order for everyone to be able to share in this initial planning stage many whole school visits were made to different parks and gardens. These visits included not only practitioners and children but also the secretary and site manager. This provided central shared experiences to which all could refer back and it provided a base from which to progress. It also provided children and adults with different perspectives on what an outside area could include and look like.

Once an initial plan began to emerge from these discussions with all concerned, professional gardeners were consulted and health and safety advice sought. When the final plan was agreed decisions were made as to how to divide the overall project into manageable steps and what the key areas of learning and teaching for each stage would be. It was at this stage that curriculum areas such as science, design and technology, information and communication technology, geography and history were incorporated into the planning cycle.

One key factor of redesigning the garden was clearly going to involve digging up large areas of the existing garden. Previous experience had confirmed to adults that there would be a variety of things to be found while digging. The question for them was how to maximise interest and learning from this opportunity. Before beginning any new phase of the work all children were involved in discussions, both to share their ideas and observations and also to be informed of some of the things adults may be focusing on. The sharing of the learning intentions set the scene and gave all children an insight as to what to expect. It in no way precluded their own interests and did not take away the excitement of expectation. The following extract shows how children were encouraged to hypothesise and predict what they might find when they dug up parts of the garden in preparation for moving plants and developing their newly designed garden.

Digging the garden

Practitioner: 'Tomorrow we are going to start digging the big part of the garden. I wonder what might be under the grass?'

At this stage care was taken to ensure that children were not being given information prior to their first hand experience. They could already see the grass but it was not assumed that they would know that there was soil underneath. This open invitation to suggest what they might find gave children the chance to share what they already knew and possibly make links with their previous experiences of digging. It also told them that we would be focusing on what we found underneath rather than in just digging. Some of the children suggested they might find treasure and what this might be and these were acknowledged alongside other children's ideas about creepy crawlies and worms.

P: What do you think we'll find?

K: Coins. Coins. My dad found five pence in our garden.

P: We might find coins. Where did you find it in the garden? Was it deep down in the soil?

K: It was in the vegetables where daddy digs lots.

C: We might dig up worms, big wiggly ones.

P: Yes we might. Has anybody else got anything else they think we might find?

M: Rubbish, old bottles.

P: Gosh yes we might. We'll have to be careful in case we find glass or anything sharp. M … Why do you think we might find rubbish?

M: Cos I have see a dustbin lorry dropping its stuff in the ground. Near my house is a dump. I go with my grandpa sometimes.

As children predicted what they thought they might find they were encouraged to give a reason why they thought that. Later they would also be given the chance to change their view in the light of their new found evidence. This type of dialogue would give children a chance to reflect on their previous experience of finding creatures, objects etc. and would also give adults a chance to begin to assess how much else they knew about what they might find. Children were encouraged to ask adults at home what they thought so that both home and school were involved in the investigation.

Other questions they were asked were:

'How will we remember what we've found?'

'How will other people know?'

Questions like this give children the chance to reflect on methods of exhibiting, displaying and sharing information and recording what was found. Once the actual digging began adult questioning continued to play a vital role. By constantly striving to ask 'open questions' children were given the chance to think, reflect, modify their views and to reason. For example, when a piece of broken pottery was found children were invited to think about how it got there, who it might have belonged to, if it was old or new. The children were very excited at the treasure they found and imaginative stories and suggestions about what it was and who it belonged to raised some interesting insights into their understanding of time past, what 'old' meant to them and how artefacts got there.

Reflection

Turner-Bisset (2002: 171) describes history as 'the imaginative reconstruction of the past using what evidence we can find'. The children in the above episode were speculating about the artefact they had found. They were exploring the past and using their imagination in full about what the piece of pottery was and where it came from and how it got there. With sensitive practitioner support, in which the practitioners understood the essence of history and the use of relevant open-ended questions, the children were helped to imagine the story or stories behind the artefact. The ability to hypothesise about what they had found enabled the children to share their understandings of time and cause and effect. As Turner-Bisset (2002) indicates, these are important concepts in developing their understanding of the past and the nature of history. The use of open-ended questions here is important in allowing children to share their own ideas and experiences and collectively build up a shared understanding of what they might find based on their experience. The questions listed above are, as Elgeest suggests 'productive questions' as they 'stimulate productive activity' (1985: 37). With children using their experiences of pieces of pottery the practitioners began a display with photographs and drawings that recorded the many finds made and the children's thoughts. Many of the things found were not very old but for the children the understanding that they had been buried for some time and therefore were left or dumped there by someone unknown, at an unknown time, provided a context for them to speculate.

In the next episode the children show how some of the same skills that they were using in exploring the artefact are being reused and developed in a context that is more scientific. This time the children were again speculating, hypothesising and raising questions as they were learning more about what it means when we say something is heavy. The real experience recounted shows how the children were stimulated by the hard work of the initial task to go further and employ their own problem solving and design and technology skills in a game that they devised for themselves.

The story of the bark chips

As part of the garden development project new bark chips were required. Adults planned for the arrival of the sacks of chips and how they perceived the children would be involved. As with any enterprise of this nature there would be numerous cross-curricular possibilities such as communication skills, mathematics, movement and physical development as well as knowledge and understanding of the world, particularly science. In terms of mathematics, estimating how many sacks we needed, tallying and counting them as they arrived were all part of the learning intentions. There would also be the very real experience of what 'heavy' really means as young children moved the big sacks. How could they do it? Moving heavy objects and developing an understanding of forces would be part of the experience children need to be able to abstract ideas at later stages in their learning and education. Communication, language and literacy would be addressed by discussions before and after the event and in making captions and commentary for displays and books. Physical development would involve the handling of large objects, manoeuvring wheeled toys and developing an awareness of themselves and their cargo within a given space. In making displays and books, that included drawings and paintings, about moving the bark chips various aspects of the creative curriculum would be brought into play.

The knowledge and understanding of the world curriculum would involve problem solving, questioning and investigating, geography, science, the appropriate selection and use of tools and use of information technology. Using the digital camera and the video by both children and practitioners enabled all to focus on their own significant events. These possibilities had all been accounted for in the planning and learning intentions relating to skills, attitudes, knowledge and understanding documented.

So far so good, but when over 100 big, heavy sacks were dumped on the pavement outside the school it was a bit daunting for adults and children alike. How do we move these before the end of school into a place where they are safe and will not be damaged or stolen? These children were used to solving problems like this and rapidly devised routes and a one-way system for wheeled vehicles to be pressed into service in the transportation of the sacks into the school garden. They regulated and controlled the flow of traffic and allowed each other time to load and move out of the way before the next group moved in to load and transport the bark chips.

In under an hour the problem was solved by the children using levers to help them lift and load the sacks onto their chosen vehicles. They developed and refined their skills of levering the sacks by trying different length pieces of wood and were soon able to move, lift and slide their sacks efficiently onto their chosen vehicle. The sacks were swiftly stacked in the garden ready for use the following day, or that's what the adults thought, but the children were only just beginning! The planned curriculum may have finished for the day with the children learning much about moving heavy loads and how to work together and take turns but the spontaneous curriculum was about to be launched.

Some children continued to count and tally the sacks, out of personal interest, but others saw their chance to develop and extend their design and technology skills. Many of them had enjoyed the physical challenge of moving the heavy sacks and it was during this enterprise that they had discovered that the sacks were really very good for jumping and sliding on. For the rest of the afternoon they designed and used their own adventure playground, sharing ideas, helping each other and taking turns to use their creation. They made route ways, paths and devised slides and jumps using the bags as they explored the properties of materials. This child-initiated activity did not mean that the adults became redundant as they still had key roles to undertake. As well as supporting the children's new activities by playing alongside and asking productive questions they observed what was happening so that future planning could incorporate, develop and extend the children's new discovery and learning.

Reflection

In this episode children were given the chance to explore the reality of forces at work. This real experience of feeling the kind of strength and effort needed to move things is very important in the children's later scientific life as it provides their own internal models of what it felt like. From this foundation it is easier for children in later learning to explore in more abstract ways some of the main theories of science and how forces work because they have a lot of experience to draw on when trying to hypothesise. As Nicholls (1999) says the real exploration experienced by these children provides a way of enhancing their cognitive abilities in science and their investigative skills. It took some groups of children longer to think out how to move their sacks but with support and working alongside the adults they were able to succeed in moving at least one sack per group.

The other significant aspect to this episode was the design technology that occurred as the children applied some of their newly learned skills to move and design their own adventure playground. Design technology, as Parkinson and Thomas (1999) suggest, can often be seen as the subject that integrates other clearly defined subject areas such as science and geography. This is clear here as the children made the route ways. The making of the pathways is an important element of being able to make and read maps. In setting up and modifying their playground as more children joined in the game and as the practitioners too became involved in the play children engaged in the design technology process. This included designing, making and evaluating the artefacts and systems they had put together. With their earlier learning of how to move the sacks and their refined skills of being able to move the sacks the children were quick to modify and extend their adventure playground.

The third episode from the garden project describes some of the issues raised as the children planned to insert a water feature in their garden.

The fountain story

When we made our initial visits with the children to parks and gardens so that they could all have some input into what we would include in our own garden development, it was agreed by adults and children alike that a 'water feature' would be good. A fountain in the far, top corner of the garden was decided upon, where it would provide a focal point for the whole of the outside area. This was the easy part of the plan.

When you think about it, exactly how does a fountain work? In planning much of the children's work around this investigation it became apparent to us as adults that we had a lot of thinking to do as well! We wanted the children to have the opportunity to experiment with a variety of equipment in the water tray so that they would begin to develop some understanding of water pressure and thus have some real working knowledge of fountains. It soon became clear to us that we were not all that sure ourselves as to the exact workings of fountains and the principles of water pressure. However, the mission statement that referred to 'a learning environment for all' was never intended to be a piece of paper that bore no relation to the day to day running of the school. Neither were staff afraid to embark on ventures to which they did not know all the answers. A community of enquiry was well on the way to being established.

Some exciting and challenging activities were set up in the water tray using tubing, funnels and rocks with holes in. At this stage some adults had clarified their own thinking as to how to support the children to try to simulate the workings of a fountain. The children themselves soon discovered that they needed to pour water from a height so that it would have enough momentum to be forced round bends in tubing and back up through holes in rocks. What do you do next? Solve the problem for the children or allow them to work it out for themselves? In this setting problems such as this were always referred back to the children but the adults would have already had some idea in their own minds as to where the investigations might lead and some possible solutions. This was not in order to give the answers but to enable practitioners to ask the appropriate open-ended questions that would allow children to try out their ideas. On this occasion the children tried various ways of raising themselves above the water tray so they could pour the water down. Eventually the climbing apparatus was brought near to the water tray so that children could climb above the water tray easily. This extra height afforded the necessary impetus for the water to rush down the tubes and be forced out of the rock or tubes but the effect was short-lived.

It is very exciting to pour large containers of water very quickly into a funnel but some children discovered that a little restraint afforded better results. Not all were this disciplined! The following short extract between two children, Ben and Aisha, illustrates some of the ideas that were explored about controlling the water and the height of the fountain.

> B: I know if you, if you pour from a high place into the tube it will go higher.
> A: Yes yes let me do it. Hold the tube.
>   The girl fills the jug and stretches up about 30cms above the tube to pour the water into the tube. She pours slowly but most of the water misses the tube.
> B: It's not doing it it's falling out. Stop. Stop. We need something like . . . (he uses his hands to show a funnel shape. (He shouts to the practitioner) Annette Annette we want a thing like this. (He uses his hands again).
>   Annette takes Ben into the hut to search for something to help. He comes out with one of the funnels and together the two children fix it to the tube. Aisha pours again and this time more water goes into the tube.
> B: It's working. It's working. Yeh. Annette it's working.

This experiment developed over a period of weeks and led to another interesting discussion that involved adults as much as children. Many of us had not really paid much attention to the difference between 'overflow' or 'overspill' and the principles of water pressure that relate to the workings of a fountain. It may be worth considering at this point why we would have ever considered it. The fact is that at this time there was a real reason to think about it and so it interested us in a real, working context. If this was important for us, how much more important it is for children as they constantly try to make sense of their world. It is also worth noting that many young children are very able to take this kind of discussion on board involving them in real thinking and discovery. During these few weeks all other areas of the curriculum were involved as children discussed, planned, illustrated and many children could describe how a fountain works. None better than one child who said at a group time, 'Well, you have to force the water up somehow and then it goes up the tube and it all

comes out and it makes a fountain, but you can buy them in a box you know.'
The children were letting us know it was time to move on so a trip to the garden
centre was planned to buy the fountain.

Reflection

The important lessons to be learned as practitioners are the significance of our
own subject knowledge in areas like science, design and technology, history and
geography to support children's learning; our willingness and openness to say we
do not know the answer and to find out alongside the children, and our ability
to know when to stop and move the children on or give them the information
needed. For the children during this episode the essential elements were being
allowed the time to explore their ideas about water and pressure. This was
developing their scientific understanding of materials and their properties, which
when combined together in certain ways and designs could control and regulate
the effects of some of the materials. Being allowed to 'wallow' in their knew-
found understanding before moving on was, as Bruce (1991) suggests, a very
important part of consolidating their learning and developing confidence as
learners, practising and refining what they knew over a period of time, until they
were ready to go and buy the fountain. Here the children were able and willing
to tell the adults when to move on.

Conclusion

These three episodes from the garden project show how over a period of time a
community that was working together learnt together through shared experiences.
The project approach Katz and Chard (1989) says encourages communities to
grow together and cultivate the life of the mind in its fullest sense, taking into
account the emotional, moral, social and aesthetic sensibilities as well as
curriculum areas. She sees the child accepting as much responsibility for the
learning and achievement as the practitioner. In this project the practitioners
worked and learnt alongside the children as they each developed their own
subject knowledge and confidence in different aspects of knowledge and
understanding of the world. At the same time practitioners documented the project
with the children using displays, books, the digital camera and the video camera
to represent the children's thoughts and ideas. This documenting of children's
ideas shows, as Scott (2001) suggests when writing about the Reggio Emilia
approach in their nurseries in Northern Italy, 'a strong belief that children are rich
and powerful learners, deserving of respect' (p. 22). The documentation also
provided an opportunity for practitioners to reflect on their practice and share and
develop their understanding of children as learners in a real situation. What was
significant and inspiring for the practitioners was the level at which the children
were able to operate and think because they were totally involved in the project.

References

Bruce, T. (1991) *Time to Play in Early Childhood Education*. London: Hodder & Stoughton.

Elgeest, J. (1985) 'The right question at the right time' in Harlen, W. (ed.) (1985) *Taking the Plunge*. London: Heinemann Educational Books.

Qualifications and Curriculum Authority/Department for Education and Employment (2000) *Curriculum Guidance for the Foundation Stage*. London: QCA.

Katz, L. and Chard, S. (1989) *Engaging Children's Minds: the project approach*. New Jersey: Ablex Publishing Corporation.

Nicholls, G. (1999) 'Children investigating: adopting a constructivist framework', in David, T. (ed.) (1999) *Teaching Young Children*. London: Paul Chapman Publishing.

Parkinson, E. and Thomas, C. (1999) 'Design and Technology: the integrator subject', in David, T. (ed.) (1999) *Teaching Young Children*. London: Paul Chapman Publishing.

Scott, W. (2001) 'Listening and learning', in Abbott, L. and Nutbrown, C. *Experiencing Reggio Emilia*, Buckingham: Open University Press.

Turner-Bisset, R. (2002) 'The essence of history in the early years', in Miller, L. *et al.* (2002) *Exploring Early Years Education and Care*. London: David Fulton Publishing.

Chapter 18

Meaningful history with young children

Rosie Turner-Bisset

What is history?

History is included in the early years curriculum as part of knowledge and understanding of the world. Children talk about where they live, their environment, their families, and past and present events in their own lives. In addition, they explore objects and events and look closely at similarities, differences, patterns and change (QCA 1999). This is a relatively new perception of what it means to do history with young children. There have been several long-standing arguments against teaching history to young children. Some educationalists argue that it is more sensible to concentrate on literacy and numeracy in the early years. Since the Plowden Report (DES 1967), there has been a widespread view that teaching subjects to young children is not appropriate because it imposes artificial divisions on their learning; it is argued that they do not learn in this way naturally. In addition, our understanding that children learn best through their own experiences seems at odds with common perceptions of the nature of history as a subject concerned with abstract ideas such as cause and effect or change over time, evidence and interpretations of evidence. There are misconceptions about the nature of history: that it is about learning facts and dates. Adults remember the kind of history they were taught at school and rightly perceive this as being unsuitable for young children. An understanding of the true nature of history is essential for doing history with young children.

History is the imaginative reconstruction of the past using what evidence we can find. We can state what we definitely know from the evidence. We can hypothesise about the things we are unsure of, and we can use other knowledge and experience to inform our interpretations. These are the processes of history. In addition, doing history involves many skills, some of which are cross-curricular: for example, observation and use of the senses, sequencing, hypothesising, reasoning and deducting, evaluating, reflecting and remembering, predicting, comparing and contrasting, sorting and classifying. Finally there are key concepts: time, change, continuity, cause and effect, interpretations, evidence, and historical situations. Young children can be introduced to the concepts, processes and skills of history providing that the evidence selected for use is appropriate for this age-range, and that suitable teaching methods are employed.

If history involves the investigation of evidence, we need to decide what are the best sources of evidence for use with young children. Evidence of the past takes many forms. It is not merely written evidence, and in any case much of this would be unsuitable for use with young children. Evidence includes artefacts, pictures and photographs, adults talking about their own past, written sources, music and dance, stories of the past, buildings and sites, as well as documentary sources. Some of these forms of evidence, in particular, artefacts and stories, are very appropriate for children in early years settings.

Using artefacts

Artefacts are ideal to use with children in early years settings. They involve first-hand experience and enquiry-based learning (Wood and Holden 1995). They are not just an interesting addition to other forms of evidence: they are an important primary source of evidence in themselves. All societies, including those who do not have written forms of evidence, such as the Australian Aborigines, use or have used artefacts in their daily lives. Study of these artefacts can tell us a great deal about people's lives in the past.

Before embarking on a play/learning session with artefacts, early years practitioners need to be aware of several points, which can influence the success or otherwise of working with artefacts. These points are: the importance of working from familiar experiences; the need to establish a framework of questions, so that the activity does not just become a guessing-game (Andreetti 1993); and the way in which young children will often flit between fantasy and reality (Wood and Holden 1995). In addition, young children will need much support and modelling from early years practitioners in observing closely and in using descriptive language. Finally, children need time to play with the objects and relate to them actively and imaginatively. Through play, children can begin to understand what an artefact is for, and what it might have been like to be the person who used it.

A group of three- and four-year-olds in a nursery setting were given a number of objects to examine and play with, including a bright yellow enamelled candle-holder of the type which has a circular tray to catch the wax and a handle to carry the holder.

Sita:	It's yellow!
Practitioner:	Yes, it's very yellow! Do you know what it is?
Oliver:	It's a wine-holder.
Practitioner:	Is it? How do you know?
Oliver:	People have these on holiday...they put the wine in there, see

(points to central part which holds the candle)…and hold it up like this, (mimes tipping it back, holding it by the handle) and drink the wine.

Practitioner: I suppose it does look a bit like that.

The artefact in question was very unfamiliar to the children. They had no knowledge of lighting before electric lighting, to inform their interpretation of the candle-holder. Oliver shows us, in his confident explanation that it was a wine-holder, that he is trying to relate the object to his previous experience, perhaps of seeing people use things of a similar shape used for drinking wine on holiday. A better preparation for investigation of the candle-holder would be to use a torch with the children first: a modern object with the same purpose as the old artefact, and one which they are more likely to have seen on camping trips or around the house. After the modern object has been handled, played with and questions asked about it, the early years practitioner can introduce the old artefact and say it was used for the same purpose.

A framework of questions is helpful to guide discussion and enquiry. The reasons for using such a framework are to avoid the tendency towards a guessing-game, noted above, to encourage the use of the senses and of descriptive language and to help the children to make some beginnings in interpreting historical evidence (see Figure 18.1).

What does this look like?
What does this feel like?
What do you think this is made of?
Have you seen anything like this?
How is/was it used?
Who uses it/who used to use it?
What would it be like to use it?

Figure 18.1 A framework of questions

Such a framework encourages children to describe what they perceive through their senses. Note there is no direct question: 'What do you think this is?' Instead the children are able to explore and use language to describe what they perceive. They may well ask this question themselves, but the 'guessing-game' type of activity is avoided. An additional problem is that once children have thought of what an object might be, their ideas are often difficult to shift, even though the physical evidence might suggest a different purpose. This was the case with Oliver, who clung to his initial idea that the candle-holder was a wine holder. There is no question in the framework about the age of the object. Young children, who may still be learning to count and sequence numbers, are not usually able to estimate how old an object might be.

The most valuable parts of this activity with the three- and four-year-olds were their playing with the artefacts and the talk which accompanied their play. Over and over again they poured pretend hot water from the kettle into the hot-water bottle and pretended to drink the 'wine' from the 'wine-holder'. As they did so they described what they were doing: 'I'm going to fill the bottle, look!' Through active engagement with the objects in play, they were able to use their imaginations as to how people in the past used these objects. Wood and Holden (1995) give an example of how artefacts such as washboards, dolly pegs, tin baths, soap and grater can be used in a role-play area, enriching children's understanding of how people washed clothes in the past.

Some young children may well have seen some old artefacts before in museums or at home. Their parents may collect such things, or they may have at home, for example, a copper kettle standing by the fire, or granny's old flat-iron. Five- and six-year-olds can record their understanding by drawing objects and either labelling the important parts, or writing a couple of sentences about their qualities and use. If necessary early years practitioners can scribe for them. Abigail, just turned six, chose a milk jug cover, a circular piece of lace work with beads hanging down from it, as her special object. Rather than tell the children its purpose directly, the teacher asked the child to fetch a jug, and she placed the cover over the rim. The children were able to say it was to keep dirt or flies out of the milk. Abigail was enchanted by the noise the beads made as it slipped over an empty mug, and thought that the sound of the beads would help to keep the flies away. She recorded her understanding in the work shown in Figure 18.2.

Using stories

Stories are an ideal way to develop an understanding of the past, of historical situations and of why people behaved how they did. Wood and Holden (1995) state that stories are central to the development of historical thinking and understanding in young children. They provide, as well as a shared experience for children and adults, a meaningful vehicle for understanding the past, and for 'introducing children to "different worlds" beyond their own experience' (Cox and Hughes 1990: 4). Wells (1986) argued that stories are one of the fundamental ways of ordering experience. We sequence events, real or imagined, into narratives which show our understanding of those events and the people to whom they happened. Story is of crucial importance as a foundation for all sense-making (Egan 1991). Cooper (1995) also argued for the centrality of stories to everyday life: she added that stories affect children's intellectual growth, through listening actively and using their imaginations to create new worlds.

Children can learn a great deal through listening to stories of the past, of other cultures in place and time. Firstly, stories are an excellent means of communicating information. The narrative structure allows the teller to convey facts, concepts, ideas and technical language in a way which holds children's attention. Recently I told a story about King Henry VIII and Thomas, a boy who

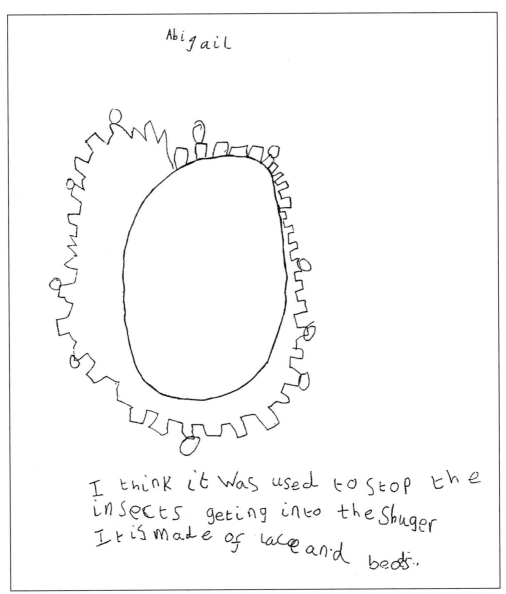

Abigail

I think it Was used to Stop the
insects geting into the Shuger
It is made of lace and beds.

Figure 18.2

wanted to be a falconer, to a group of five- and six-year-olds (story adapted from 'The King's Feather' in Fines and Nichol (1997)). They were rapt from beginning to end, in spite of the fact that some of the ideas and vocabulary were new to them. They did not know 'falcon', or 'falconry', yet by the end of the story, they had some idea of what falconers do. Neil asked, to confirm his knowledge of the new word, 'What did you call that bird thing again?' I asked them what else they had learned, and they said: people travelled on foot or by horse in the olden days.

Stories create a context for abstract ideas such as kingship, loyalty, authority, community and duty, as well as for the overarching historical concepts such as change and continuity. They create a sense of wonder: for example in the story used above, the moments spent describing the richly dressed King Henry VIII not only showed how wealthy people dressed in Tudor times, but also allowed the children to exercise their imaginations in picturing the gorgeousness of his clothing. Stories also help in relating the past to the present. In the story of Thomas, the children were able to relate his longing to be a falconer to aims and ambitions of their own, though admittedly these can change very frequently in such young children.

It is important to tell stories as well as to read them. There is something very special about telling stories. It is almost as if human beings are programmed to listen to stories. In the telling of a story one can make eye-contact with the children. Eyes convey meaning very powerfully: emotions can be understood in this way. Storytelling also allows one to use gesture and movement. In this way, one can act out part of a story. Stories can help children understand how and why people behaved as they did. In this particular story of 'The King's Feather' I stopped the telling just before the end, and asked the children what they thought Thomas would do next. They were able to predict that he asked to be a falconer, having understood the story within the context.

Many different kinds of story can be used to develop historical understanding, say of life in the past, or simply to develop skills of sequencing, or understanding cause and effect. Early years practitioners can use well-known stories such as 'Little Red Riding Hood', 'Three Little Pigs' or 'Goldilocks' as a means of teaching sequencing of events, cause and effect, and as a way of approaching moral issues about behaviour, right and wrong. In a story one action leads to another: 'Goldilocks lay down *because* she was tired.' This is an illustration of cause and effect. Through a story such as 'Three Little Pigs' children can begin to understand the processes of reasoning which led the third pig to build his house of bricks.

Such stories are not necessarily historical stories, but can be used for the development of some historical skills and concepts, for understanding of human behaviour, and for personal and social development. All kinds of stories: fairy tales, myths and legends, folk tales from other cultures and from our own culture, as well as stories based on evidence of real people and events in the past, can be used in this way. One example of an historical process which can be developed through story is that of interpretations of history.

The process of interpretation of evidence would seem to be too sophisticated to develop with very young children, but stories can be used to begin some interpretation. Children can begin to understand that there are versions of stories and of past events. Cooper (1995) describes how through telling different versions of well-known stories from the point of view of other characters, for example the wolf in the 'Three Little Pigs', four- and five-year-olds can begin to see that different people would report the same events in different ways. This does not happen spontaneously: such young children need discussion and adult intervention to move from thinking that two versions are two unlinked stories, to thinking that there are two versions.

Play

Play can be linked to both stories and artefacts. It is an excellent way of developing historical understanding in young children. They can re-enact stories or parts of stories they have been told. Such play helps to reinforce understanding of people's actions and behaviour: children can internalise the kinds of feelings the people in the stories experienced. Cooper (1995) suggests that stories from the past have a structure which children can reinvent through play, recreating and internalising their meanings. In play the boundaries between imagination and reality are blurred: children can hypothesise about what might happen if events took a different turn. They can be in control, shutting out of the play any events or characters which may be too threatening or beyond their understanding.

However, this kind of play needs input and inspiration from the practitioner. A story or artefact such as an old doll or teddy can be the initial starting point, but the early years practitioner has an essential role in ensuring maximum value in play (Sylva *et al.* 1980; Bateson 1985). In examining an old teddy with a group of five-year-olds, the practitioner asked where Teddy might have been before she had him. The price tag still attached gave the clue that he had been in a shop or on a stall. This led to speculation about who might have owned and played with the teddy before he was in the shop. Thus the children and practitioner collectively made a story about the artefact.

A group of three- and four-year-olds were provided with a setting and toy animals for the children to 'play' the story of the 'Three Billy Goats Gruff'. In evaluating the activity afterwards, the practitioner stated that the props were essential to get the children started. Simple costumes, such as long skirts, cloaks and hats can help to fire imaginations, and the home corner can be turned into a variety of settings: a castle, a ship's cabin, or a Victorian kitchen, for example.

It is important that adult intervention and interaction is sensitive: early years practitioners should observe the children and supply information or ideas based on observation. Sometimes this can be in the form of questions, to advance the children's ideas, for example: 'What will you do when the Romans attack your village', or 'What do you think Red Riding Hood should do next?' All the time the children are making narrative structures through enactment of stories, and coming to understand how such structures work.

Meaningful history

There are many different sources of evidence and approaches to teaching and learning from which one could choose in planning for young children's learning in and through history. In this chapter, I have selected just three: artefacts, stories and play, because they are the most suitable for children in early years settings. Pictures and storybooks, photos, buildings and adults talking about their lives can all be used, but the three approaches presented here are of great value in promoting historical understanding in young children; and in developing the beginnings of key historical concepts, skills and processes.

References

Andreetti, K. (1993) *Teaching History from Primary Evidence.* London: David Fulton Publishers.

Bateson, G. (1985) 'A theory of play and fantasy', in Bruner, J. S. *et al.* (eds) *Play, its Role, Development and Evolution.* London: Penguin.

Cooper, H. (1995) *History in the Early Years.* London and New York: Routledge.

Cox, K. and Hughes, P. (1990) *Early Years History: an approach through story.* Liverpool: Liverpool Institute of Higher Education.

Department of Education and Science (DES) (1967) *Children and their Primary Schools: A report of the Central Advisory Council for Education* (The Plowden Report). London: HMSO.

Egan, K. (1991) *Primary Understanding: education in early childhood.* London: Routledge.

Fines, J. (1997) *Teaching Primary History.* Oxford: Heinemann.

Qualifications and Curriculum Authority (1999) *Early Learning Goals.* London: Qualifications and Curriculum Authority.

Sylva, K. *et al.* (1980) *Childwatching in Playgroup and Nursery School.* London: Grant McIntyre.

Wells, G. (1986) *The Meaning Makers: children and using language to learn.* London: Hodder & Stoughton.

Wood, L. and Holden, C. (1995) *Teaching Early Years History.* Cambridge: Chris Kington Publishing.

Part 3
Positive learning environments: children and adults

Linda Miller

Introduction

The preceding sections of this book focused on the importance of both the process and the content of the early years curriculum: that is, on both what and how young children learn. In this section the chapters are concerned with the emotional aspects of learning and how the people with whom we learn and the physical environment in which we learn can affect the emotional wellbeing of both children and adults. As Drummond (1998) argues, we are concerned about high standards and quality of provision for our children. We want well trained practitioners, and buildings and resources which are not part of a 'jumble sale' mentality and which are respectful of the children who play and learn in them. Rouse (1991) discusses the need for practitioners to take care of themselves and believes that quality provision is dependent upon adults being responsible for their own wellbeing – their welfare, care and health. She recalled a visit to the Italian nurseries of Reggio Emilia, which are renowned for the quality of the environment, relationships with parents and carers and pedagogic practices. She describes how cooks, guests and teachers had 'A relaxed and delicious meal' (p. 13) during which 'banter, news and views were exchanged' (p. 13). In addition six hours each week were set aside for in-service training. It is important that adults working in early years settings have systems that allow time for planning, for talking in teams and for assessing and evaluating their work collaboratively, issues that are explored in chapter 23 of this book. Practitioners who feel hard pressed and who are responding to external changes and pressures, may view such practices with a degree of scepticism and doubt the possibility of adopting such a philosophy here in the UK. However, Margy Whalley (2001), at Penn Green Centre for the under-fives and their families, describes how all staff, including ancillary, support staff and parents, take part in training opportunities and how they are involved in decision making. She explains how time is created for this, which involves the closure of the centre at certain times, a policy supported by the parents. Such inclusive training opportunities and practices are a way of showing staff that they are valued and this in turn will contribute to their wellbeing.

Positive learning environments: children and adults

In the first chapter in this section Marion Dowling explores the importance of 'Emotional wellbeing' – the title of her chapter. She cites Pascal and Bertram's (1998) view that emotional wellbeing is one of four important factors in children who have the potential to be effective learners. Dowling highlights the role of adults as key players in children's emotional development and suggests ways in which they can support children through significant stages such as transitions and loss. Peter Elfer's chapter 'Building intimacy in relationships with young children in early years settings' complements Dowling's chapter and explores the importance of warm and responsive relationships in early years settings. He discusses how the quality of children's learning is dependent upon the quality of relationships they form with adults; he acknowledges the challenge of achieving such relationships in practice and explores possible solutions. Sue Robson's chapter on 'The physical environment' considers how the actual environment of the setting can give very strong messages to children about how they are respected and valued as individuals. She argues for enabling both children and adults to contribute to the way in which their space is, and can be, configured. She also looks at some of the basic entitlements that any early years setting should consider. Jenny Linden's short but important chapter considers 'The future of childhood' and voices the growing concern that children and their environments are becoming too safe for their own good. She identifies strategies to encourage children to learn about risk taking so that they can become confident and competent learners.

Practitioners who feel good about themselves and their professional practice will be in a position to provide challenging opportunities and experiences for children and will have the time, confidence and energy to respond to the needs of children and their families. In chapter 23, 'Creating contexts for professional educare', Angela Anning and Anne Edwards report on a collaborative project in which a group of practitioners were supported in developing a community of practice, which helped them to explore their own professional development and in so doing enhanced the development and learning of the children in their care. In the final chapter of this book, which is aimed at an audience of early years practitioners, we appropriately hear the voice of one practitioner, Sharon Ellis. Sharon charts her own professional development, beginning with her early desire to work with children through to her current role as deputy officer in a nursery centre. Roger Hancock, as co-author of this chapter, notes the impact of recent policy and funding developments upon the practice, training and professionalism of early years practitioners such as Sharon. However, he also acknowledges, as do Anning and Edwards in their chapter, the powerful combination of personally acquired knowledge and what he describes as codified and published knowledge in empowering practitioners in their work with young children and families. Empowering practitioners is also a key aim of this book.

References

Drummond, M. (1998) 'Warning: words can bite', *Coordinate* (July), 4–5.
Rouse, D. (1991) *The Italian Experience.* London: National Children's Bureau.
Whalley, M. (2001) 'Working as a team', in Pugh, G. (ed.) *Contemporary Issues in the Early Years: working collaboratively for children*, 3rd edn, 125–45. London: Paul Chapman Publishing.

Chapter 19

Emotional wellbeing

Marion Dowling

In this chapter we concentrate on the importance of regard to feelings. Laever's work is strongly echoed in the current important action research project 'Accounting Early for Life-Long Learning'. Pascal and Bertram claim that emotional wellbeing is one of four factors seen in children who have potential to be effective learners.[1]

Emotional wellbeing is also prominent in curriculum documents. In the New Zealand Early Childhood Curriculum document *Te Whaariki*, the section on wellbeing states that two of the entitlements for children are: 'an expectation that the early childhood education setting is an enjoyable place to be; a place where they have fun; and to develop a trust that their emotional needs will be responded to'.[2] The reference to emotional development is a significant addition in the new Early Learning Goals for children in the Foundation Stage of education.[3] Emotional wellbeing is reflected in the Department for Education and Skills (Sure Start Unit 2002) guidance for the very youngest children in *Birth to Three Matters*, where one strand of the component 'A Healthy Child' is emotional wellbeing.[4]

Experiencing and expressing emotion

Children's experiences and expressions of feelings develop tremendously during the early years of life. Most of a child's basic emotions are in place by the time he or she is two years old. Young children also quickly develop their unique means of expressing their feelings and then use them deliberately to suit the occasion.[5]

Case study

Maggie's emotions change frequently and rapidly. She can be furious one moment when her block construction collapses, but jump for joy the next moment when her childminder announces they are going out to the shops. By contrast, Kirsty's feelings are more long lasting and even. She rarely shows excitement, but plays equably by herself for most of the time. When Kirsty is upset or angry it is difficult to cheer her up. Her angry feelings (or mood) remain with her, sometimes for a whole day.

> **Comment**
> Linda, the childminder, was aware that these two three-year-old girls had different emotional styles which required a different approach. Maggie was often easier to deal with, although unpredictable. Kirsty's feelings were less easy to 'read'.

In certain situations young children may cope with their feelings in ways which are puzzling to adults. On experiencing the death of a loved relative or a close family friend, children will show their grieving through withdrawal, anger or denial. Paula Alexander, a parent at the Pen Green Centre of Excellence, describes how her three-year-old son went back to bed-wetting at home after being told that his father had died:

> At nursery he kept taking things to the sandpit, burying them and digging them up to bring them back to life again. Then he'd say out of the blue 'My daddy's dead.' You have to pay close attention to what they are trying to express. The nursery did a lot of work with him through play.

Adults are usually very prepared to cope with a child's grief in the short term but may not recognise that the impact of bereavement is not always immediate. In the same article, Woolfson, a child psychologist, suggests that while adults feel the need to recover from their grief,

> there is no urgency in children. You tell them the news and their immediate reaction is to go and play, but it all takes time to work through. One minute a three-year-old will say granny's dead and the next minute will ask you not to forget to set a place at table for her.

It is important for adults not to have any preconceptions about how children will react to grief. However, there is likely to be a time, once children have absorbed the news, when they will want to talk about their loss and to recreate their understanding through play. Early years practitioners can play a critical role in responding to each child's needs at a time when the child's family members are likely to be distressed and vulnerable themselves.

Despite important differences in expressive style, most young children are full of raw emotion and feel acutely. The power of their emotion is heightened as their feelings are not tempered by experience. Most things are happening for the first time; as a consequence children can be desolate in their distress, pent up with fury and overbrimming with joy. They are receptive to all experiences that are offered to them. The effect of this responsiveness for those children who live turbulent lives is that they may live their lives on an emotional roller-coaster. In situations like this children can be ruled by their emotions. This is particularly noticeable with those young children who find it hard to express themselves in spoken language. It is difficult for adults to be fluent and articulate when they are angry or distressed – how much more so for a three- or four-year-old when emotions overwhelm them.

Young children's feelings, positive and negative, will initially be best reflected from actions. An early years curriculum should actively help all children to make this transition to using symbols. However, children's readiness cannot be pre-empted. Requiring all children to do things for which only some are ready will result in only some of them making any sense of what they are doing.

The effect of transition on children's feelings

A young child on familiar territory at home or in an early years setting is likely to feel secure and to be confident and competent. Any move means that a child is emotionally challenged. The initial effect on young children's confidence and independence of moving from a known setting is well known to early years practitioners. Children experience many complex and often conflicting feelings. Excitement and anticipation of the move are tempered by anxiety, distress and confusion about the unknown. In these circumstances children's emotional wellbeing is not secure; this affects their ability to learn.

Although children will initially show their feelings through what they do, their spoken language is important for them to learn to deal with emotions. In order to cope with such momentous experiences as starting school, children need to talk to express their feelings and also to make sense of what is happening to them during the school day. The following moving extract is from a teacher's informal diary of Joanne's response to starting school; it reflects the child's skills and her coping strategy with the obvious emotional difficulties that she faced.

Case study

Joanne was one of 25 four-and-a-half- to five-year-olds who started school in a reception class.

Phase 1 (about a week): Joanne is very upset all the time in school. Clings to her mum and sobs when she eventually leaves. Cries for most of the day. Will try activities but joins in with tears rolling down her face. Finds out-of-class activities – music, assembly, playtime – especially difficult. She doesn't know the other children very well as yet... and she's too distressed to start making friends. Typical extracts of transcripts: *'I want to go home now. Why do we have to go out? When are you coming back? I want my mum to come.'*

Phase 2 (about two weeks): Joanne seems to be starting to come to grips with school. She's begun to repeat, almost obsessively, the daily routine out loud. *'This is assembly now, and then we go back to our class and we have a little play. Then it's playtime, outside isn't it? Are you going to come and play today?...And then we come back for, we do... have a story and another play and then it's time for my mum to come.'*

She appears to be internalising school structures and systems through verbalising her experience. She is breaking down the whole overwhelming

---

school experience into manageable chunks, using spoken language. She is still quick to tears, especially in out-of-class activities, but seems to be becoming more philosophical about her daily endurance test.

Phase 3 (about a month): Joanne is starting to talk more positively about school life and, by altering the pattern of her language, she seems to be changing the nature of her actual experience. *'This is assembly but it doesn't last long and then we can all go back to our room don't we?'*

A constant oral delivery of her new fluctuating emotional state accompanies every new situation she is presented with. *'Oh, good...today it's the office. I like doing the office. I'm going to go there. (Later) Mrs Knight is in the office. I'm writing, gonna do a letter for my mum. This is good. (After) I liked that Mrs Knight. I'm gonna take my letter home, give it to my mum.'*

Even more disconcerting: *'Ah...now this is the bit I don't like but I 'spect it won't be very long will it? And then you'll come back and get us.'* (Music time with the school specialist).

By keeping her language cheery and optimistic in tone she's coping much better during the school day. Seems to be talking herself into acceptance of school attendance, sometimes talking cheerily with tears in her eyes: *'Now it's playtime again. I'm putting my coat on but I bet it's cold out there. Are you coming to play? (No) Oh...(pause) then I'll just have to be Mrs Baker's friend and it's only for a little while and then we can come back.'*

She is keeping verbal control of an almost unbearable situation and seems thereby to exercise control over her emotional responses.

Phase 4 (last five weeks of term to Christmas): Becoming less verbal now and more relaxed in school. Only major changes in routine (like class assembly) are overtly distressing, although physical education is still a difficult time. Still the occasional disconcerting outburst: *'I was cross with you then Mrs Knight. I knew the answer then and I was sitting nice and you didn't ask me at all.'*

I thought that the (Joanne's) problem was just about resolved so was somewhat taken aback when retrieving my talk box tapes. Joanne offered this prayer: *'Dear God, I hope it's soon time for my mummy to come and get me...love from Joanne'!*

Obviously still uncomfortable and anxious at school but less need for an active listener to provide comfort now. She's turned to the tape recorder to express her anxieties. She's now able to take a full part in all class activities and is becoming interested in all areas of the curriculum. Actively participating – not just sitting it out and surviving.

Phase 5 (the new term – Jan): Joanne seems much happier and more settled in school. She is proud of her achievements and is making good relationships with her peers. She is especially supportive and caring when others are injured or upset and tearful. She was delighted when a younger class started after Christmas. I was encouraging my class to be extra helpful and friendly to help the new children settle in. Joanne's comment was: *'Oh, the poor things. I'm gonna be friendly, specially in the playtime outside. Do you remember when it was me that was the new one?'* (Only too well!)[7]

Comment
Joanne's fluent use of language made her difficulties instantly recognisable. Less fluent children may experience the same agonies which may not be picked up so easily. Joanne's teacher's sensitive observations made her recognise what more she could do to help children come to terms with their feelings on starting school.

The influence of the family

Young children's understandings and use of their feelings will be heavily influenced by the significant people around them, initially their parents. An important part of knowing about ourselves is to be able to recognise the different feelings that we have and that other people experience. Dunn vividly highlights the remarkable insights that babies develop during their first year of life, as a result of noticing the emotional behaviour of family members. By the time they are two years old, children recognise that their mum, dad or brother can change from being angry to showing caring behaviour, or can be worried one moment and relaxed and smiling the next. At this early age children are learning rapidly what is required to alter these emotional states; for example, by comforting an unhappy younger brother.[8] These studies show that even toddlers can show care and empathy in families where this is demonstrated. By stark contrast, there is evidence of how less fortunate children learn different lessons. Goleman provides case studies of the dire emotional effects on small children who have been repeatedly physically abused.[9] The most noticeable result is that these children who have suffered so much completely lack care and concern for others. At two and three years of age they typically ignore any distress shown by other children; often their responses may be violent. All they are doing is mirroring the behaviour that they have received themselves.

In families where feelings are not only expressed but are openly discussed, a young child is helped to recognise and accept his emotions and those of others. In these circumstances children are also more likely to talk freely about what they feel. These intimate contacts between parents and child involve shared experiences and loving attention over a period of time. Some parents lack this as a result of the busy lives they lead. While the early years setting would never claim to be able to replace these family interactions, it can play a crucial role in working with parents and sharing the task of helping children understand what they feel.

Children's emotional understandings are dependent not only on the degree of family support but also on what sex they happen to be. Different messages about emotions are given to boys and girls. In one small study, mothers talked more often to their 18-month-old daughters about feelings than they did to their sons at this age. By the time they were two years old these little girls were seen as more likely to be interested in and articulate about feelings than the boys.[10] Other studies offer further evidence. When parents make up stories for their small children they use more emotion words for their daughters than their sons; when mothers play with their children they show a wider range of emotions to girls than to boys. Brody and Hall, who summarised these studies, suggest that as a result of the experiences they have, and because girls become more competent at an early age with language than do boys, this results in the girls being able to use words to explore feelings. By contrast boys are not helped so well to verbalise and so tend to be confrontational with their feelings and become less tuned in to their own and others' emotions.[11] These early experiences and consequent emotional differences can very often continue into adulthood and be seen in relationships. Goleman suggests that women are well prepared to cope with the emotional aspects of a relationship; conversely, men are more inclined to minimise emotions and are less aware of the importance of discussing and expressing feelings as a way of sustaining a partnership. He argues that this emotional imbalance between the sexes is a significant factor in the break-up of marriages.[12]

Young children's developing understandings of emotion

Young children need to have experienced a range of emotions before they begin to understand them. Using puppets with children, Denham found that those who showed both positive and negative feelings in their play were more likely to recognise and comprehend what others were feeling in different situations.[13] Moreover, using puppets again, Denham suggests that children are beginning to recognise that in a given situation people may feel differently. For example, many children could understand that a puppet could be sad about going to nursery, while they would be happy.[14] This ties in with other studies which indicate that young children are able to appreciate another viewpoint and are not only focused on themselves.[15]

However, it is much more difficult for children to recognise that emotions can be mixed. When six-year-olds were asked to predict the feelings of a person who eventually found his lost dog, but it was injured, they typically said that the owner would feel totally happy or sad, but not a mixture of both. Children at ten years acknowledged that it was possible to feel both emotions.[16] Furthermore, although they may show complex feelings, they cannot predict them. However, it seems that social convention plays a part; from a young age children can be influenced to show feelings which are socially acceptable but are not genuine. In one study, four-year-old girls responded to social pressures by smiling when the researcher presented them with a disappointing toy, although when they examined their toy alone they showed their disappointment. (Interestingly, boys did not attempt to mask their feelings in the same way.) Questioned later, when they were able to swap their disappointing gift for a more exciting one, the little girls admitted to being disappointed, but thought that this would not have been recognised because of their polite words of thanks. These children made no reference to their smiling faces or the control of their real emotions and despite their behaviour were unaware of how their displayed emotion could beguile observers.[17] As children grow older they begin to understand that the feelings that they show to others may not be the same as their true feelings. This lesson is a necessary one as part of becoming socialised. Nevertheless, where young children are pressurised or coerced into constantly masking their true feelings and substituting socially acceptable responses, this could lead to them misunderstanding the function of emotions in life.

Seizing opportunities for emotional learning

We see and hear a great deal about how those adults with emotional problems can track them back to some difficulties in childhood. Goleman suggests that because early childhood is one of the very critical times for nurturing emotional growth, if this opportunity is missed or the nurturing becomes abuse it becomes progressively harder to compensate for this at a later date. If early years practitioners are to aim to prevent these problems in adulthood they must take advantage of the receptive nature of young children and positively help them to achieve emotional health. This means looking at a climate in the setting which helps children to feel, think and talk about feelings. They will think carefully about how to organise this climate. For example, circle time has become a common means of encouraging children to converse about things that matter to them. Sometimes, though, even where staffing ratios are good, these occasions are organised for the whole group of children. Even though the adult has very good relationships with all of the children, a large group involves a degree of formality and does not provide an atmosphere conducive to sharing intimate thoughts.

A group of early years practitioners made a study of the times when children in reception classes were more likely to share personal thoughts and feelings. These included:

- circle times in small groups (with eight to ten children)
- times when the child could approach an adult individually, particularly during outdoor play or when an adult was helping a child get ready for PE
- during conversations with small groups in the book area, and on the dough and drawing tables.

Less effective times were after children had had physical activity such as swimming and PE and whole group times, particularly when these were conducted on a formal question-and-answer basis.[18] Children, like adults, are more likely to talk about things that affect them with people who show that they are genuinely interested and who are prepared to give time to listen.

Children's feelings will be stirred by sensory experiences such as listening to music, looking and touching beautiful things, tasting and smelling. If they can talk about their reactions to these positive experiences, it will alert them to recognise similar feelings on another occasion. In the same way they need to recognise negative emotions. Anger and fury which results in loss of control can be extremely frightening for a three- or four-year-old. Sensitive adults can provide safety and reassurance and encourage children to try to see patterns in their behaviour and reasons for their strong reactions. In this way children will come to accept and regulate their feelings.

Children who are emotionally vulnerable desperately need a calm and safe environment. However, occasionally the setting that emphasises calm therapy can be in danger of repressing emotions. Children have the right both to witness and to experience different feelings. Living in a calm, bland atmosphere can produce dull people. Children's feelings should also be respected.[19] It is questionable whether adults should attempt to jolly children along when they are bereft at being left in the nursery, or their friend won't play with them. This sorrow and desolation is more devastating than that experienced by an adult in a comparable situation for the simple reason that the child does not have the life experience which tells her that the cause of the distress is only temporary. A simple acknowledgement of sympathy will at least show the child that he or she is being taken seriously. As always, practitioners themselves play a very important role as models. A strong relationship between adults and children is founded on feeling. In such a setting children recognise that the adults care for them, laugh with them, share their tragedies and excitements and also become angry when boundaries of behaviour are broken. So long as the love and care are prevalent, children will flourish and grow given this healthy emotional repertoire.

Summary

People's emotional lives are seen to be critical factors in their success in life. Young children's emotional development is rapid and closely tied to other areas of development. In order to achieve emotional health, children need to experience and be able to express a range of emotions in their own way through a broad curriculum. They need to talk through negative emotions, particularly during times of stress, as when moving into school. Children's understandings about their feelings are heavily dependent on the support they receive from their families and also whether they happen to be a boy or a girl. Given support, they start to show empathy as toddlers and then learn to understand that people can feel differently from them. Early years settings can play an important role in aiding children's emotional wellbeing through their curriculum and organisation and the ways in which early educators work with children and act as role models.

References

1. Pascal, C. and Bertram, T. (1998) Accounting Early for Life-Long Learning. Keynote talk at Early Years Conference, Dorchester, July.
2. New Zealand Ministry of Education (1996) *Te Whaariki, Early Childhood Curriculum.* Wellington: Learning Media.
3. Qualifications and Curriculum Authority/Department for Education and Employment (2000) *Curriculum Guidance for the Foundation Stage.* London: QCA/DfEE.
4. Sure Start Unit (2002) *Birth to Three Matters: a framework to support children in their earliest years.* London: DfES.
5. Denham, S. (1986) *Emotional Development in Young Children.* New York: Guilford Press.
6. Williams, E. (1997) 'It's not bad to be sad', *TES Primary*, 12 September, 13.
7. Knight, A. (1992) 'Starting school – a painful process', *T.A.L.K., The Journal of the National Oracy Project*, **5** (Autumn), 3, 4.
8. Dunn, J. (1988) *The Beginnings of Social Understanding.* Oxford: Blackwell.
9. Goleman, D. (1996) *Emotional Intelligence.* London: Bloomsbury.
10. Dunn, J., Bretherton, I. and Munn, P. (1987) 'Conversations about feeling states between mothers and their young children', *Developmental Pscyhology*, **23**, 1–8.
11. Brody, L. R. and Hall, J. A. (1993) 'Gender and emotion', in M. Lewis and J. Haviland (eds) *Handbook of Emotions.* New York: Guilford Press.
12. Goleman, D. (1996) *op. cit.* (note 9).
13. Denham, S. A. (1986) 'Social cognition, social behaviour, and emotion in pre-schoolers: contextual validation', *Child Development* **57**, 194–201.
14. Denham, S. A. and Couchard, E. A. (1990) 'Young pre-schoolers' understanding of emotion', *Child Study Journal* **20**, 171–92.
15. Borke, H. (1983) 'Piaget's mountains revisited: changes in the egocentric landscape', in M. Donaldson (ed.) *Early Childhood Development and Education.* Oxford: Blackwell.
16. Harris, P. L. (1983) 'Children's understanding of the link between situation and emotion', *Journal of Experimental Child Psychology* **36**, 490–509.
17. Cole, P. M. (1986) 'Children's spontaneous control of facial expression', *Child Development* **57**, 1309–21.
18. Dorset In-Service Group (1994)
19. Scott, W. (1996) 'Choices in learning', in C. Nutbrown (ed.) *Childrens Rights and Early Education.* London: Paul Chapman.

Chapter 20

Building intimacy in relationships with young children in early years settings

Peter Elfer

Introduction

In this chapter, I want to argue that while most people working in a variety of early years settings would agree that warm and responsive relationships are of great importance in supporting children's learning and development, such relationships may not be happening very reliably in practice.

I then want to suggest that while much work has been done on the ways in which young children develop cognitively, comparatively little work appears to have been done in the early years field on the emotional content of children's relationships with adults and its importance to their learning.

The implication of this is that if close and emotionally responsive and responsible relationships with young children are to be formed and maintained within a professional and accountable context, then this will require an organisational culture that expects and supports these relationships. Such a culture should include, as a minimum, developed systems and processes of supervision and mentoring.

Close relationships in theory

Many early years writers and trainers emphasise the importance of children's emotional life as an integral part of early learning (Bruce 1987; Lally 1991; Drummond 1993; Nutbrown 1994). So too does research (Hennessey *et al.* 1992; Sylva 1994).

Beyond this basic consensus there has recently opened up a sharp divergence in how different writers see the emotional life of young children being met and sustained in early childhood settings. On the one hand, Dahlberg, Moss and Pence have argued that while intimacy may be an important and necessary characteristic of family relationships in order to promote the healthy development of the young child, it is neither necessary nor desirable in early childhood settings:

If we approach early childhood institutions as forums in civil society, the concept of closeness and intimacy becomes problematic. It can turn public situations and institutions private. As such, it not only creates a 'false closeness' and risks trying to duplicate, necessarily unsuccessfully...it also hinders the ability of the institution to realise its own social life and relationships...

To abandon ideas of intimacy, closeness and cosiness does not leave indifference, callousness or coldness. It does not mean being uncaring. Instead...a contrasting concept to closeness, the concept of *intensity of relationships* implying a complex and dense web or network connecting people, environments and activities which opens up many opportunities for the young child.

(Dalhberg, Moss and Pence, 1999: 81–2)

On the other hand, Elinor Goldschmied, Dorothy Selleck and I have argued that the evidence from four different branches of psychology: neuroscience, psychiatry, developmental psychology and psychotherapy, come together to build an overwhelming case for children's crucial need for intimate relationships with adults (Elfer, Goldschmied and Selleck 2003). By 'intimate' we mean relationships that are sufficiently consistent and emotionally close to allow an adult to notice and respond to the fine details of young children's communications, vocally, through body language and through the feelings the young child is able to evoke in the adult.

National Standards and National Guidance

The early years practitioner who is sensitive and responsive in this way (and such a role, in order to be both respectful of children's rights and professional in the way it is conducted, requires a context of supervision and detailed accountability) might be described as playing a key role in a child's overall development. It is hardly surprising that the term 'key person' or 'key worker' has therefore gained wide currency in early years practice over the last twenty years. Further, there are references to a key person role throughout the guidance to the National Standards issued by Ofsted (2001). More recently, the *Birth to Three Matters* framework (Sure Start Unit 2002) enshrines the key person role as an underpinning principle of the Framework: 'A relationship with a key person at home and in the setting is essential to a young child's emotional well being.'

Close relationships in practice

How well do we offer such relationships in practice? An accumulating body of evidence suggests that there may be both quite complex organisational and psychological issues to be addressed. Organisationally, many nurseries, particularly in the private sector where economic competition is a sharp pressure, rely on flexible deployment of staff in order to be able to use staff as economically and efficiently as possible. This may directly conflict with an approach that prioritises continuity of staff–child relationships and limits the movement of staff between one room and another or even between one nursery and another. Beyond these economic considerations, there appear to be psychological ones too.

Juliet Hopkins (1988) identifies four reasons why nursery nurses in local authority day nursery settings avoided close relationships:

- many nursery nurses had made close relationships in the past with children and recalled how painful it was for both them and the child when they parted;
- where children had become very attached, sometimes they had become very demanding, jealous and possessive;
- in order to feel they were behaving professionally, the nursery nurses were determined to treat all the children the same and it was difficult to do this if relationships were close and you liked some children more than others;
- some nursery nurses acknowledged that they were afraid they might form happier relationships with the children than the children had with their own parents.

Two other studies suggest the formation of close relationships with children is problematic:

> We have often seen in nurseries a child's supposed 'key worker' attending to impersonal tasks while he was fed or comforted by another staff member. Unless the key person system is given primacy in the organisation of the day the child may have no more contact with his designated worker than with any of the other adults. In that case the relationship can have no real meaning for him.
>
> (Goldschmied and Jackson 1994: 36)

Whilst Smith and Vernon (1994), in their study of policy, commissioned by the Midland Bank, concluded that in only one nursery of 15 studied in depth,

> did key workers take on all of the following responsibilities: welcoming and saying goodbye to children; having meals with key children; undertaking routine care tasks such as toileting, as well as being involved in play and other creative activities; linking with parents, and assessing, planning for and writing reports on individual children … a child could spend the day in the company of more than six different adults, none of whom might have any specific responsibilities regarding that particular child.
>
> (ibid: 62)

Why should it be that despite the emphasis given in theory to the importance of close emotional relationships with children they do not appear to occur reliably in practice? There are perhaps a number of interrelated reasons.

First, there seems to be a fear held by parents and early years practitioners that a child's attachment to a worker may somehow undermine or weaken the child's attachment to her or his parents.

Second, there seems to exist within the very culture of the caring professions a concern not to be 'over-involved'. This concern is quite appropriate as over-involvement may at best be unhelpful to children and at worst abusive. But a high concern does seem to be placed on the importance of 'not being over-involved' in contrast to the dangers of being 'under-involved' with children.

Third, it seems to be quite difficult in practice to discuss the emotional content of professional relationships with children. Discussions about the emotional content of professional relationships with children seem to be at risk of becoming quite emotional in their own right. If close relationships with children are really as important as the early years literature suggests we need to look closer at what makes them so difficult to sustain. Three concepts from ethological and psychoanalytic studies of children may assist.

Attachment

In its original formulation, attachment theory provided a model of human development that argued it is essential for infants to have a single primary relationship with one key caregiver. The theory suggested that this prime relationship provided the foundation for all later development and that if it was not secure and consistent then the infant was likely to grow up subject to adult psychiatric disease (Holmes 1993). The idea that very young children can only develop healthily if they have one and only one caretaker, the mother, throughout the day, has now been clearly rejected by research.

However, while there is still disagreement amongst researchers as to whether day care for infants of less than a year is detrimental to their later development (Sylva 1994), the importance of reliable and responsive adults is still strongly supported by research as well as clinical evidence (Murray and Trevarthen 1992; Miller *et al.* 1993). Professionals in nursery settings who are reliable and responsive to young children provide a 'secure base, the essence of which is that it provides a springboard for curiosity and exploration' (Holmes 1993: 70).

When young children feel confident, their energy for curiosity and exploration is considerable. When they are anxious, perhaps because of a new situation or maybe a situation that is beyond their developmental stage, they need to return to their secure base. If this is not available (mother, father, childminder) then they need to return to an alternative secure base, for example, a teacher or nursery nurse with whom they feel connected and held. If to the children the practitioner feels detached or remote – not like a secure base – then their energy for exploration and curiosity is very reduced or disappears. We see this in children who may be described as clingy or a little withdrawn.

Isobel entered reception class at the age of four years and three months and had been there for nearly seven months. She found it difficult to settle but what always made a big difference to her was if she could literally be 'handed over' from her mother to the teacher. She seemed to need the teacher to actually take her hand so she was attached to someone during her transition to school. When her mother had gone she could let go of the teacher's hand and explore a little. This is not an easy thing for a teacher to do with 30 or so children all requiring her to be something of a secure base. So for Isobel, it was not a 'handover' she could rely on and managing to go to school in her first year was difficult for her and her teacher. For many educators, acting as a 'secure base' for children seems to happen almost instinctively and automatically:

> one day a girl looked unwilling to settle at an activity and let her mother leave her. A member of staff approached her, took her hand, led her to an activity and sat and worked with her. The adult's body language and her intonation were supportive and sensitive to the girl's needs, and helped her to settle without tears.
>
> (Marsh 1995: 35)

Others are sufficiently secure and sensitive enough to facilitate and accommodate the individual parting routines of young children and parents. Mary Jane Drummond (1993: 44) illustrates this in relation to James, aged six, and his mother:

> The route they took to school led down a narrow road through some trees to a spot where the school drive branched off to the right, leading uphill again to the school front door, about 50 yards away. James and his mother stopped at this spot and kissed each other goodbye. James bolted up the drive to the front door, while his mother waited on the same spot. From the doorstep of the school, James waved and blew kisses, which were warmly returned. His mother then started walking uphill, and as soon as she walked away, James came into school, and flew down the corridor to his classroom. He stood on the classroom windowsill (luckily a low one), and waited until he could see his mother corning back into sight through the trees, as she walked homewards up the hill behind the school. When she saw him at the window, a second round of waves and kisses ensued, and then, satisfied. James was ready to join the class.

Of course, it is not only parents and children who sometimes find it hard to cope with partings. Those working with our youngest children may find it hard to let them move on, to playgroup, to school, or even into the next 'age group' room of the nursery. This account concerns Shayma:

> Shayma, aged two, had been in the room since she was 12 weeks old. During her first year and a half of life, her key worker has ensured that she was there to meet Shayma's every need, and had gained great satisfaction from feeling indispensable to her. The observations showed, however, that Shayma's growing independence had affected the relationship between child and key worker. In one observation, Shayma was seen to spend sustained periods with other adults in the room. When she returned to her key worker, Shayma found her engrossed in the care of a new baby who had just joined the group. Shayma attempted more than once to attract her key worker's attention, but with little response. Shayma remained close to her key worker for the rest of the session. Occasionally she stroked her arm, or tapped her leg. She did not continue her exploration of other areas of the room.
>
> (Early Childhood Education Forum 1998: 70)

A skilled professional will be aware of those feelings in themselves and talk about them. A skilled manager will also be sensitive to these difficulties and will be available to give support.

Containment

This is the capacity of an adult to help a child manage feelings that may worry, frighten or threaten to overwhelm the child – the adult acts as a container for these feelings (Shuttleworth 1989).

At its most simple, a child may be frightened of a dog. An adult may dismiss this fear as silly – 'it's only a dog – it won't bite you!' This is not an adult that is containing the child's feelings of anxiety but is rather rejecting them. In so doing she does not assist the child to think about his fears or begin to make judgements about which dogs may be dangerous and which may be friendly.

A baby is continually 'pouring' all kinds of fears and anxieties into her mother or other key figure as an important container for these fears and anxieties. A baby crying has a disturbing impact on adults around provided they are sufficiently tuned to the baby's needs. This disturbance is fully intended to 'disturb' the mother or carer. If she can contain her own feelings, she can be with the baby in his or her distress without becoming too distressed or disturbed in herself (Miller *et al.* 1993). She is then able to think about and respond to the baby's needs.

Adults who immediately shout at the two-year-olds fighting over a tricycle do not contain their angry feelings or help them think about the possibility of turn taking (of course two-year-olds may not be able to give up their rage at having to wait or be susceptible to the idea that turn taking is a way of sharing the tricycle. Their anger may then need to be contained in a more direct way perhaps by firm but gentle holding!).

An example I came across recently was of a four-year-old boy trying to get to grips with life in a reception class. The little boy, anxious to make contact with the member of staff in charge and who obviously felt he couldn't do so directly, made a telephone out of stickle bricks. He brought the telephone to the busy teacher and said, 'Look what I've made.' The teacher responded, 'We're not having the stickle bricks out today'. The boy replied. 'But look, I've made a phone.' The teacher repeated that the stickle bricks were not to be used today and the little boy turned sadly away and broke up his telephone, returning the component bricks to the box. Despite the very great difficulties staff are faced with in working with large numbers of four-year-olds in reception class settings, the teacher could not accommodate or 'contain' this four-year-old's independent initiative. It is possible to imagine all kinds of responses that the teacher might have made. She might have commented on how skilful he had been in making the telephone and this perhaps could have been developed to asking who he would like to ring and what he might like to say to the person he telephoned.

Transference

In a general sense, transference is the phenomenon whereby we seem to respond in our relationships with other adults or with children, according to patterns from the past. We transfer feelings and attitudes developed, or 'left over', from earlier experiences. Readers may have found themselves watching a film or television programme and experiencing quite powerful emotions of sadness, distress or anger that do not seem to have their origin entirely in the programme.

In a similar way, certain children, sometimes for no obvious reason, get on our nerves or under our skin. It is hard to identify exactly what it is that child does that is so infuriating. It just may be that the child is doing something that we longed to do but were never allowed to. Our fury at our own childhood denial is transferred to the child in front of us.

Recently, in a working group looking at the needs of under threes, one person in the group, a nursery manager, said despairingly that she did not know what to do with a member of staff who refused to respond quickly to babies crying. That member of staff seemed to take the view that it is wrong to respond to babies as soon as they cried – they needed to learn to wait. This is perhaps an example of both containment, or lack of it and transference. The member of staff is not containing the baby's cries and distress, but is refusing to respond to them. The baby's crying may trigger feelings from her own childhood. Perhaps she was made to wait before she was allowed food or attention – why should this baby have an immediate response when she had to wait? These processes are of course unconscious and not deliberate. The staff member may be acting with the best intentions, trying to help prepare the baby for a world in which he or she will have to wait for things.

The baby may not yet have much past experience or trust to draw on that adults will reliably remember she is there and that they will not forget about her. It is not surprising, then, that a baby who is not responded to reasonably quickly begins to show signs of real anxiety and distress. It is hard to fail to see this in babies who have had to wait too long – their bodies shake with distress and they are clearly distraught. If our arrangements for providing and enabling adults to respond quickly to this distress fails, we very much fail the infant. Consider this example of not making the baby wait:

> Martin, a five-month-old baby boy, had been fed mostly on a demand schedule and was accustomed to waking in the morning, crying or gurgling for a little while until his mother heard him and came into his room to lift him up and feed him. He was accustomed, that is, to drawing his mother to him with his voice. However, on one occasion, the mother heard the child stirring before he was fully awake and waited by his cot side till he awoke. When he opened his eyes he saw her face and slowly revealed absolute and astonished delight.
>
> (Alvarez 1992: 62–3)

Of course babies and young children often have to wait. This is not an ideal world and parents and professional workers are human too, with needs and many demands on them. The point is, that although we may not always be able to respond to children's emotional needs as quickly or as much as we would like, we can know about these needs, rather than deny them. Within the constraints of our work setting we can then at least think about how we can respond in the most creative and sensitive way.

Thinking about our relationships with children, how can we as individuals and in teams begin to do this? I think it is difficult alone. Ideally we need the assistance of another adult. That other adult may be a manager, or colleague, or a group of people working in a similar way or in a similar setting. The other adult may even be ourselves, the reflective practitioner, able to take time to stand back from our immediate involvement with children in order to think a little more objectively about our relationships with them than we can when they are right beside us. Failure to do this seems to risk feelings of 'burn out', an experience that is increasingly referred to (Hawkins and Shohet 2000; Rodd 1994).

The process of talking about feelings, however painful, does seem to pay off. Listen to this account of changes in the nursery nurses' approach to their job after some time discussing their relationships with children:

> (nursery nurses) became increasingly aware of the impossibility of fully meeting the infants' needs, because of the inadequate staff/child ratio and the special needs of disturbed and disadvantaged infants. Greater awareness of the children's needs was accompanied by a greater response to them and more pleasure in doing so; in this way the job became more rewarding. But greater awareness of the impossibility of providing sufficient care made the job more painful and frustrating...Some nurses stopped using distraction as the main technique to deal with children on the brink of tears, and began to find that there were benefits in picking them up and allowing them to have a good cry. [For] example, Peter, aged 18 months, had appeared to pass each day during the month he had spent at the nursery tremulously on the brink of tears, When his nurse stopped diverting him with toys on his arrival, but picked him up for a cuddle when his mother left him, he sobbed on her shoulder and then for the first time settled down to play. Nurses were surprised to recognise that tears and fuss could be a sign of a child's security in his relationship with his nurse, and not simply a sign of her failure.
>
> (Hopkins 1988: 104)

We need to move from a culture where the main beliefs might be:

- 'anyone can care for children'
- 'I'm very experienced – I don't get over-involved'
- 'I treat all children the same.'

to a culture that recognises that for practitioners' relationships with children to take account of children's emotional learning and development a culture of reflective practice is crucial. This in turn depends on a culture that supports the learning of skills to talk to one another about how we make children feel and how children make us feel.

This shift needs building up in training days, in team days, in consultation and appraisal meetings – it cannot just be switched on.

To conclude: we know infants are learning through relationships and exploration from the earliest age:

> ...the infant is no longer just a sensual, appetitive little animal seeking gratification, and a passionately loving and destructive creature, finding and losing love and

nurture. He is also, when the conditions allow, a little music student listening to the patterning of his auditory experience, a little art student studying the play and pattern of light and shade and its changes, a little dance student watching and feeling his mother's soothing movements or playful vitalising activities, a little conversationalist taking part in pre-speech dialogues with his mother in the early weeks of life, a little scientist working to yoke his experiences together and understand them.

(Alvarez 1992: 76)

The quality of this learning depends intimately on the quality of relationships that can be formed with adults. The challenge is to think about how early years practitioners can support and extend the emotional development of children as an integral part of their overall learning. The development of this aspect of early years practice, and its theoretical underpinning, needs to be as rigorous and detailed as the early years literature on supporting and extending children's cognitive development.

This chapter is based on a previous article published in Elfer, P. (1996) 'Building intimacy in relationships with young children in nurseries', *Early Years* **2**, 30–4.

References

Alvarez, A. (1992) *Live Company Psychoanalytic Psychotherapy with Autistic, Borderline, Deprived and Abused Children.* London: Routledge.

Bruce, T. (1987) *Early Childhood Education.* London: Hodder & Stoughton.

Dahlberg, G., Moss, P. and Pence, A. (1999) *Beyond Quality in Early Childhood Education and Care: postmodern perspectives.* London: Falmer Press.

Drummond M. J. (1993) *Assessing Children's Learning.* London: David Fulton Publishers.

Early Childhood Education Forum (1998) *Quality in Diversity in Early Learning: a framework for early childhood practitioners.* London: National Children's Bureau.

Elfer, P., Goldschmied, E. and Selleck, D. (2003) *Key Persons in the Nursery: building relationships for quality provision.* London: David Fulton Publishers.

Goldschmied, E. and Jackson, S. (1994) *People Under Three: young children in day care.* London: Routledge.

Hawkins, P. and Shohet, R. (2000) *Supervision in the Helping Professions: an individual, group and organizational approach*, 2nd edn. Buckingham: Open University Press.

Hennessey, E., Martin, S., Moss, P. and Melhuish, P. (1992) *Children and Day Care: lessons from research.* London: Paul Chapman Publishing.

Holmes, J. (1993) *John Bowlby and Attachment Theory.* London: Routledge.

Hopkins, J. (1988) 'Facilitating the development of intimacy between nurses and infants in day nurseries', *Early Child Development and Care* **33**, 99–111.

Lally, M. (1991) *The Nursery Teacher in Action.* London: Paul Chapman Publishing.

Leach, P. (1994) *Children First.* Harmondsworth: Penguin Books.

Marsh, C. (1995) 'Quality Relationships and quality practice', *International Journal of Early Years Education* **3**, 29–45.

Miller, L., Rustin, M. and Shuttleworth, A. (eds) (1993) *Closely Observed Infants.* London: Duckworth.

Murray, L. and Trevarthen, C. 'Emotional regulation of interactions between two month olds and their mothers', in Alvarez, A. (1992) *Live Company Psychoanalytic Psychotherapy with Autistic, Borderline, Deprived and Abused Children.* London: Routledge.

Nutbrown, C (1994) *Threads of Thinking: young children learning and the role of early education.* London: Paul Chapman Publishing.

Office for Standards in Education (Ofsted) (2001) *Full Day Care: guidance to the National Standards.* London: DfES.

Rodd, J. (1994) *Leadership in Early Childhood.* Buckingham: Open University Press.

Shuttleworth, A. (1989) 'Psychoanalytic theory and infant development', in Miller, L., Rustin, M. and Shuttleworth, A. (eds) (1989) *Closely Observed Infants.* London: Duckworth.

Smith, C. and Vernon, J. (1994) *Day Nurseries at a Crossroads: meeting the challenge of child care in the nineties.* London: National Children's Bureau.

Sure Start Unit (DfES) (2002) *Birth to Three Matters: a framework for supporting early years practitioners.* London: DfES.

Sylva, K. (1994) 'The importance of early learning', in Ball, C. *Start Right: the importance of early learning.* London: Royal Society of Arts.

Chapter 21

The physical environment

Sue Robson

Introduction

> Until this matter of environment is settled no method can save us.
>
> (McMillan 1930)

The nursery and school classroom environments within which we 'live' (McLean 1991) have an effect upon us all. Underlying the ways in which these spaces are organised are the philosophies of early years settings and early years practitioners, and their beliefs about care and learning, and the most effective ways of organising for them. Many early years settings will contain similar apparatus, and may be organised in what seem to be physically quite similar ways. Any similarities may, however, end there. The provision we make comes to life through the ways in which it is used, and it would be very wrong to equate *provision* with *curriculum*. It is what we *do*, or, more importantly, what the *children* do with the environment and materials in it which matters. As Hartley demonstrates, things have the potential to be used in very different ways, depending on our beliefs, and the ways in which those beliefs are enacted in our planning. He describes two nurseries, each containing much the same basic equipment, and each espousing broadly similar reasons for the physical organisation they favoured: 'To be structured so they [the children] can be unstructured' and 'The freedom to control themselves' (Hartley 1987: 63) In practice, their appearance, and what went on in both, was quite different.

It is this *difference* which is crucial. Blenkin and Whitehead suggest that the creation of an environment or setting is 'the most neglected and misunderstood dimension of the planned curriculum' (1988: 36) because it is often seen as peripheral to the *real* task of curriculum planning. In reality, attention to the environment in which we live and work is central to the task of teaching, providing the physical context to working with young children. Practitioners in Reggio Emilia talk of space as the 'third educator', and as an active force with the capacity to support children's social, emotional, physical and intellectual development (Edwards *et al.* 1998). Clarke-Stewart (1991) has identified several indicators of quality that impinge upon children's development, including a well organised and stimulating physical environment. The potential exists, then, for the physical setting to have a positive impact upon the children in it. By implication the converse is also possible: that the physical features of the places in which young children are expected to live and learn can lead to poorer quality for them (Stephen and Wilkinson 1995).

Undoubtedly (and unfortunately) some aspects of these environments can be beyond our power to change. You may be working in a purpose-built centre with sufficient indoor and outdoor space, good equipment and appropriate furnishings. On the other hand, many of us may find ourselves in less suitable spaces: rooms converted for young children, no outdoor space, toilets a long trek away, little appropriate equipment, and furnishings which have all the appearance of having been collected by a committee at a jumble sale. As Goldschmied and Jackson (1994) point out, commercial organisation soften spend huge sums of money in order to create an attractive environment for customers during their brief stay, while children are often condemned to pass their most formative years in less than ideal surroundings.

A seemingly poor environment can never be an excuse for offering poor quality to children. The research project 'Principles into Practice: improving the quality of children's early learning' finding is 'that quality is a matter of well-qualified professional people and their commitment to young children; it is not simply appropriate resources, and it is certainly not bureaucratic structures' (Whitehead 1994: 28). Here I look at the ways in which we, as 'professional people', can make the most of the spaces we do have, to provide an environment in which adults and children alike can live and work happily, and which has a positive impact upon each child's development. We shall consider why it is so important to plan our environment, and how this can contribute to our aims for young children, and then look at some aspects of this organisation. While you are reading, you may find it useful to think about settings with which you are familiar, looking particularly at what seem to be the underlying assumptions and beliefs about teaching, learning and the care of young children.

Why do we need to plan our environment?

The chief reason we need to consider how early years settings are physically organised is one which underpins all aspects of working with young children, that what we do should never become 'a standard practice beyond...reflection' (Hartley 1987: 66) This is particularly important when considering the organisation of space and resources, because the 'givens' (Wood *et al.* 1980) are so many. Opportunities to alter the physical construction of buildings, removing walls, for example, are rare, and we cannot just go and buy whatever equipment we think we need because money is often limited. All this can lead us towards focusing on limitations rather than possibilities: 'I can't do that, because...', rather than 'how can I do that with what I've got, or what I can get hold of?' While this should not be taken to mean that working with young children is about 'make do and mend' (for it certainly is not), it does imply the importance of continued reappraisal of the environment, and its appropriacy for the children concerned and their needs and interests. The needs of four-year-old children in a nursery or reception class may be very different from those of one-year-olds in a nursery setting or six-year-olds in an infant class, and organisation must reflect these differences.

Some features of learning and young children

What must always drive this reappraisal are our aims for the children in our care, our beliefs about what will be most appropriate for them, and about the nature of learning. Concern for the physical dimension of the setting is a means to these ends, and not an end in itself. What, then, do we know about how young children learn? Gura (1996) described what she called 'the two contexts of learning', commenting that curriculum arrangements must acknowledge both the inner, or individual, context and the outer, or social, context of learning: 'They interpenetrate and together make up the human experience of learning' (p. 149). This emphasis, supported by much research and writing in recent years, suggests the need for an environment which facilitates and supports children's efforts as social beings, and the idea of learning as a social process. Alongside this, Blenkin and Whitehead suggest that 'The underlying principle which should guide the establishment of such an environment is that it must enable the children to be active in learning' (1988: 47). Taken together, they imply a need to ensure that young children have opportunities to be physically and mentally active, in an environment which allows them to collaborate with others, both adults and children, as well as offering them opportunities to play and work alone.

Tizard and Hughes (2002) suggest that what characterises young children is their relative ignorance and a limited conceptual framework with which to organise their experience and thought. Part of our energies will need to be directed towards providing a wide range of worthwhile experiences which reflect children's own interests, and acknowledge their importance for them. In so doing, it is worth bearing in mind that young children may often learn most from self-chosen play activities (Siraj-Blatchford *et al.* 2002) and opportunities for children to choose and develop those experiences for themselves will be of particular importance. There is now considerable consensus (Clark 1988), supported by HMI (1989), Ofsted (1993) and QCA/DfEE (2000), that the quality of opportunities young children have for both play and talk will be crucial to their development, and that these two are the chief vehicles by which young children learn. The environment, then, must offer high-quality opportunities for children to be playful and engage in play, alone and with others, and to develop their linguistic skills with a range of talk partners.

All these aims are essentially cognitive ones related to young children's intellectual growth. Others are also central to their development. The social, emotional and physical development of young children are all concerns for the professionals working with them, and will be reflected in the provision made. Socially, for example, the aim of developing children's capacity to share and to collaborate with others will affect the organisation set up. Other aims may be more particular to individual centres or places. Karrby and Giota, for example, commenting on Swedish day-care centres, stress the goal of creating 'a stimulating social environment for the children in which democratic values are expressed in the practice and relationships within the preschool' (1994: 4). Moss and Petrie suggest that 'children's spaces' should be central to everyday life in society, for both adults and children, and seen as 'environments of many possibilities – cultural and social, but also economic, political, ethical, aesthetic, physical' (Moss and Petrie 2002: 9).

How do children 'read' the environment?

What of the children themselves? Gura (1996) has commented on the way in which arrangements of time and space send messages to the children. These messages may be about a range of issues. They will be about the valuing of self and others, they may also tell children much about what is sanctioned and prized in the setting (Dudek 2000: 23). The space given to particular types of activity, the presence or absence of adults in particular areas of the room, the proximity of different areas and materials, all say much to children about what has value and status in a particular unit. Jackson (1987) makes a strong case for suggesting that children's capacity to make sense of these messages and to grasp the organisational procedures of the setting will condition their access to the learning opportunities within it. Not only that, but if they fail to do so and remain unaware of routines and expectations, they may be regarded a unsuccessful by the adults concerned, with all that this can imply for those adults' future expectations of them.

Settings, and the ways in which we organise them, have an effect on all those within them. Dowling (1992) maintains that they affect the ways in which we work, and the evidence of Sylva *et al.* (1980) and Smith and Connelly (1981) suggests that the quality of children's play is affected by design and layout of space. Pascal provides a poignant reminder that it can affect not just what children do, but, importantly, how they feel, in her record of a teacher's comment:

> I have just moved with a group of children from the nursery class to the reception class and the difference was so dramatic. Gone was the wonderful space, the large apparatus, jigsaws, construction toys...I felt frustrated and disappointed – can you imagine how the children felt?
>
> (Pascal 1990: 23)

How can these underpinning principles and beliefs be reflected in the ways in which the environment is organised? The environment is, of course, ultimately the totality of children's experience in a setting, but in order to look closely it can be considered in particular areas, beginning with basic structure and organisation.

Fitness and flexibility

In considering the way in which the space is to be used, it is worth borrowing a phrase given prominence in Alexander *et al.* (1992), that of 'fitness for purpose'. In the present context this means thinking about developing spaces appropriate to the ages and stages of the children who are to use them. This involves a recognition of the differing needs of young children. Provision appropriate for the under-threes will differ from that we make for four-year-olds. If one of our intentions is for children to develop a disposition to work and play collaboratively, we shall need to reflect this in aspects such as seating arrangements. In setting out room arrangements for the youngest children, Whalley (1994) and Goldschmied and Jackson (1994) put forward cases for two different types of organisation. Whalley documents the decision made by staff at Pen Green Family Centre, not to separate the under- and over-three-year-olds, and to have family groups rather than a baby room, toddler room and preschool room. Their decision was based on ideological as well as physical grounds (p. 36). By contrast, Goldschmied and Jackson suggest the desirability of age grouping in day-care centres (p. 19). This well illustrates that, ultimately, there are no universally applicable answers, only solutions that are right for a particular situation, at a particular time.

Appraising the environment

Above all, it will be necessary to be familiar with the space available, and all that it contains, to be clear about the possibilities it holds and to appraise the worth of equipment. The only way to do this is to have first-hand experience of using the space and its contents, relying neither on the fact that it is already there, nor on an idea that something is so much a part of the early years 'tradition' that we cannot *not* have it. Goldschmied and Jackson suggest that it can be worthwhile holding a meeting for all who use a particular space, adults and children alike, where the theme is 'What I would like to keep in this room and what I would like to get rid of' (1994: 22), as a way of appraising the fitness for purpose of materials, equipment and spaces. Gura (1996b) describes an experiment where, in a nursery classroom, all of the equipment was removed and taken to a central hall. The children were then allowed to bring things back into the space, as they wished. After several weeks, most things (apart from the piano and the table and chairs) had been returned, with the children arranging all of the large equipment around the walls, leaving a large central space for play.

Arranging space

Many settings opt for an arrangement of space into distinct areas, for example, a role play area, small and large construction, malleable materials, graphics, sand and water, 'creative workshop', etc. (Edgington 1998). Harms and Clifford (1998) refer to these as 'interest centers' (sic). What may be most important is to see the space, and the areas within it, both inside and out, as flexible, with the potential for combination across areas, as well as within each area.

One feature of successful learning is the capability to transfer knowledge and understanding from one area to another, and the making of useful connections between ideas. If we wish to develop such competence in young children, a material provision which reflects this flexibility is vital.

What may be most useful is to consider the space available as a range of clearly defined different areas, ordered partly according to necessary 'housekeeping' criteria (there are, after all, very good reasons for siting art areas near a sink and on an easily cleaned floor surface, and similarly books and construction areas may not be good neighbours), and partly with a view to facilitating interesting associations and creative transformations of materials. Thus, physical proximity of areas, for example home corners and block play areas, may enrich children's play through the combination of materials from both, but children can also be encouraged to feel able to move a whole range of materials and equipment about to suit their purposes (Edgington 1998: 115). Cleave and Brown illustrate this well:

> A group of children observed playing in the home corner first kitted themselves out with shoes from the 'shoe shop'. They made a vehicle from the large construction blocks and went on a journey. It was a hot day so the children used paper provided from the painting and writing tables to make a fan to cool themselves. They returned to the 'vehicle' fanning themselves as they travelled back to the home corner for 'lunch'.
>
> (1991: 151)

A 'transparent structure' (Hutt *et al.* 1989: 230) which encourages neither the children nor the adults involved to view the spaces in rigid terms is most desirable. Hutt and colleagues concluded that, where rigidity was a feature, children's play tended to be more stereotypical, and less innovative. The dry sand and water trays, for example, they found to be places where children could, essentially, be alone. Play was usually in parallel, and 'one can shut out some of the hustle and bustle endemic to nurseries' (p. 98). There is, of course, a need for quiet niches in the setting, where children can be alone if they so choose. However, to see an element of provision such as the dry sand as a haven of solitude may not be using it to its full potential. There is a need for different 'micro-environments' (p. 98), but, as McAuley and Jackson conclude: 'Adult involvement together with reflection on the purpose and value of all areas of provision should enhance the quality of *all* "micro-environments"' (1992–68).

Freedom of access

Implicit in this sort of organisation is freedom of access for children, with opportunities for them to develop autonomy and a sense of control. Gura (1996) commented on the provision in nurseries in Reggio Emilia of low 'sleep nests' for babies and toddlers, containing their own belongings, into which they can crawl, by themselves, to take a nap. Older children can be helped to take responsibility for themselves, making decisions and selecting resources as they need them. So, materials, equipment and all areas of the setting, both indoor and out, need, as far as possible, to be freely accessible to children at all times. What messages might we be giving to children, and how much more dependent upon us are we making them, if we have decided beforehand everything that can be out for them to use, with other things kept behind closed doors to which they have no access? Pragmatically, too, such a system will increase the number of low-level demands made upon adults, to service requests for materials (McLean 1991: 168).

In practice, staff attitudes will condition children's feelings of 'permission' to use equipment, the timetable will need to ensure that children can have access, and materials and equipment will need to be stored in such a way that children can not only retrieve what they need when they need it but they can also put it back ready for someone else. Shelves and containers clearly labelled (with words and pictures) at child height can contribute to this independence. The attitudes of adults, in giving children responsibility, and in helping them to take on some of the routines which assist this independence, will be crucial to its success as a strategy (Edgington 1998).

Organising time

Time is an important resource which needs to be organised with the same care as any other aspect of provision. Children's time in early years settings is often fragmented by organisational aspects outside their, and sometimes practitioners', control. Children may not start an activity, knowing, from past experience, that they will not have the chance to complete it because of the restricted time available. What need, then, is there to break up the time available any more than is necessary?

If children are to feel enabled to take on challenges, and to sustain their interest over a long period, then they will need to have the opportunity for continuous uninterrupted activity, and to know that this will be possible. This includes opportunities to carry on with an activity or project from one day to another.

Careful observation of what children are taking where, of how they are using and transforming materials, and to what purposes they are putting equipment, can be invaluable in deciding future provision, and in making adjustments to space.

Equal opportunities: access to the classroom

All professionals working with young children have the obligation for ensuring equality of opportunity. One factor which will condition the ways in which such aims can be realised is the quality and type of material provision made, to ensure that all children have access to the events of the setting, and to counter stereotyping and prejudice. A wide range of resources, representing many cultures and not supportive of stereotypes of race, gender, class and disability, is one element of this provision, but it must be complemented by the ways in which that provision is used. Much research (see, for example, Davies and Brember 1994; Hutt *et al.* 1989) points to the attraction of different types of activities for boys and girls with consequent effects upon practitioners' perceptions of their maturity, adjustment to school, and behaviour.

The culture of the setting will need to encompass many viewpoints and experiences if all children are to derive most benefit from it.

Safety and security

None of us ever has what we might think of as the 'perfect' space, so using what we do have to the very best advantage is vital. Before thinking about what you are going to do with the furniture and equipment look long and hard at the basic space, indoor and out, and think about its possibilities and its constraints.

The first consideration in looking at the space available is to ensure children's safety and security. Outside, for example, are all exits secure, with latches on gates placed so that children inside cannot undo them? Is large climbing apparatus safe? Where are the fire exits? Inside, are electrical sockets covered? Do radiators have guards on them? Is the equipment in good repair? It is important to feel sure that you have kept a check on all possible hazards, as well as ones you have not even thought of! Young children are curious and keen to explore their surroundings, while also being unaware sometimes of the dangers it poses. Helping children to develop the skills they need to use things is an important responsibility for all adults working with them, and their competence in handling woodwork tools, for example, often surprises parents and those working with older children. As a message about the capabilities of young children it is hard to beat. Issues of safety, security, and the development of children's skills in using a range of tools is discussed in Edgington (1998).

In and out of doors

In their study of four-year-olds in reception classes, Cleave and Brown (1991) are adamant that young children need space both indoors and out. Edgington (1998) stresses the need for practitioners to see both inside and outside as one learning environment.

By the time children are six or seven years old, outdoor play at school has invariably become a way of 'letting off steam' rather than an opportunity for learning and development. In the early years, the indoor and outdoor environments can, and should, both be seen as central, with 'no firm distinction between indoors and out' (McLean 1991: 71). Sadly, not all early years settings have dedicated outdoor areas, but where they do, the space can be planned with as much care as indoors (Bilton 2002), to provide a complete learning environment, where children have opportunities for gross motor play, for investigations, for gardening, and using much of the equipment from indoors. In short, the vast majority of activities and experiences that take place inside can easily occur outside, alongside others, such as running, jumping, bicycle riding, environmental studies and digging. In talking to children throughout the primary age range, Titman (1994) found that children of all ages sought a broadly similar range of opportunities from the school outdoor environment: 'a place for *doing*...a place for *thinking*...a place for *feeling*...a place for *being* (her emphasis) (p. 58). She adds one other quality, too: 'In addition, and of overriding importance perhaps, was the need for school grounds to be "a place for fun"!' (p. 58).

Alongside the potential of outdoor spaces for young children's development, there are other reasons why opportunities for them to play outside at school may be important, more now perhaps than ever before. Many children now live in densely populated urban areas, with little access to gardens and outdoor spaces at home. Increased fears about traffic and danger from strangers mean that parents are reluctant to allow their children to play outside. A survey by McNeish and Roberts (1995) found that the great majority of parents perceived their children to be at far greater risk from these dangers than they had been when they were children themselves. As a consequence, children are often obliged to play indoors, with activities such as watching television and playing board games featuring high on the list. While in themselves these are not bad ways for children to spend their time, if they predominate then children are clearly getting less opportunity for physical exercise, for learning about their environment and for social interaction. These same parental fears have led to even less independence for children, as more and more parents take them, often by car, to and from school and other activities. The consequent implications for their future health (and their present development and enjoyment) are clear. So, the availability of richly provisioned, challenging outdoor space in school is a real priority.

Principles in organising outdoor space are similar to those guiding the provision made indoors. Children need opportunities to experience a wide range of activities, to play alone and with others, to be private, to be active, to make choices and decisions for themselves. Again, as with indoor spaces, this necessitates seeing the space as a series of 'micro-environments', where what is on offer is easily accessible to the children, without adult help, and where children feel able to move materials from one place to another, as it suits their purposes.

Conclusion

This chapter stresses the importance of the physical environment. It points out that:

- practitioners' beliefs about and aims for young children's learning and development are visible in the way the environment is organised
- the environment can facilitate learning and development or conversely foster a 'learned helplessness'
- there is a need for versatile materials and spaces which extend children's understanding and imaginations and which can be adapted to their needs.

It concludes that only by providing a quality environment for children can we hope to ensure a quality experience for them, and thus have high quality expectations of them.

This chapter is adapted from an earlier work – 'The physical environment', in Robson, S. and Smedley, S. (eds) (1996) *Education in Early Childhood*. London: David Fulton Publishers in association with the Roehampton Institute.

References

Alexander, R., Rose, J. and Woodhead, C. (1992) *Curriculum Organisation and Classroom Practice: a discussion paper*. London: DES.

Bilton, H. (2002) *Outdoor Play in the Early Years*, 2nd edn. London: David Fulton Publishers.

Blenkin, G. M. and Whitehead, M. R. (1988) 'Creating a context for development', in Blenkin, G. M. and Kelly, A. V. (eds) *Early Childhood Education: a development curriculum*. London: Paul Chapman.

Clark, M. M. (1988) *Children Under Five: educational research and evidence*. London: Gordon & Breach.

Clarke-Stewart, A. (1991) 'Day Care in the USA', in Moss, P. and Melhuish, E. (eds) *Current Issues in Day Care for Young Children*. London: HMSO.

Cleave, S. and Brown, S. (1991) *Early to School: four year olds in infant class*. Windsor, Berks: NFER-Nelson.

Davies, J. and Brember, I. (1994) 'Morning and afternoon nursery sessions: can they be equally effective in giving children a positive start to school?' *International Journal of Early Years Education* **2** (2).

Dowling, M. (1992) *Education 3–5*, 2nd edn. London: Paul Chapman.

Dudek. M. (2000) *Kindergarten Architecture: space for the imagination*, 2nd edn. London: E & F. N. Spon.

Edgington, M. (1998) *The Nursery Teacher in Action*, 2nd edn. London: Paul Chapman.

Edwards, C. *et al.* (1998) *The Hundred Languages of Children*, 2nd edn. Norwood, NJ: Ablex.

Goldschmied, E. and Jackson, S. (1994) *People Under Three: young children in daycare*. London: Routledge.

Gura, P. (1996) 'An entitlement curriculum for early childhood', in Robson, S. and Smedley, S. (eds) *Education in Early Childhood*. London: David Fulton Publishers in association with the Roehampton Institute.

Gura, P. (1996b) *Resources for Early Learning*. London: Hodder & Stoughton.

Harms, T., Clifford, R. M. and Cryer, D. (1998) *Early Childhood Environment Rating Scale*. New York: Teacher's College Press.

Hartley, D. (1987) 'The time of their lives: bureaucracy and the nursery school', in Pollard, A. (ed.) *Children and their Primary Schools*. Lewes: Falmer Press.

HMI (1989) *The Education of Children Under Five*. London: HMSO.

Hutt, S. J, Tyler, S., Hutt, C. and Christopherson, H. (1989) *Play, Exploration and Learning: a natural history of the preschool*. London: Routledge.

Jackson, M. (1987) 'Making sense of school', in Pollard A. (ed.) *Children and their Primary Schools*. Lewes: Falmer Press.

Karrby, G. and Giota, J. (1994) 'Dimensions of quality in Swedish day care centres – an analysis of the Early Childhood Environment Rating Scale', *Early Childhood Development and Care* **104**, 1–32.

McAuley, H. and Jackson, P. (1992) *Educating Young Children: a structural approach*. London: David Fulton Publishers.

McLean, S. V. (1991) *The Human Encounter: teachers and children living together in preschools*. London: Falmer Press:

McMillan, M. (1930) *The Nursery School*. London: J. M. Dent.

McNeish, D. and Roberts, H. (1995) *Playing it Safe*. Ilford, Essex: Barnardo's.

Moss, P. and Petrie, P. (2002) *From Children's Services to Children's Spaces*. London: Routledge Falmer.

Office for Standards in Education (1993) *Framework for the Inspection of Schools*. London: HMSO.

Pascal, C. (1990) *Under Fives in the Infant Classroom*. Stoke-on-Trent: Trentham Books.

QCA/DfEE (2000) *Curriculum Guidance for the Foundation stage*. London: QCA.

Siraj-Blatchford, I., Sylva, K., Muttock, S., Gilden, R. and Bell, D. (2002) *Researching Effective Pedagogy in the Early Years*. London: DfES.

Smith, P. K. and Connelly, K. J. (1981) *The Ecology of Pre-School Behaviour*. London: Cambridge University Press.

Stephen, C. and Wilkinson, J. E. (1995) 'Assessing the quality of provision in community nurseries', *Early Childhood Development and Care* **108**, 83–98.

Sylva, K., Roy, C. and Painter, M. (1980) *Child Watching at Playgroup and Nursery School*. London: Grant McIntyre.

Titman, W. (1994) *Special Places, Special People*. Godalming, Surrey: WWF/Learning through Landscapes.

Tizard, B. and Hughes, M. (2002) *Young Children Learning*, 2nd edn. Oxford: Blackwell.

Whalley, M. (1994) *Learning to be Strong*. London: Hodder & Stoughton.

Whitehead, M. (1994) 'Stories from a research project: towards an analysis of data', *Early Years* **15**, 23–9.

Wood, D., McMahon, L. and Cranstoun, Y. (1980) *Working with Under Fives.* London: Grant McIntyre.

Chapter 22

The future of childhood

Jennie Lindon

Children matter. Their emotional wellbeing is of importance to every member of society, not just their own families, because children are a vital and irreplaceable resource for everybody's future.

Children are not babies for ever, any more than they remain members of a nursery or primary school community. We need to remember that for each individual child an important point of their childhood – their own positive outcome of those years – is that they are enabled to emerge as competent and confident adults.

Let children take risks

Children's learning has to be grounded in their own personal, social and emotional development. Their ability to continue to learn rests on the development of a positive view of themselves as people who can learn, who can deal with mistakes or setbacks and draw on the support of adults who care about them as individuals. Helpful adults do not shield children from all risk, whether this is physical, emotional or intellectual. Children need to explore new experiences in order to extend their skills of problem solving, planning and reflection. They learn a great deal through play but play is definitely not their only medium for learning. Children and young people want to learn from adults who share their own skills, both in a specific practical how-to-do-this context and in more general ways, such as talking around a problem or voicing feelings.

There is a growing concern that our approach to children and young people in the UK is too much on the side of identification and avoidance of problems rather than supporting children to develop a sense of competence in the face of the normal ups and downs of life. Children cannot develop properly in an environment in which adults look only to the short term and to what could go wrong.

The Mental Health Foundation's report *Bright Futures: promoting children and young people's mental health* (1999) addressed the need for adults to consider a positive sense of mental health and not just the absence of specific problems. The report draws on the research into *resilience* that emerged from American studies of children from disadvantaged backgrounds who overcame unpromising early circumstances. The insights from these studies, as well as the ideas of children learning a *mastery* rather than a *helplessness* orientation, alert us to our adult role in helping children to learn positive skills and outlooks, rather than a focus on children as passive victims whom adults have to protect.

Children need to be enabled to take risks within a caring environment that offers support if they need it. Risks will sometimes be within the arena of physical skills, but they are just as often within emotional and intellectual learning. Children's lives are full of puzzling new ideas and the possibility of making mistakes. The children who develop resilience towards everyday adversity seem to share experience in the following areas:

- They have a secure attachment to parents and other consistent carers. So their learning can be grounded in relationships that last over time.
- Children learn step-by-step a problem-solving approach which boosts their confidence that initial difficulties with skills or in relationships can be resolved.
- They grow in their broad communication skills, enabling them to express concerns, to reflect and to share happy experiences with people whom they trust to be interested in them and not to belittle any difficulties.
- What important adults say to and do with children enables them to develop a 'can-do' approach that is realistic. Adults offer constructive feedback that helps children to work out what has gone awry. Helpful adults do not simply drench children in unconditional praise that fails to help them to address mistakes or struggles. Children gain in confidence and a sense of competence that they can, with help if they wish, face and deal with situations in which the answer is not obvious.

Learning from adults' experience

The final goal of childhood is to emerge as a competent and confident adult. Adults need to consider how best to share their grown-up skills, experience and insights with children.

Step-by-step coaching

Coaching is a way of supporting children's learning of any life skills, especially those in which there are safety implications. The idea of coaching children is positive because it locates adult expertise in specific areas rather than depending on an image of adults who always know more than the children. As children grow older, they soon have areas of expertise, knowledge and specific skills that they can share, in their turn, with adults. The relationship of coaching, skill sharing and exchange of knowledge can become a pleasurable two-way process.

Tell-show-do

The essence of coaching, so that children can learn as well as possible, has been summed up as 'tell-show-do'.

- *Tell* children what you are doing and explain why, as and when this is appropriate. Describe your actions in words and phrases that are simple enough for these children. Be prepared to explain again or several times, if necessary.
- *Show* children clearly what you mean through demonstration. Children need to see how to do something and be able to make a clear link between what you say and do.
- Give children an opportunity to *do* it themselves, as soon as you have completed 'tell' and 'show'. Encourage them to ask for help as and when they want. Offer guidance as they wish . . .

Encouragement and constructive feedback

Children will gain in skills and satisfaction far more effectively if adults offer plenty of encouragement with constructive and accurate feedback. Encourage children with the following approaches:

- Acknowledgement of children's efforts that does not always focus on the end-product. Children learn from 'well done' for what they have managed so far, as this acknowledges the fact that they had the sense to come and ask for more help and another explanation.
- Warm words of encouragement will help a child to persevere or to try another method. You might say: 'You've done really well so far, let's see how you've got stuck here' or 'I can see you're frustrated, let's see if it will work this way.'
- Children are encouraged by appropriate compliments from adults such as: 'I'm so pleased I can trust you all to do this on your own' or 'That's worked so well: I wouldn't have thought of doing it this way.'
- Constructive feedback works alongside encouragement by providing honest and accurate information to the children. Children do not benefit from being given indiscriminate praise or actually told something is 'fine' when it is not. When children realise that things have not gone right, but an adult is still saying 'lovely', then the child loses confidence in that adult's judgement . . .

Children can learn if you 'tell-show-do' about any safety implications . . .

- Share useful tips and techniques in how to do a practical activity. Children can learn a great deal through discovery but it is unhelpful to leave them to reinvent the wheel, when there are tried and tested ways to undertake an activity.
- Good technique is also likely to be safer as well as leading to a more satisfying end-product for children. You might say, 'It works better if you do

little sawing movements like this...' or 'This kind of sewing goes up and down again into the material. It doesn't go over the side.'
- Take opportunities as they arise to be explicit about safety but obviously don't overdo the message. You risk losing children's attention through excessive repetition or by harping on possible dangers rather than practical approaches such as 'This will work better if we...' or 'I've found this is a good way to...'

Raising children is a long term project in which ideally children's own parents will provide the essential continuity as the years of childhood pass into adolescence. Early years practitioners of all backgrounds have an essential role to play over those months or years, when you share with parents the care and learning of their children. You have a responsibility to ensure that the children are indeed safe enough in your setting. However, you have an equally strong responsibility that children are enabled to experience and negotiate challenges appropriate to their age and ability level.

[This chapter is adapted from an article in the September 1999 issue of the journal *Coordinate: the journal of the National Early Years Network*]

Chapter 23

Creating contexts for professional development in educare

Angela Anning and Anne Edwards

In this chapter Annings and Edwards report on a project involving a collaboration between higher education, local authority officers and early years practitioners in creating an informed community of practice.

In this chapter we look at professional learning for educare in a changing system: the learning of individuals; the contexts in which their learning takes place; and what this learning means for practice, training and management. We use the term 'learning' rather than 'coping' not simply because we want to avoid the rather negative tone of coping, but also because we believe that dealing with change is a matter of simply learning something new and taking a positive approach to that learning. We are therefore optimistic that an area of provision that has expertise in helping children learn will also be good at helping adults learn.

Sound quality interactions with adults are central to the development of children's dispositions to learn. It is a truism, but nonetheless a powerful one, that children learn to love learning through being with adults who also love to learn, and are themselves in contexts that encourage their learning. This truism, therefore, means that children deserve to be supported by adults who are driven by their own intellectual curiosity to understand their practice better. Children's learning, we would argue, is supported by a system that has the learning of both children and adults as a priority.

Educare as a community of practice?

The goal of an informed community of practice is important for the development of educare as a new form of professional practice. The idea of a community of practice comes from the work of psychologists and anthropologists who have researched how knowledge is used and shared in communities of practitioners (Lave and Wenger 1991; Chaiklin and Lave 1993).

Communities of practice are seen as knowledge communities that create and use their understandings of practice in quite specific ways. For example, the knowledge community of children's nursing is very different from the knowledge community of children's welfare work and both are different from early years teaching. The knowledge found in communities of practice is often tacit and therefore not open to public scrutiny. Instead, knowledge of practice is understood, used and developed in the context of the practice. New members of a knowledge community are brought into established practices by learning to participate in the practices. For example, student nursery nurses become members of the community of practice of nursery nursing, first through observation, then through some marginal activities and finally by working alongside experts to use the knowledge of the practices they have been gaining through observation and simple tasks.

Learning through participation in traditional practices is a very powerful model of learning and one that has dominated in the training of nursery nurses and, more recently, teachers. It makes a great deal of sense when we are helping people learn to work as professionals in complex settings such as preschool. However, the idea of a community of practice as a place for passing on traditions also reveals some of the problems facing early years providers. If educare is to have any currency it needs to have coherence, have a knowledge base that can be scrutinised, and draw on only the best of recent traditions to meet new challenges. Above all, educare as a form of professional practice has to be forward looking and not simply rely on the passing on of existing ideas of what good practice is.

Therefore, if understandings of practice come through practice itself, forward-looking change has to start simultaneously with changes in practice as well as changes in ways of thinking about practice. The challenge is therefore to create a new community of practice while supporting those who are learning as they develop new practices.

Supporting the learning of practitioners

In our project the learning goals for practitioners, like those for the children, focused on the *who* as much as on the *what* of learning and particularly on helping participants develop a capacity to interpret and respond to the learning opportunities available for children. The goals included:

- developing the capacity to see the educational potential in experiences shared with children;
- developing the capacity to respond to the demands they have identified as they work with children;
- developing dispositions for enquiry and learning;
- developing ways of seeing and being which draw on the knowledge base of educare.

Like children, adults learn best in safe and well-supported contexts where they are able to learn through a form of *guided participation*. Guided participation is important because we are suggesting that learning the practice of educare is a question of learning to interpret familiar events in fresh ways and developing a repertoire of responses to new interpretations. Fresh interpretations and responses usually need to be modelled or guided and can seem quite risky. Interpretations might be wrong and responses may misfire. Practitioners need support if they are to change their practices.

During the project practitioners' learning was *scaffolded* by:

- the modelling of strategies with children by more expert practitioners – for example, when Mollie worked with children on mark-making and was observed by a colleague;
- discussions for planning and reviewing;
- joint data collection and analysis;
- shared frameworks for data collection – for example, observation schedules;
- a shared focus on children's learning in numeracy and literacy.

Practitioners' learning through those scaffolding processes became evident in how they used language and in how the familiar materials of pre-school provision took on new educational meanings as, for example, the construction area became a site for children's early mark-making in one setting and their mathematical thinking and action in another.

In the structured and non-threatening learning contexts provided by the action research projects practitioners were able, in their discussions, to *appropriate* the frameworks and language of early learning shared in the workshops and readings. Similarly, while they worked with these new ideas with children they were able to identify the educational potential of familiar materials – such as how blocks and play people could be used together to develop children's use of mathematical language in a fantasy play context – and respond knowledgeably.

Participants did not identify a need for new resources as a result of an increased emphasis on curricula. Instead, existing materials were being given new (educational) meanings by practitioners. The changes appeared to be in how the adults were interpreting events and responding while working with children. The professional learning that occurred through well-supported participation in new forms of practice seemed considerable. Like the children, the adults learnt through participating in experiences which demanded specific (i.e. in this case educational) ways of thinking and acting. But like children, adults can only change their ways of thinking and acting in contexts that allow these changes to occur. Learning contexts for adults, therefore, need careful management.

Current work on educational settings as learning organisations

We intended that the project would give key participants experiences of frameworks for evidence-based practice which would help them develop their colleagues as educarers. Our focus was therefore as much on the adults as learners as on the pupils. Because of the focus, our concern was the development of the pre-school settings as learning communities.

Louis *et al.* (1996) identified five components which they found to be significant in schools as learning communities which in turn supported children as learners. These components were:

1. a shared sense of purpose;
2. a collective focus on pupil learning;
3. collaborative activity;
4. deprivatised activity;
5. reflective dialogues.

A shared sense of purpose takes time to achieve and can't be imposed. Quite often a sense of coherent purpose only emerges in the processes of discussion and action as colleagues clarify exactly what they mean by, for example, the community values underpinning the work of a preschool centre. Fullan (1991, 1993) points out that one sign that change is not really happening is when people demonstrate 'false clarity' – for example, the rhetoric is spoken and accepted but the implications for practice are barely explored. Parental involvement is an area where false clarity is frequently seen. False clarity is evident, for example, when parental involvement is discussed as a 'good thing' without anyone being clear about what they really think parents can do to help their children learn. In our study, as we shall see later in this chapter, our colleagues took the time necessary to move way beyond any sense of false clarity in their work with parents and identified coherent rationales for parental involvement.

A collective focus on pupil learning allows the development of a professional discourse which centres on the professional actions of colleagues as they create contexts and plan and evaluate actions taken to support children's learning. In our study two strong themes in the collective focus on children's learning were (i) detailed and clearly focused observations of how children were making sense of the opportunities available to them and (ii) careful consideration of how adults interacted with children while they engaged with the materials provided.

Collaborative activity is essential for the development of a professional discourse of educare and the professional learning of educarers. We have proposed that learning occurs as people take action and interpret and react to events in increasingly informed ways – i.e. as they become people who see and act differently. Knowledge, we have therefore argued, is constructed in action as well as in discussions of action. Collaborative activity was central to our study.

Deprivatised activity links closely to both a collective focus on learning and taking action together. Most preschool settings are well placed for ensuring that adults' activities are visible. What did have to be worked at was finding space for the open discussion of activities in which new practices were tried out or modelled. Key activities became the focus of frequent staff meetings in which areas for action were identified, strategies selected and the evidence gathered during the activities was discussed. Early childhood services in Reggio Emilia similarly emphasise deprivatised activity in the stress they place on documenting their work to ensure that their practices are visible to colleagues and parents (Edwards *et al.* 1993). These documents not only render expert practice visible but enable colleagues to respond more coherently to children.

Reflective dialogues, in which evidence either about the settings or action taken is discussed, encourage careful observation and analysis and the sharing of insights and information. But above all they ensure that the tacit expertise of professionals is revealed. Reflective dialogues were the vehicles for knowledge exchange and joint knowledge construction and were carefully built into project planning in every step.

There is evidence to suggest that supervisory practices which focus on professional issues, attend to the personal development of practitioners, emphasise the learning of individuals and groups and allow roles and practices to develop responsively are found in cultures usually described as developmental or learning (Hawkins and Shohet 1989). We would argue that supervisory systems for educarers in many ways parallel key worker systems for children. Good quality supervision which focuses on how adults are helping children develop as learners and encourages reflective dialogue based on evidence and joint activities may prove to be one important driver of change in educare.

Let us now look in a little more detail at how learning relationships were sustained through links between settings, other agencies, the community, adult education, higher education, parents, and other types of preschool provision.

Working with other agencies

Speech therapy. Ivy's project involved her learning while working alongside speech therapists while she herself guided the learning of the mothers on whom her project was focused. Ivy collaborated with speech therapists in devising a tightly focused learning programme for the mothers which aimed at developing their interaction skills with their children. The speech therapists' specialist expertise, their experience in developing communication skills and their familiarity with the nursery were invaluable in both planning and carrying out the programme.

A local multicultural service. Bernie and Reza work for the multicultural services section of one of the collaborating local authorities. They were also project members who collaborated with teachers in two inner-city nurseries. Bernie's collaboration focused on number use. Working with a group of practitioners in one nursery, he was able to advise practitioners on how to make the most of the cultural strengths that the children, from up to 11 different ethnic backgrounds, brought to the nursery.

For Reza, the project allowed him to explore a long-held professional hunch: that children's musical experiences at home vary across ethnic groups and that this may have an impact on how they are able to engage with learning experiences in number in nurseries. As we outlined, he learnt through the interviews undertaken with parents at home about what the parents from a range of ethnic groupings thought about children's early number experiences at home and in the nursery, and how music was used within each home.

Partnership in early literacy. Meg and her staff at her children's centre on a large outer-city council estate had, for a long time, been keen to involve parents in supporting their children as learners. Meg started with an unstructured book loan scheme for the three- and four-year-olds which brought the parents into the centre to choose books with their children. Our advice was that Meg should work with the parents' strengths, i.e. the strong emotional links they have with their children, and make sure that anything they asked parents to do was easily managed and was fun. We discussed nursery rhyme cards that we had seen in use in another project and Meg took up the idea.

Meg produced simple cards with rhymes on one side and suggestions on the reverse. These suggestions included actions to accompany the rhyme, help with finding familiar words in the rhyme, help on how to point to print and ideas for using the same sounds to make up your own rhymes. Parents shared their children's enjoyment with staff when they exchanged cards and appeared to have lost their earlier diffidence about how they might support their children as learners. It seemed that the book and card loan schemes, with their realistic expectations, broke a barrier between home and nursery that had been troubling Meg.

These brief outlines of some of the individual projects illustrate four key features found in each of them:

1. a coherent sense of purpose;
2. a strong sense of the possible;
3. an openness to new possibilities;
4. an openness to new relationships.

We would suggest that these features are essential in preschool settings in order for them to deal with the rapidly changing contexts in which they are operating.

The project as a learning network

We designed the project with relationships very firmly in mind. A new knowledge community could not be developed unless relationships across boundaries were possible and new forms of practical knowledge could be generated in joint action. We were influenced in our thinking by the idea of learning networks. We thought that networks would allow participants to bring together the best of current practice, refreshed by external insights, and develop understandings that would allow them to make informed decisions about future practice. In this section we look at how we operated as a network for learning.

We were aware that our roles as higher education-based researchers in the action research of settings-based practitioners, and in the project as a network, needed exploring. Elliott's (1994) work on teachers' knowledge and action research reminds us of the place of theory and the role of higher education in action research networks. He argues that the ideas of theorists don't threaten practitioners if these ideas can be translated into concrete curriculum proposals that can be scrutinised in action by practitioners who then decide what should be ultimately absorbed into practice. Action research, he suggests, gives the university-based 'theorist' a role as supplier of theoretical resources for practitioners to draw on when analysing and developing practice. However, he emphasises that the practitioner is the ultimate judge of what is useful knowledge.

Elliott's summary of the role of university-based staff in teachers' action research projects is a useful starting point. However, our project as a network did more than simply focus on how individual practitioners developed practical reasoning. Our role involved us in working at three organisational levels: the local authority, the preschool setting and groups of practitioners. Key stakeholders in each of these levels were crucial to the success of the project and we could not have found ourselves with better collaborators. Each level in turn enabled the next. The senior local authority officers with whom we planned the project shared our vision and identified experienced and responsible stakeholders at the level of the settings and then did all they could to support the activities at settings level. The experienced settings-based staff became our research partners and, in turn, enabled the responsive activities of their colleagues as they worked with new strategies with children and with other agencies or parents.

This strong, multi-level commitment to the project then served as a sound basis for the learning network we established. Learning a new form of professional practice in the acts of practice can be highly challenging. Part of the difficulty lies in the need for practitioners to experience a destabilisation of current understandings before new ones are recognised as necessary. The destabilising can be professionally threatening when working publicly with children.

Going slowly was therefore essential. At Step 1 we gained agreement on (i) the purposes of the project and (ii) that we would work slowly from evidence gathered in the settings. During Step 1 we spent time at workshops, building relationships through sharing current understandings and concerns, and everyone visited each others' settings. We cannot over-estimate the importance of the time taken to establish sound relationships across the network. At two residential meetings and workshops at Steps 2 and 3, participants provided each other with both enthusiastic interest in progress and informed support at times of glitch. Mutual support was an extremely important feature and gives us some confidence in the sustainability of the network we helped to establish.

Our roles changed over the duration of the project as the practitioners gained control of the presentation of knowledge in discussions and written texts.

Conceptual framings were increasingly represented in texts of practice by our research partners who appropriated the frameworks we shared and used them in discussions of practice. Experience sharing occurred regularly in workshops and, as we visited each setting, we carried information about developments from one setting to another and shared experiences and practical ideas we had gained elsewhere in similar projects. Help with observations came through advice on observational methods for both exploring practice and formatively assessing children. Analysis of observations also occurred during our visits and in workshops. Most settings were eventually managing their own evaluations of their work in their own settings.

We saw the network as a set of overlapping communities of practice, all with the interests of children as learners as a central concern. As researchers we belonged primarily to the research community. Our research partners were primarily practitioners, who themselves belonged to the communities of, for example, either care or education. The senior managers were led by the concerns of that role. We all brought a range of strengths and experiences to the project. We learnt from each other as we moved in and out of the overlapping communities, gathering information and sharing insights drawn from our particular expertise.

Contexts for the development of educare

Educare professionals, working together, need to see the possibilities for informed responsive action that are available to them in their settings, and use those possibilities. They need to talk about what they are doing and why they are doing it and so take responsibility for the generation of their own knowledge base.

The development of educare will depend upon the continuous development, in action, of a common store of practical knowledge which is itself constantly open to scrutiny. Such scrutiny can only occur in a professional climate that encourages the confidence to value openness and collaboration across boundaries of profession and location so that the best interests of children are served.

References

Chaiklin, S. and Lave, J. (eds) (1993) *Understanding Practice: perspectives on activity and context.* Cambridge: Cambridge University Press.

Edwards, A. and Brunton, D. (1993) 'Supporting reflection in teachers' learning', in J. Calderhead and P. Gates (eds) *Conceptualising Reflection in Teacher Development.* London: Falmer.

Elliott, J. (1994) 'Research on teachers' knowledge in action research', *Educational Action Research* **2** (1), 133–7.

Fullan, M. (1991) *The New Meaning of Educational Change*. London: Cassell.

Fullan, M. (1993) *Change Forces*. London: Falmer.

Hawkins, P. and Shohet, R. (1989) *Supervision in the Helping Professions*. Milton Keynes: Open University Press.

Lave, J. and Wenger, E. (1991) *Situated Learning: legitimate peripheral participation*. Cambridge: Cambridge University Press.

Louis, K. S., Marks, H. and Kruse, S. (1996) 'Teachers' professional communities in restructuring schools', *American Educational Research Journal* **33** (4), 757–98.

Chapter 24

Developing the role of a senior practitioner: a personal perspective

Sharon Ellis and Roger Hancock

A number of recent policy and funding developments have impacted upon the practice, training and professionalism of early years practitioners. Notable landmarks in the last five years of reform include: the National Childcare Strategy; Curriculum Guidance for the Foundation Stage (QCA 2001) (3 to 5 years); Birth to three matters: a framework to support children in their earliest years (Sure Start Unit 2002); Sure Start initiatives to support families in disadvantaged areas; and Early Excellence Centres (now Children's Centres) to explore integrated approaches to education and care.

In the wake of these initiatives, there has been a gathering emphasis on training. Abbott and Hevey (2001) conceptualise a 'climbing frame' of nationally accredited qualifications for early years practitioners ranging from basic to advanced study. They believe this framework should be flexible, allowing individual practitioners to choose pathways that are meaningful to them. Thus, there can be movement 'across' for specialist study (e.g. working with children with complex needs) as well as 'upwards' to NVQ Level 4, Foundation Degrees or qualified teacher status (QCA 2001).

The practitioner account in this chapter comes from Sharon Ellis, who works at Rowland Hill Centre, Haringey, London. Sharon writes about many aspects of her work, but especially the interrelationships between learning through her practice, formal training and professionalism.

Professionalism is not a fixed concept. What it means to act 'professionally' at any point in time is determined by a web of social, economic, practice and political considerations. These influences and expectations change over time according to priorities and beliefs as to how best public services can serve their clients. This developmental feature of professionalism requires that practitioners continually examine their practice (Harrison 2003).

It is important for practitioners themselves to have a major input into the development of an early years knowledge base. Meade (1999), however, expresses concern that their voices can be left out of the debate. Honest practitioner feedback is vital to ensure that policies, recommended curricula and theories make sense when put into practice. Children and parents too must be helped to provide feedback – in a similar way, their voices are essential to the integrity, relevance and success of early years provision. Highly regulated structures and requirements can make it difficult for people to 'view themselves as originators of knowledge' (Woods 1990: 28).

Sharon's account engages with these issues. It arises from a number of conversations over several months. It gives a strong sense of what she believes is valuable to her practice and senior practitioner role, but also draws out the personal and professional principles that underpin her daily interactions with children, parents and staff colleagues at Rowland Hill. Four themes in her account are of particular interest.

First, Sharon made an early career choice to work with children. There is another group of early practitioners (also mainly women) who tend to be recruited once they have had children of their own. There's a sense in which Sharon, through having a daughter, has become a member of both recruitment groups. The extent to which the great majority of practitioners also carry out unpaid work as mothers and homemakers should not be overlooked by the move to increase their training and professionalism (see Hatt, 1997). Their career choices, decisions about part-time or full-time employment, and the ability to engage with training opportunities are often mediated through a mother's commitment to the 'first shift' (Hochschild 1997).

Second, Sharon gives a strong sense of the intuitive aspects of her professionalism – the pleasure of being with children, her orientation towards families, and her wish to create a truly inclusive early years centre for children, families and all those who work at Rowland Hill. As she says in her concluding paragraph: 'I believe that everyone has a right to feel that they belong.' Instinctive professional attitudes located within a 'community of practice' can serve to ground, humanise and supplement formal training [see Chapter 23 by Anning and Edwards in this volume, and also Anning and Edwards (1999)].

Third, her commitment to inclusion for children and parents has resonance in her approach to leadership, co-ordination, staff support and supervision – all rapidly expanding areas of responsibilities in terms of her senior role. She characterises her approach to leadership as 'democratic' (see Leithwood *et al.* 1999); and, like Rodd (1998), she stresses the part played by vision in her leadership style. This growth in leadership and management tasks has resulted in Sharon seeking further training to support her knowledge and abilities.

Lastly, throughout her piece, Sharon gives an indication of the extent to which she feels she can learn in a day-to-day way at her centre. Eraut (1994) believes we should not underestimate the degree to which 'unsystematised personal experience affects the knowledge-creation process' (p. 55). He suggests that new knowledge can be created by practitioners solving problems that arise from individual cases. This knowledge is different, however, from the codified and published knowledge of researchers. For Sharon, the combination of personally acquired knowledge and formal training knowledge seems a very powerful force for her professional development.

At the time of writing, the notion of a senior practitioner exists more in concept than in terms of an officially specified role. Sharon's experience, her formal qualifications, her personal and professional values, and her considerable skills and abilities appear to give an indication as to some of the essential elements of this role.

Sharon Ellis

My early career and interests

I've always wanted to work with children. At primary school I thought about being a children's nurse but decided against it. When I was 14 I worked in a children's nursery as a volunteer and during this time I took a City and Guilds pre-vocational course in child-care. I left school in 1987 and worked as a nursery assistant in a day nursery. I learnt a lot from the nursery nurses about ways of communicating with children. The staff said I 'talked naturally' to children. I'm a playful person and I believe it helps if adults can enter into children's play, but we need to learn how. During this time I developed a strong belief in the importance of close practitioner contact with parents and carers. A lot of my learning came from careful observation of the practice of others – both staff and parents, and also the reactions of children. I think I learnt a lot from watching others. I still do.

I worked as a nursery assistant for nearly three years and found I could do a great deal that qualified nursery nurses were doing. I thought if I can do all this I ought to study to become a qualified nursery nurse. So, at 19, with a small grant, I studied full-time for a Nursery Nurses Education Board (NNEB) qualification. It was two years of hard work because I shared a flat with a friend and I needed a regular income. I found some part-time work as a cleaner and as a cook. In my second year I moved back home as finances were very tight. Towards the end of the course I took an English GCSE and a full first-aid course – both necessary for the NNEB qualification.

The NNEB gave me important insights into children's development and their learning needs. It helped me understand how adults, and the wider environment, play an immense part in children's lives and learning opportunities. It helped me to know how to release creativity in children, and to stretch my mind in order to accommodate to their needs.

When I got the NNEB qualification I worked as a nursery officer in a children's centre in Barnet. I was based in a room with one other member of staff and around ten to 12 children aged 3 to 4 years. I also gained experience of working with children aged from birth to 5. This was my first real experience of working with the whole family as a social unit and it brought a new light to my understanding, particularly the way in which parents are often represented as 'good' or 'bad' in the media.

At Barnet I had my first experience of working with children with physical disabilities. This gave opportunities to work alongside other professionals. At first, this was very scary because you think you know where other professions are coming from. For instance, you think the police aren't there to help families but to pursue crime. However, I discovered they could have similar family support interests to my own. I suppose, however, that every profession has its own agenda with regard to where they want the family to be in terms of being 'normal'.

My next job, in Enfield, was related to my growing interest in families. My experience of case conferences in Barnet gave me an insight into what the family's role in a child's development was really about. I felt my own experiences, and particularly my developing skills of listening and empathising, were very important in this work. I was able to appreciate some of the root causes of family unhappiness and breakdown. This included the effect of physical, emotional and drug abuse on carers and children. My involvement in running parent education courses served to increase my knowledge and enhance my interpersonal skills. I also developed insights into counselling adults and therapeutic work with children.

My current post at Rowland Hill

I returned to Haringey in November 1997 as a nursery nurse at the Rowland Hill Centre. My daughter had started primary school in the Borough and I wanted more personal time for her during the school holidays. As a mother I felt I was missing out on her early years and was therefore feeling stressed. I felt work always had me – whether I was there or not.

The following year, my role at the Centre expanded. Haringey LEA wanted us to provide a centre for all families from the local community. My hours of work and contract changed and I became a nursery officer. We merged with a special needs nursery next door and worked towards being genuinely inclusive. A position for an acting deputy nursery officer came up. The Head of Centre was encouraging. I felt she valued my previous experience and believed this would enable me to bring a breadth to the deputy's role.

In July 1998 I was appointed deputy nursery officer as a job share on a temporary basis whilst continuing to work as a nursery officer for the other half of my job. The merger with the nursery wasn't an easy process for some members of staff. Also some people were uncomfortable with the idea that I should take on a senior role because they felt my experience was not extensive. This brought on feelings of conflict within me. In the following year the deputy's post was advertised, I applied and was made permanent, but still as a job share. I was told that the position had scope for growth and it was up to me how much I took on. At this point I dived in! In February 2000, my job share colleague left and I took on the full-time deputy post.

Rowland Hill offers part-time and full-time nursery places for 84 children aged 3 to 4 years and TOPS (Toddler Opportunities and Parent Support) and drop-in groups for around 70 families. We provide extended day provision consisting of a breakfast club and an after-school club. Children referred to the 'Early Intervention Panel' are allocated places within the nursery and the TOPS groups. We also arrange adult training sessions and play schemes during half term break. We are open from 8.00 am to 6.00 pm for forty-eight weeks of the year. This level of extended provision can be very exhausting for staff. However, seeing the family as a whole, including children who may have disabilities, is very important for me.

The Centre was awarded 'excellence' status in 1999. This, however, is a considerable responsibility and it makes many demands on us. For instance, it brings a surprising amount of interest from people in England but also other countries like Japan, America and Canada. As a networked (with two other Haringey centres) and designated centre of excellence, we are asked to closely monitor the services on offer to our 'clients', i.e. children, parents, and those on training courses. Additionally, we need to keep clear records of the children coming into and leaving the Centre. I help to ensure children's safety by writing health care plans with their parents, carers and health professionals. Children's dietary needs are my responsibility after discussions with parents and other agencies involved with the child.

We have a number of policies related to our practice and the life and welfare of the Centre more generally. These are important in terms of establishing shared procedures and practices and are also required by Ofsted. I am involved in helping staff to draft and review these and I'm directly responsible for health and safety, healthy food, and extended day policies.

The staff are very committed to detailed observation of children, which happens mainly in an ongoing way, and in more concerted ways during non-contact time. Every two weeks, we have LIOT ('life in our teams') meetings when we discuss issues related to working effectively together. In addition, there are fortnightly team meetings when we focus more on the children – their targets, parental involvement, and wider agency involvement. These two-weekly meetings also aim to help individual team members to feel supported.

Being a leader

Much of my work involves acting as a co-ordinator, manager, facilitator and leader. So, what kind of a leader am I? I think it's important for a leader to have a clear vision of how things need to be done and where education and care should go. Leaders need the interpersonal skills to enable others to share in and develop the vision so that it doesn't become stale or stuck. I strive to be an inclusive and 'democratic' leader but I recognise that there will be times when I must take the lead in a reassuring way. The wish to be a skilled leader lies at the heart of my sense of being a professional.

My deputy's role involves direct work with children, staff, parents and other professionals, but there are also management, personnel and administrative duties. Recently there has been an expansion in my administrative role, which reflects my position in the Centre as a senior practitioner. The Centre is large so it has a substantial core budget plus external funding streams. The Centre head manages this, however, some aspects need extra support so the deputy head teacher and I provide this.

I help support 28 staff, and work with the head and deputy to keep the organisational front going. This includes delegating work – such as the family lunch with parents, carers and children, and the staff – as well as attending meetings with other professionals. I organise and manage the extended day provision, which includes play-schemes, breakfast clubs and after-school clubs. I am, at times, involved in interviewing new staff. This was daunting at first because of making a decision about somebody's life. I deal with staff personnel issues like sickness monitoring, annual leave, and staff leaving, as well as inducting new staff, disseminating information about the Centre, and keeping my line manager (the head teacher) informed. As a team leader, I am responsible for the appraisal of five members of staff.

I am the accident-reporting officer and I am responsible for the follow-up to accidents. It's very easy to do a risk assessment when it's something fairly straightforward like clearing the exits. However, when there is something wrong with the building, for instance, and money is needed, that generates a lot more work in terms of prioritising when and how things can be funded. Health and safety communications can be time consuming and I sometimes feel they take me away from my work with children and parents.

In 2002, I applied to do an NVQ Level 4 which, I felt, would enable me to look more closely into my leading and managing roles, develop my insights into teaching and increase my study skills. I am confident with the practical side of teaching but not so confident at talking and writing about it. Unfortunately, although I found an assessor, I was unable to find an accredited teacher so I withdrew.

I recently attended a management and leadership course at Penn Green Centre, Corby. There I noticed they had a 10-day introduction to the MA (Management and Leadership). If I took this higher degree on, my Centre head would need to mentor me. It would help me too with my increasing leadership role and also give me a wider understanding of management theories and approaches. I feel hesitant about enrolling because I don't have a teaching degree. One option would be to complete an early years Foundation Degree before going on to this MA.

In the meantime, I've been accepted for a 12-week Leadership and Management course at The Tavistock Centre in Swiss Cottage, London. I have also continued to develop professionally by taking part in other courses, e.g. child protection, health and safety management, attachment theory. All courses I do tend to result in me taking on more responsibilities within the Centre.

Working with parents

For me, a vital aspect of being professional involves working with the families and helping them to become powerful. This is in addition to enabling staff members in their development. All communications require consistency and trust. This it what keeps me going – this is the core of what I do.

Rowland Hill is inclusive in terms of the way in which we aim to meet the wide range of children's and parents' needs through the curriculum. We have a number of children with physical disabilities who are not mobile and this can surprise some parents when they first visit.

I believe the curriculum for young children is primarily about enhancing growth and development and a sense of self in all areas of their lives, with a strong emphasis on fostering the wellbeing and values of children within the community. Many of the experiences we provide at the Centre enable children to learn through play. We feel our curriculum is part of their play and this educational philosophy is shared and discussed with parents.

We approach our work with a high regard for the contribution of parents to children's development and learning. Much of what we do takes account of this and often involves working alongside parents and learning from them. This partnership begins when we make a home visit before children start. Parents then visit us with their children, but also on their own when we hold an open afternoon. The afternoon enables us to talk about the way in which we approach the curriculum and the way in which we structure play activities to foster learning in the six areas of the Foundation Stage.

Examples of how we develop a close partnership with parents include working together to establish learning goals for children and valuing parental insights. A substantial number of our parents are learning English as an additional language. We have parents from Turkish, Albanian and Kurdish backgrounds. This, however, can change as families move in and out of the area. When parents come to the Centre we encourage them to bring an English speaking friend if they wish, or we provide an interpreter. Children from these families are supported within the Centre by their key workers and a language support worker.

Professional challenges

There's a lot in my work that gives me pleasure but there are many challenges too. For instance, I was very involved in our recent Ofsted inspection. I was interviewed about the Centre's family support and childcare provision, and our aims and my ideas for the future. I was asked about finance and what we might do with an increased budget. Here I spoke about parents wanting an affordable childcare service so that they could return back to work or pursue further studies. We had a good report and retained our 'excellence' status.

A further area of challenge is the growth of my role within a developing network of Haringey excellence centres. My administrative tasks have expanded considerably with the data collection and evaluations that are needed to monitor the services we provide, and to oversee their cost effectiveness. Owing to current budget restraints, additional administrative help has been difficult to get, so my knowledge of ICT has greatly increased as well as my typing speed! If I'm honest, it is hard to keep on top of my workload. Therefore it is important to keep things in perspective and initiate a 'to do' list in order to prioritise my work each week.

Dealing with payments from parents is an increasing difficulty in an urban borough where debts are very much a part of family life. This is a sensitive issue, which requires a great deal of patience, practicality and knowledge of household budgeting as well as being an attentive listener. For some families managing money seems to be more difficult than is sometimes acknowledged.

Lastly, there can be feelings of uncertainty for me when I manage staff who are also my friends. Very occasionally there is a need to take disciplinary action. This can be stressful and painful for all.

What I contribute and what I enjoy

On most days, I come into work with excitement and enthusiasm. I try to arrive with ideas of where I want to be and where I would like to lead others. My current wish is for growth in my management role and my effectiveness, but I know I must take on one thing at a time.

I enjoy our weekly strategic management team meetings when we attend to our own thoughts and feelings – time to be truly reflective. We achieve this by 'releasing' how we're feeling. We go around the group and take turns to say what's on our minds and what we've been experiencing. This is so important because we could end up being 'containers' with adults and children off-loading their feelings into us. We therefore need this time to unpack what we've received.

It is heartening to see children and their families develop in ways that others thought were not possible. I come into contact with people, both young and old, who experience life as another day of struggle with very little joy or fun. As I go around the Centre, if I see a smile on the face of a baby, a child or an adult, it warms me. The trust that is built up through the people that I have worked with teaches me about different 'walks of life', but also highlights my professional strengths and weaknesses.

Rowland Hill is a good place for adults and children to develop. We work collaboratively with parents and also encourage them to apply for posts which means they formally work alongside us as colleagues. I'm learning a lot about people. Often you think you know about them but then you get a new set of parents and children. There are so many aspects of human life that engage me at the Centre so I can't stop learning at Rowland Hill! I feel valued and I work with a committed group of people. My professional convictions and beliefs help me to be tolerant, to enjoy what I do, and to foster my deep commitment to my work. I believe that everyone has a right to feel that they belong to our Centre.

References

Abbott, L. and Hevey, D. (2001) 'Training to work in the early years: developing the climbing frame' in Pugh, G. *Contemporary Issues in the Early Years*, 3rd edn. London: Paul Chapman.

Anning, A. and Edwards, A. (1999) *Promoting Children's Learning from Birth to Five: developing the new early years professional.* Buckingham: Open University Press.

Anning, A. and Edwards, A. (2004) 'Creating contexts for professional development in educare' in Miller, L. and Devereux, J. *Supporting Children's Learning in the Early Years.* London: David Fulton Publishers.

Eraut, M. (1994) *Developing Professional Knowledge and Competence.* London: Falmer Press.

Harrison, R. (2003) 'Learning for professional development', in L. Kydd, L. Anderson and W. Newton (eds) *Leading and Managing People and Teams.* London: Paul Chapman.

Hatt, S. (1997) *Gender, Work and Labour Markets.* London: Macmillan Press.

Hochschild, A. (1997) *The Second Shift.* New York: Quill.

Leithwood, K., Jantzi, D. and Steinbach, R. (1999) *Changing Leadership for Changing Times*. Buckingham: Open University Press.

Meade, A. (1999) 'If you say it three times, is it true? Critical use of research in early childhood education'. Keynote address to the Third International Early Years Research Conference, University of Warwick.

QCA (Qualifications and Curriculum Authority) (2001) http://www.qca.org.uk/news/circulars/1202001.asp (Accessed 8th July 2003)

Rodd, J. (1998) *Leadership in Early Childhood*, 2nd edn. Buckingham: Open University Press.

Sure Start Unit (DfES) (2002) *Birth to Three Matters: a framework to support children in their earliest years*. London: DfES.

Woods, P. (1990) *Teacher Skills and Strategies*. Basingstoke: Falmer Press.

Index